# GOVERNMENT IN REPUBLICAN CHINA

# GOVERNMENT IN REPUBLICAN CHINA

BY
PAUL MYRON ANTHONY LINEBARGER
*The Department of Political Science*
*Duke University*

FOREWORD BY
FRITZ MORSTEIN MARX

FIRST EDITION

**WILDSIDE PRESS**

*Dedicated with filial affection*

*to*

PAUL MYRON WENTWORTH LINEBARGER

United States Judge in the Philippines,
Counselor to and Biographer of President
Sun Yat-sen, Formerly Legal Adviser to
the National Government of China

# FOREWORD

To the cynic, two nations clasped in murderous embrace yet nominally living in peace with each other might well be one of the miracles of our century. No less miraculous has been for many the tenacity of Chinese resistance to Japan's invasion ever since the first bullets whizzed through the night near the Marco Polo Bridge southwest of Peking early in July, 1937. The undeclared war has spread disaster through an area larger than that immediately affected in Europe's battles from 1914 to 1918; hundreds of thousands have died in action; for months China's capital has been in the hands of the enemy. But China is not on her knees.

The explanation is simple. For the first time in her history, China fights as a nation. More is involved than can be attributed to Generalissimo Chiang K'ai-shek's personal leadership or the strategic and organizational services rendered, until his recent recall to Germany, by Alexander von Falkenhausen, chief of staff of the Turkish armies during the World War. A people without allegiance to its government and without faith in itself would have been incapable of braving the ordeal of retreat, massacre, and occupation as successfully as have the Chinese. That China fights today as a nation is no small tribute to the National Government of the Kuomintang established at Nanking in 1927. How long she will be able to fight as a nation is a question to be answered only by reference to the national mentality and political institutions which have emerged since the collapse of the Manchu Empire in 1911–1912. It is the purpose of this volume to appraise the record of China's republican era.

The author was compelled to beat his own path. Only a few books on modern government in China are available in English, and these, written by Chinese, are modeled in their presentation on Western prototypes to an extent of obscuring, though unintentionally, the very substance of Chinese politics. In Dr. Linebarger's pioneer venture the dynamics of internal instability, typical of the earlier phases of the Republic, and the gradual consolidation under the Nanking regime are analyzed with extraordinary penetration. Instead of being confronted with meaningless form and empty legality, the reader is placed in a position to view step by step the evolution of conflicting and merging forces: political movements and their contest for the loyalty of the masses, the rough and ready rule of military might, and the official hierarchies representing organized governments. Throughout this work, as in Dr. Linebarger's earlier *Political Doctrines of Sun Yat-sen,* the broad stream of Confucian thought fertilizing age after age of China's social existence and Sun's purposeful ideological adaptations combined in his *San Min Chu I* are shown in fundamental harmony. One distinction, however, stands out clearly. The Confucian tradition applied itself to a vaguely conceived but essentially unified world order. In the *San Min Chu I* we encounter the elements of a national credo, self-assertive and militant.

The role of ideology in modern government has suffered curious neglect among students of politics for a considerable time. In periods of relative ideational saturation or stagnation, the mechanics of constitutional law or the give and take of legislative barter may distract from the basic framework of values and objectives giving shape to the political order. The rise of totalitarian systems relying heavily on ideological appeal and propaganda techniques has laid new stress upon those factors which predetermine political behavior. In China's vast experience we have the supreme example of ideological guidance so firmly established as to reduce to a minimum direct governmental intervention in the affairs of the individual. It is perhaps Sun Yat-sen's tragedy that for years he placed his faith in the magic of democratic verbiage imported from the West; a new orientation came to prevail after 1923, when at Sun's instance tested practitioners of mass organization from the Soviet Union began to overhaul and streamline the Kuomintang apparatus.

Government in China has become migratory as a result of Japan's advance. A mere description of its previous structure and functions would today have little relevance. But Dr. Linebarger has probed deeply enough into the foundations of Chinese political life to distinguish with uncommon discernment between the ephemeral and the durable. His long-range exposition transcends the exigencies of the hour and delineates the issues of China's future.

FRITZ MORSTEIN MARX.

ADAMS HOUSE,
HARVARD UNIVERSITY.

# ACKNOWLEDGMENTS

I am deeply indebted to the five gentlemen who have read the entire manuscript in some one of its stages. My father, Judge Paul Myron Wentworth Linebarger, has given me tireless help in this as in all my projects, for which I shall never be able to tender sufficient thanks. My teacher, Professor Harley Farnsworth MacNair of the University of Chicago, supplied numerous addenda and corrigenda of great value from his knowledge of modern Chinese history. Professor Arthur N. Holcombe of Harvard University suggested changes which have made the work more realistic. Assistance offered me by the Sinologue and philosopher, Professor H. H. Dubs of Duke University, was of the utmost value. Professor Paul H. Clyde, Duke University, provided many useful and significant hints, especially in the field of Sino-foreign relations.

I am also under obligation to Mr. J. C. Yang, Library of Congress, and Professor James R. Ware, Harvard University, for further suggestions; to Professor Charles Sidney Gardner and Dr. John Fairbank, Harvard University, and Professor George Kennedy, Yale University, for aid in the general course of my Chinese studies; to Professor Maria Magdalena Schoch, until recently of the University of Hamburg, Germany, for a critical reading of the revised manuscript; and to Miss Hazel Foster and Mr. M. F. Nelson for similar assistance. Mrs. W. M. Gibson, Miss Whitty Daniel, and my wife have helped in the preparation of the manuscript.

P. M. A. L.

Durham, N. C.,
*August*, 1938.

# CONTENTS

|  | PAGE |
|---|---|
| FOREWORD BY FRITZ MORSTEIN MARX | vii |
| ACKNOWLEDGMENTS | xi |
| INTRODUCTION | 1 |
|     Duality or Confluence? | 1 |
|     The Peculiarities of Old China | 2 |
|     The Peculiarities of Modern China | 6 |
|     The World Significance of Chinese Government | 7 |
|     The Main Factors in Modern Chinese Government | 9 |
|     The Approach | 11 |

## FIRST PART
## MOVEMENTS

### CHAPTER I

| CONFUCIANISM | 13 |
|---|---|
|     The Ages before Confucius | 13 |
|     The Ideology Called Confucian | 15 |
|     Government in the Confucian Ideology | 18 |
|     The Replacement of the Confucian Ideology | 22 |
|     The Chief Movements in the Rebuilding of China | 24 |
|     Confucianism in the Republic | 26 |

### CHAPTER II

| THE RISE OF NATIONALISM | 31 |
|---|---|
|     Nationalism: Patriotic Anti-Manchu Phase | 31 |
|     Nationalism: Revolutionary Modernist Phase | 34 |
|     Nationalism: Republican Phase | 36 |
|     Nationalism: Constitutionalist Phase | 38 |
|     The Political Doctrines of Sun Yat-sen | 41 |
|     Opportunist Movements and Their Anticonstitutional Effects | 44 |
|     Christianity as a Political Force | 48 |
|     Nationalism: Social Revolutionary Phase | 50 |

### CHAPTER III

| BATTLING CREEDS | 57 |
|---|---|
|     Nationalism: Governing Phase | 57 |
|     Independent Marxism in China | 63 |

## CONTENTS

|  | PAGE |
|---|---|
| Japanese Efforts to Participate in Creating a New China | 69 |
| Patriotism: The United Front | 72 |

# SECOND PART
# ARMIES

## CHAPTER IV
WARRIORS. . . . . . . . . . . . . . . . . . . . . . . . . . 76
  Military Rule and Political Economy . . . . . . . . . . . . . 76
  The Downfall of the Charioteers . . . . . . . . . . . . . . . 79
  Military Elements in Chinese Imperial History. . . . . . . . 83
  The Military Organization of the Manchu Dynasty. . . . . . 86
  The Army and the Republican Revolution. . . . . . . . . . . 97

## CHAPTER V
CAUSES . . . . . . . . . . . . . . . . . . . . . . . . . . . 102
  The Age of the War Lords. . . . . . . . . . . . . . . . . . 102
  The Age of Air Conquest . . . . . . . . . . . . . . . . . . 108
  Governmental and Political Role of the Armies. . . . . . . 113
  War and the Agrarian Economy . . . . . . . . . . . . . . . 115
  Imperialism and Chinese Wars. . . . . . . . . . . . . . . . 119

# THIRD PART
# GOVERNMENTS

## CHAPTER VI
THE EMPIRE. . . . . . . . . . . . . . . . . . . . . . . . . 126
  Government to the End of the Warring States . . . . . . . 126
  The Chinese Imperial Government . . . . . . . . . . . . . 129
  Family, Village, and *Hui* . . . . . . . . . . . . . . . . 136
  Governmental Changes Foreshadowing the Republic . . . . . 139

## CHAPTER VII
THE REVOLUTION. . . . . . . . . . . . . . . . . . . . . . . 145
  The Presidency of Sun Yat-sen and the Republican Revolution. 145
  The Parliamentary Republic. . . . . . . . . . . . . . . . . 149
  The Presidential Dictatorship of Yüan Shih-k'ai . . . . . . 152
  The Phantom Republic in Peking. . . . . . . . . . . . . . . 155
  The Governments of Sun Yat-sen in Canton. . . . . . . . . . 160
  The Nationalist Government, Soviet in Form. . . . . . . . . 162

## CHAPTER VIII
RECONSTRUCTION. . . . . . . . . . . . . . . . . . . . . . . 167
  The National Government of China. . . . . . . . . . . . . . 167
  The Chinese Soviet Republic. . . . . . . . . . . . . . . . . 182

CONTENTS xv

|  | PAGE |
|---|---|
| Other Governments in China | 184 |
| The Growth of Government in China | 186 |

CONCLUSION . . . . . . . . . . . . . . . . . . . . . . 191
    The Collapse of the Imperial Society . . . . . . . . . . . 191
    The Nature of the Transformation . . . . . . . . . . . . 192
    The Problems of Government in China . . . . . . . . . . 193
    The Question of Chinese Political Survival . . . . . . . . . 195

CHRONOLOGY OF DYNASTIES . . . . . . . . . . . . . . . . 197

INDEX . . . . . . . . . . . . . . . . . . . . . . . . . . 199

# INTRODUCTION

The origins of Chinese society may reach half a million years into the past. Anthropologists have suggested that Sinanthropus Pekinensis, among the earliest forms of man, resembles the modern Chinese more closely than he does any other modern race. In what specific period the earliest ancestors of the Chinese came to China is not known. It is certain, however, that about 1500 B. C. there existed a well-developed civilized society in the Yellow River valley, and that this same society has lived on—modified by the centuries, but in unbroken continuity—down into the present. China has outlasted Crete, Tyre, Greece, and Rome. The Aztec empire, which arose in Mexico when China was already ancient, has become only a memory, while China is still vital. How is it that China's institutions survive, while those of other nations did not? How real are Chinese institutions today? What, precisely, is the Republic of China?

## *Duality or Confluence?*

The phrase *Republican China* indicates an era rather than a system. The preceding ages of China have been known by the names of great dynasties. T'ang China (620-906 A. D.) overawed and instructed all eastern Asia. Sung China (A. D. 960-1279) flourished, civilian and tolerant, in a world marked by bigotry and arms. Well into the past century the West remained distant and vague. Republican China struggles in the presence of the modern world and subject to its superior force; her very name is a capitulation to the twentieth century. The problems of the Republican era are not merely the problems of republican government; they involve the broad question of the meeting and interpenetration of civilizations. How are the Chinese, schooled for thousands of years in the effective operation of their own political system, to adapt themselves fast enough to the Western scheme? What happens when they must and yet cannot effectuate such adaptation? These are not queries to be answered simply in the routine terms of Western politics.

For the past three thousand years and more the eastern end of the European-Asiatic land mass has formed a world to itself. Most of this time it was larger, richer, and more civilized than the European world. Down to the nineteenth century of the Christian era the Chinese had no reason to suppose that theirs was not the most advanced and powerful of civilized societies. They looked upon the Far East as the all-inclusive universe of civilization; to them, their way of life was the common-sense way. The Europeans did likewise, with reference to their own sphere. When the European realm expanded so as to include the whole planet, when Western civilization began to dominate the earth, and the Christian family of nations became the world-wide international system, the Chinese were forced to concede that the Far East could not be kept to itself. They have found it indispensable to respond, as individuals and as a people, to the new environment closing in on them. Doing so has necessitated the reexamination and restatement of nearly all basic values of Chinese life.

Since the nineteenth century the Chinese have been faced with the alternative of adhering to their own traditions or accepting those of the West. Institutions and practices which are so well established that they seem to rest on sheer common sense in each of the competing civilizations have been placed in juxtaposition. As a result, the Chinese now know two kinds of common sense to justify a course of action. The ensuing difficulty at times goes deeper; for they may be said to have even two kinds of sanity. In old China a man who wanted no sons seemed a patent lunatic; in the Western world he might be perfectly sane. A modern Chinese faces thousands of such choices.

*The Peculiarities of Old China*

Obviously, government in Republican China cannot be understood without analysis of the foundations upon which it is built. Such an analysis requires an inquiry, however cursory, into the peculiarities of old China and those of contemporary China. Some of the difficulties of modern China arise from the very adequacy of the old system. Had the Chinese of the past been less satisfied with their society, they might have become more accustomed to change and transience.

China from the first millennium B. C. occupied the central position in the Far East. No other country in that part of the earth was so powerful or so civilized. India, despite important contributions to Chinese religious thought, was too far away to impinge greatly upon the Chinese. Japan was heavily indebted to the Chinese, and encouraged the Chinese in viewing themselves as the most civilized of peoples. This had important consequences. As China was unified most of the time, and as there was no other polity to compare with the Chinese, their political system took on the appearance of a universal empire. The neighboring states paid formal tribute, and the Chinese were unprepared to meet another people who might claim political equality as an organized state. Even today, in the attitudes of the Chinese and Japanese toward one another, there are strong traces of this traditional point of view and indications that the Japanese would like to restore a closed Far Eastern order with themselves in supremacy.

Since old China was rarely confronted with international problems, the Chinese were not aware of their realm as a nation-state. There was no sharp territorial limit to the Chinese polity, and no requirement that within certain boundaries one authority be defined as supreme. The Chinese were able to make their adjustments in the interplay of social and political controls with less frequent resort to theory than the Westerners. Nor was the Chinese ruler ever so firmly entrenched as to eliminate the chance of being overthrown or to preclude the existence of other—pluralistic—independent social controls. The power of government was indeed limited. It maintained the peace of the Chinese world, directed education, supported the social proprieties, and was ornamental rather than efficient for the greater part of its activities.

The Chinese lived primarily under the dominance of non-political agencies. These were the family (comparable to the Western clan), the village and district, and the *hui* (association, guild, society—in the narrowest sense of the term). The family was intimately bound up with the Chinese religious system, which stressed the continuity of each individual in the flesh. A personal immortality was to be secured with greatest certainty through the survival of one's own blood. The village was the main economic unit, and the union of villages into districts (*hsien*) provided an administrative division of importance: below the *hsien* level, common interests were fostered by community home rule; above it, by the government. This meant that elders, clans in council, village bosses, and other nongovernmental agencies carried on police work, all local public construction, and most of the activities which are regarded in the modern West as falling under the jurisdiction of the state. The *hui* was able to supplement the family and the village; in guild form, it provided the chief framework of commercial and industrial organization.

If the government was weak and limited, and social control ensured primarily by nongovernmental agencies, how did the Chinese achieve so great a political stability? Why did their polity not break up into a wilderness of tiny social groups, each jealous and particularistic, like medieval Europe? The answer is to be found in the psychological controls which the Chinese established. They devised a system of indoctrination unequaled by that of any other people.

The Chinese sought to guide men through the guidance of their ideas: government by education, or government by propaganda. For this purpose scholarship and administration were closely allied. The government was made up of scholars, who thereby occupied the position of greatest prestige in the society; the scholars were trained to serve as government officials. Few officials were not scholars; few scholars pursued a nonpolitical course. This led to a profound uniformity of thought, and was in accord with the dictates of the Confucian tradition.[1]

From the earliest times Chinese thought was social and political in emphasis, rather than metaphysical and scientific. For thousands of years scholars studied problems of society, government, and ethics. They appealed to tradition, and interpreted it. They organized the primitive religion of the Chinese into a sophisticated social philosophy, and over the centuries their work took effect. Chinese of different racial backgrounds, using different spoken languages and unable to communicate with one another by writing, living under different climatic and economic conditions, came to show a startling uniformity of behavior. Custom and common sense were woven into a solid pattern by the scholars and accepted by the masses. Everything in human life bore some relation to everything else, and the life of man was related to the world of nature. There was no sharp distinction between natural science and social philosophy.

The educational integration of government, mores, and physical existence created a system of control which has exceeded all others in lasting power. The group in command was the scholastic bureaucracy, but membership in it was not hereditary. Scholar-officials were recruited by civil service examinations, and to this degree the society was a democratic one. Every child in the society had the theoretical opportunity of becoming prime minister. Furthermore, the power exercised by the scholar-officials was different in its nature from that of legal rulers in the West. Government was preventive rather than remedial. Constitutionality was not confined to legal matters; in a broader sense it extended to all subjects. The scholars were as much subject to established tradition as the humblest Chinese, and everyone knew the tradition. The scholars excelled only in knowing it more thoroughly.

It may be stated as a truism that under any government the actual scope of its intervention is confined to a certain category of affairs, bounded on the one hand by matters which are so trivial or so unexplored that they are left to the citizen's free choice and on the other by subjects in which there is such general agreement as to make political action unnecessary. This latter sphere might be called ideological compliance—control of men brought about by the inculcation of broad uniform patterns of belief and behavior. If men are induced to agree upon a traditionally fixed mode of behavior, they will unite in persecuting dissenters and will not be conscious of the tyranny of ideological doctrine. But if they think in many different ways, they will be able to gain security only by promises of mutual noninterference. Liberty—as absence of governmental restraint—may thus result either from a complete concord, in which every man is free to do as he wishes since all men wish to do basically the same, or from a specific guarantee of each individual's freedom to follow his own interest or caprice within a defined limit. The old system of China was a free society in so far as dissent calling for government interference was relatively negligible, and at the same time a society rigidly controlled with respect to the uniformity of individual behavior.

This tradition was pragmatic and realistic. The Chinese ideological controls operated successfully because they corresponded reasonably well with the actualities of social and economic existence. With the coming of the West, the old Chinese system was affected in two ways: First, the amorphous Chinese society was threatened by the strong, effectively organized states of the West. Secondly, the competitive accomplishments of Western civilization destroyed, in large part, the assumption of universality upon which much Chinese tradition depended, and thereby impaired the power of the scholar-officials. The twentieth century brought China a new freedom, unaccustomed and unsought. The old system was threatened with ruin, and modern China faced the problem: replacement or reconstitution? Or, more dangerously: chaos or political extinction?

*The Peculiarities of Modern China*

The lifetime of one man can span the gap between old China and new. There are men living in Peking today who can remember when the Forbidden City (the palace-city of the emperors) was sacred and inviolate, and when the mandarinate ruled in accordance with immemorial usage. These may regard all Western science as a confusion, a wild torrent of exotic words, which answers no problems, gives human life no aim and no dignity, and is bound to return to the alien dust whence it came. Opposing them are younger Chinese who hate the dead hand of the past and look forward to a Westernized, scientific, industrial China which will differ from Europe and America only in being even more modern than they.

Most Chinese fall into neither of these groups. Many of them, however, have a definite conception of the West and of the benefits which Western civilization has to bestow. They also realize the threat which it contains for those who do not master it. Yet they have been nurtured in the serene humanity of ancient custom and hold to it with the effortlessness of habit long transmitted. Out of this dual standard there spring daily problems of ethics and conduct, of private life and public policy. Administrative organization versus family loyalty and nepotism, promptness versus leisureliness, discipline versus courtesy: these and many others are omnipresent antitheses.

Anachronism is China's second self. There is no set scheme of things. Modern Western civilization has not been adopted so fully as to make the traditional habits seem outmoded, nor has the past survived to an extent as to make everything modern appear ridiculous. The notion of world government, for example, is gone from China, and the notion of multi-national government not yet clear. The relation of the individual to society and of the parts of society to the whole are not yet reformulated; this affects such matters as criminal law, political organization, and economic development. Virtually every adaptation in China must be thought through from the beginning by the Chinese; and even in thinking there are varying styles. Are the Chinese to think after the fashion of the West—scientifically and logically —or are they to think in their accustomed traditional and empirical manner?

It is thus patent that the new Chinese world which is appearing must grow out of the background of the past and the necessities of the present. It cannot readily be planned because there are not enough formulas common to the old Far Eastern and the new Western worlds. New China must be a blending, from use, from habit, from new skills imposed upon old. Out of the dangers and misfortunes of the years since 1912 the Chinese have developed a small body of political methods which is temporarily workable. But the greater part of their social and governmental thought and custom has yet to go through the process of reevaluation by practice. Chinese political development has perforce to be emergent and not planned.

According to either time scheme, that of her long past or of the modern world, modern China is anachronistic. The transformation of the Chinese world of the past to the China of the future involves the creation of a whole set of transitional institutions designed to lead from one to the other. Contemporary Chinese institutions are neither those of the past nor those of the future; they are a peculiar scheme of more recent origin and bound to be replaced. Old China is gone. Modern China is novel and unstable; in time it too will yield to a China of which prophecy affords but few glimpses.

*The World Significance of Chinese Government*

If government in Republican China is an extemporized and doomed system, rooted in no past, committed to no future, why should it be scrutinized at all? A number of reasons for examining Chinese government suggest themselves. Some of these are of sufficient significance to merit statement, so as to suggest facts and issues worthy of special notice. If certain points of key importance are kept in mind, they may serve as references whereby the relative ranking of any specific topic may be ascertained.

First, the mere geographic extent of China is such as to make her government necessary to a picture of contemporary governments. At least every fifth human being now living is a Chinese.

Second, in international relations China has been of great passive importance. The wars between Western and Far Eastern nations have all been fought over the so-called Chinese question. The partition of China and the open door in China have been issues of international concern. Since 1931 the Chinese have been active participants in the struggle for the control of China, and the nature of their government determines in large part the effectiveness of their resistance. China is a vast market, and an even vaster reserve of man power—for troops or for industrial labor.

Third, the pathology of government deserves attention. Chronic social disorder may provide a great variety of political facts wherewith to gauge the nature of political power. Well-governed societies do not supply similar material because they rarely need to probe political fundamentals.

Fourth, old China offers a challenging demonstration of secular, civilian, pacific world government. The Chinese commonwealth of the past was supernational; it seemed to the Chinese like unified civilized humanity. Among the conflicting currents of present world politics, there are some which drift toward world unity; old China may present significant analogies to the international institutions of today.

Fifth, the universal features of government may be more fruitfully scrutinized in a novel cultural and social setting. China presents a background radically different from the Western one, and affords a unique test whereby Western political patterns and those of world-wide significance may be distinguished from one another.

Sixth, the question of method in political science may meet qualifications after being applied to Chinese political thought. The Chinese did not seek that illusory precision which has been one of the chief goals of Western thought ever since logical procedure was established by the Greeks. The Western man in the street, however, depends very little on mathematics or logic in his everyday thinking. Indirectly, the effect of inductive and deductive method has been revolutionary, but their importance in routine operation or unspecialized thought is open to question —especially in view of the findings of modern psychology. It may well be that Chinese thought can assist in the interpretation of everyday experience in the West, precisely because it is not too specialized or scientific.

Seventh, the Chinese may contribute in a practical way to political knowledge and leadership throughout the world. These contributions may be anticipated by a consideration of past and present Chinese government.

Eighth, the Chinese have lived in a peculiar historical environment, consideration of which may broaden our outlook. Most Western "world histories"—with few exceptions such as H. G. Wells's brilliant *Outline*—are histories of the West Asiatic and European worlds, with only perfunctory references to China.

The relative novelty of Chinese materials to Western research explains in great part the neglect accorded them in the Western social sciences. With the narrowing of the world by modern means of transport and communication the situation is changing. The science of Sinology (systematic study of China through Chinese texts) has won its place among the archaeological disciplines. Sinologists have made available to Westerners a great deal of material, but its value depends in large part upon the degree to which it is incorporated into the generally accessible and usable body of knowledge.

*The Main Factors in Modern Chinese Government*

In the consideration of modern Chinese government a somewhat novel approach to government is called for: one which distinguishes different elements and levels of control and makes plain their interrelation. The narrow consideration of the formal structure would be puzzling and discouraging, since the various governments of modern China have been the ornaments rather than the engines of political power. An attempt to explain modern China in terms of constitutional legal development alone would lead to exasperation or frustration; the ideological and institutional context which might convey meaning would be lost.

How can government be studied when politics are antecedent to government? If the rulers make and unmake the form of government almost at will, where is the real source of their power? If armies can dissolve overnight and be reassembled under different banners on the morrow, military power may seem tenuous and dependent on other factors. What are these? If property is insecure and the standards of wealth subject to variation, how can economic power be treated as an ultimate determinant? How do men wield authority of any sort, while they create or destroy the machinery of authority?

For centuries China had been held together by a close-knit system dependent upon tradition. This tradition, the ideology called *Confucian*, was the device whereby the scholar-officials of the old imperial bureaucracy controlled society. Government itself was subordinate to the moral and social leadership of the intellectuals, who relegated the economic and military professions to the less honored categories of society. The whole fabric of Chinese life was made up of interlocking patterns; the West, by destroying a part, tore the whole asunder. Modern China faces more than political problems; a totalitarian revolution has engulfed it. China has been proceeding not from partial control to complete control, as are Italy,[2] Germany,[3] and the Soviets,[4] but from complete control to something not far from universal license—freedom all-pervading, unwanted, and terrifying. The problem of modern Chinese government is the problem of re-creating government out of its raw materials: land, people, doctrine, force, and law.

In this problem certain factors stand forth as preeminent: ideological movements, military and economic factors, governments.

First, the movements. These supplant the ancient tradition and the old hierarchy of scholars. In the place of one settled authority over all subjects, there suddenly appeared thousands of little authorities. Anarchism, dress reform, Christianity, feminism, nationalism, pro-Japanism, communism, atheism, capitalism—discordant and partially contradictory, these all compete for the authority or a part of the authority once held by the old system. China undergoes intellectual, moral, educational, political, economic, military, scientific, and industrial revolutions all at once, and all for the same reason—the passing of the old unified order. Imagine the Renaissance, the Reformation, the French Revolution, the industrial revolution, the Gold Rush of '49, the World War, and the Russian Revolution all happening in the same country in the same generation! This is a commonplace comparison, frequently made. Movements determined the loyalty of troops, the title to property, the form of government. Power inhered in them, since they determined the conditions under which men would seek and wield power. A great part of the control of China has been exerted directly, by means of the movements themselves.

Second, the armies took the power which goes with military force, simply because theirs was military force. They did not have to seek power. It accrued to them, out of the disorder of society. Along with military power went economic power as the most tangible and negotiable. Guns and property seem very realistic indices of power, as long as the troops are loyal and the property safe from confiscation or devaluation.

Third, the governments. Between ideological movements, which sought to rebuild the ideas and habits of men, and armies wielding a brief but nearly unrestricted authority, government played its tertiary role. It was at times of ludicrous unimportance, and on some occasions possessed power in its own right. It leaped to a sharply improved position after 1928, but never possessed the generality of assent or the monopoly of force to the degree common in the West.

*The Approach*

Government may mean the control (or attempted control) of society by men professing to act in the name of all society. In this sense it includes propagandists and educators who seek to reconstitute society, leaders of movements, soldiers, economic leaders of all classes, and government leaders (so far as they use government establishments as an actual means of control). Viewed thus, the political processes of modern China are manifold and significant. Here is power stripped naked, power without ornament, power resting squarely upon the brains or guns of men. Men rise and fall in the contest for power; they rise and fall absolutely, not in a fictitious scheme which establishes a fictitious order of constitutional offices sometimes providing asylum for popular leaders in eclipse.

Government may also mean the structure and function of that formally organized group in society which claims to act upon the mandate of legal sovereignty. When the concept of sovereignty itself is vague, confused, or absent, government by title may be merely one among several factors of power. Government in China is broader than the governments of China; the two should be distinguished from one another.

In outlining government in Republican China, the present analysis follows the broader construction of the word *government*. The governments proper are accordingly discussed in the last part, the first two being devoted to the ideological movements and to the military and economic factors. For the purpose of defining the three sets of controls as clearly as possible, each is treated separately. This has necessitated a corresponding arrangement of the historical data, though in each part presented from a different point of view. But it is highly desirable that the long-range Chinese chronology be kept in mind. To this end a table of Chinese dynasties has been provided.[5] As a result of separate analysis the movements, the armies, and the governments may appear in bolder relief than would otherwise be possible, and the role of government in the broadest sense may be made clearer, not only for China but for the West as well.

### NOTES

1. For a description of this system see below, pp. 18 ff.
2. *Cf.* H. Arthur Steiner, *Government in Fascist Italy*, New York and London, 1938.
3. *Cf.* Fritz Morstein Marx, *Government in the Third Reich*, 2d ed., New York and London, 1937.
4. *Cf.* Sidney and Beatrice Webb, *Soviet Communism*, 2d ed., New York, 1937.
5. See below, p. 197.

# FIRST PART
## MOVEMENTS

### Chapter I
### CONFUCIANISM

The continuity of Chinese civilization depends not alone upon its political virtues, but upon its working effectiveness in all relevant spheres of human activity. In emphasizing certain aspects of old China, it is impossible to trace the entire broad evolution.[1] In fact, the emergence of those devices which, along with government in the narrow sense, guided China in her long past dates back to prehistory. Throughout the ages, however, Chinese life has preserved its identity.

Chinese culture is unique in its continuity. Its most striking characteristic is a capacity for change without disruption. It would appear that that characteristic goes back even to [those] cultures which preceded the Shang in northeast China. Shang culture, like all great cultures, was eclectic, fertilized by influences from many quarters. But these influences and techniques, when they were accepted, met the same fate which has overtaken every people, every religion, every philosophy which has invaded China. They were taken up, developed to accord with Chinese conditions, and transmuted into organic parts of a culture which remained fundamentally and characteristically Chinese.[2]

This is the comment of H. G. Creel, an American Sinologue who has helped to explain the archaeological sites of a Chinese civilization considerably older than any other. Even in its historical beginnings the civilization of man in China displayed features corresponding to that of the modern Chinese.

*The Ages before Confucius*

The earliest Chinese state known is the Hsia, which is traditionally termed a dynasty in the Chinese chronicles and given the dates 2205–1765 B. C. More critical examination of the materials of Chinese tradition, the excavation of the engraved bones and bronzes from succeeding periods, and an interpretation of Chinese history with the technique of modern archaeology have upset the credibility of the records of the earliest periods. All that is established is the fact that the Hsia was a state before the Shang. It is unlikely that Hsia exercised any imperial hegemony over other peoples, since the empire system did not rise till Chou times.

Of the Shang dynasty (traditionally 1765–1123 B. C.) much more is known. Thirty years ago most Western scholars thought the Shang chronicles to be myth, but excavations in northeast China have located a Shang capital and have unearthed a large body of inscriptions on bone.[3] The Shang culture must have been highly developed, possessing an urban life, writing, and a definite system of monarchical government. The germs of scholastic leadership were present. Power was in the hands of a single ruler (*wang*, or king), who claimed hegemony for an undetermined distance beyond the walls of the capital.

In the twelfth century B. C. the Shang dynasty was overthrown by conquerors from the west, the Chou. The Chou dynasty bridges the gap between the semihistoric and the definitely historic period of Chinese antiquity. Under the Chou the chief features of Chinese social and intellectual existence took on clear form. From the Chou conquest and their attempts to establish stable government China derived striking social and political characteristics. One of the astonishing facts about early Chinese history is the manner in which the Chou rulers utilized propaganda to make their conquest secure, and in which their propaganda furnished dynamic concepts of Chinese social thought and development.

The most important of these widely propagandized concepts was that of the Chinese Empire. The city of Shang had been the center of a dominion which could not possibly have included more than a fraction of what is known today as China. The civilized areas along the Yellow River were probably no larger than Palestine. Most of what is now China was conquered in succeeding centuries. Even in this small area, it is not known what relationship existed between the ruler of Shang and other rulers. The Chou monarchs built up the legend that the Shang rulers had occupied a position of primacy among the rulers of the civilized world, and then claimed the position themselves by right of succession through conquest. There was thus fostered the notion of one ruler, central and supreme.

Secondly, the Chou themselves taught the doctrine of the right of revolution. They identified their god with the Shang god instead of declaring that their god had overwhelmed the other. They asserted that this one god had been displeased by the profligacy and wickedness of the Shang and had called upon the Chou to overthrow the Shang rulers. Both these theories, refined and amplified, became fundamentals of Chinese political thought in later ages.[4]

The Chou established a system of government which left an imprint on Chinese politics for three thousand years. In relating their metropolitan administration to their occupation of the lands of North and Central China they were less successful. Lacking any other device of government, they turned to feudalism, and on the quasi-feudal foundations of the Shang they imposed a fief system. This led first to the division of China into many small feudal units and later to the appearance of powerful territorial states. The first of these periods—that in which feudalism predominated—was known as the Ch'un Ch'iu, or Spring and Autumn epoch (770–473 B. C.). The second—in which the states developed—was known as the Chan Kuo, or Warring States epoch (473–221 B. C.).

The rise of the Chou provided China with her first government on an imperial scale and with the beginnings of a theory concerning the nature of imperial government. The increasing disorganization during the Ch'un Ch'iu and Chan Kuo periods led to the development of the Confucian and other philosophies, wherein the Chinese, conscious of political shortcomings, sought the good society.

*The Ideology Called Confucian*

551 B. C. is most commonly given as the year of Confucius' birth. Confucius (K'ung Ch'iu; also Master K'ung—K'ung Fu-tzŭ, from which Confucius is derived) was a wandering scholar and would-be official whose life was spent in the advocacy of political and social reform. He was important because of his part in establishing the profession of teaching and for his doctrines upholding good government. Discontented with the present, he turned to the past—becoming conservative and aristocratic in outlook. His position in the history of political thought he owes to the bent which he gave aristocratic con-

servatism. He sought the leadership of the *chün-tzŭ* (the upright, superior, or aristocratic man) rather than the domination of laws. He developed an ethical system secular and practical in its orientation and humane in its tenets. He emphasized the necessity of the individual's appropriate self-consciousness in the society, and the need for following *li* (propriety), the established values. He stressed family loyalty above all others, and insisted on respect for tradition. After his death in 479 B. C. his ideas were elaborated, clarified, and revised into what is known as the *Confucian system*.[5]

This system underwent many changes. The Confucian influences came to prevail in the Han dynasty, in the second and first centuries B. C., but lost its official preeminence with the fall of the Han in the third century. It nevertheless retained a great share of intellectual leadership. In the Sung period (960–1279) the philosopher Chu Hsi developed Confucianism into its most recent accepted form. Others joined him in sharpening and refining Confucianism.

The Sung philosophers evolved a Confucianism which showed the influence of the Taoist and Buddhist philosophies. They reinterpreted the classics by emphasizing works other than those hitherto regarded as preeminent. With reference to the concept *li*, they developed the notion of a truly complete order running through both spirit and matter. Metaphysics, alien to the mind of Confucius himself, became an operative part of Confucian thought. Through their ethical and psychological studies the Sung Confucians translated the Confucian rationale into an effective ideological technique for domination. It is not inconsistent to find them opposing any action definitely governmental. Furthermore, they showed themselves to be conservatives in politics, and through their commentaries on the classics—which were studied in succeeding centuries along with the texts themselves—imprinted their conservatism upon the Chinese mind.

The ideology called *Confucian* is not identical with Confucianism as the philosophic system proper. In the first place, it is not known how much of the social doctrines taught by Confucius and his successors was original and how much mere transmission of preexisting beliefs. Confucius himself regarded his work as that of a transmitter and not a creator. Secondly, the whole Chinese culture contributed elements of strength to the ideology to which the name of Confucius became attached by Westerners. Thirdly, the system developed in practice to an extent which Confucius could not have anticipated. The Confucian ideology and society bear the relation to Confucius which Christendom bears to Jesus Christ; both founders would scarcely recognize the derivations to which their teachings have led.

The Confucian ideology came to prevail in China just before the day of Christ. At the time of Christ, Wang Mang, a usurper and a zealous Confucian, shook the Han Empire with his experiments. A period of reaction against Confucianism set in. Taoism and Buddhism provided rival cults. After the twelfth century, Confucianism rose slowly to power over men's minds again—although it had never been wholly superseded by other doctrines, it had long lacked its all-compelling primacy. Not until the Ming dynasty (1368-1643) did it become the state philosophy of China, the ideology whereby China lived politically and whereby she was governed.

Descriptions of Confucian China apply, therefore, with particular cogency to the past five hundred years, if account is taken of the role of Confucianism as a state philosophy. But if those elements of Chinese culture which are subsumed under the name of Confucianism are considered apart from Confucian philosophy, the time may be extended indefinitely. Confucian doctrine is one aspect of Chinese culture which has in various centuries risen to the forefront. Underneath this doctrine there are tenets, near the level of unconscious habit, which apply to almost all ages of China. It is difficult to separate the two phenomena and to distinguish between Chinese culture and its most representative philosophy. An analogy, remote but suggestive, is the influence of Aristotle in the West. Periods of Aristotelian predominance can be distinguished from the general history of Western thought, in which Aristotle plays a consistent but lesser role. As Aristotle was interpreted by Aquinas, so was Confucianism by the Sung philosophers. Aristotelian politics are far removed from the specific problems of representative or modern authoritarian government; nevertheless they possess great value and exercise an indeterminable influence upon the entire West. The analogy holds for China if left in its loosest terms. Confucianism is far from oblivion. The

China which met the Western impact—"old China" in the eyes of the twentieth century—was in fact more Confucian than was the West Aristotelian. She was permeated by an ideology in which Confucius' teachings were the key pattern, though not one which he had made up in its entirety.

*Government in the Confucian Ideology*

In Confucian China, government was reduced to a minimum. There existed a set of institutions which in many respects afforded a remarkable although misleading parallel to the governments of the West. In fact, the earliest Western visitors to China found no difficulty in applying their own political language to China. The supreme Chinese leader they called the *emperor,* despite the inevitable Caesarian connotations of the term and the fact that it erased the peculiar significance of the Chinese title. Subordinate areas were called *provinces.* All the way through, the use of European concepts compelled whole series of unwarranted parallels. The term *mandarin* forced its way into Western tongues, however, since there was no existing term to describe the members of the curious hierarchy of scholar-bureaucrats occupying a position of hegemony among the institutions of Chinese society. Unfortunately for Chinese as well as Westerners, both were so poorly informed in the beginnings of intercourse that the Chinese could not secure an adequate picture of Europe, while the Europeans assumed that the Chinese were more, rather than less, like themselves. The Chinese society, with a single supreme ritual leader, was termed an *empire,* and the predominant hierarchy of that society a *government.*

Actually, modern political scientists would have to hestitate before applying the term *government* to the hierarchy of old China. In many respects that hierarchy was more like Europe's medieval universities and our fraternal societies than the governments of the West. The prestige accruing to positions in the system was not derived so much from political power as from the status which the system offered to its members. An official, although he might value his power, was regarded in the society at large almost as much for what he was as for the dignity with which the office invested him. This arose from his peculiar role, in which his function was to provide a model of propriety in his private and public life rather than to interfere in the lives of others. Interference, to be sure, occurred—sharply, Draconically, directed more against the social group of the offender than against the offender himself, on the theory that it was the function of the group to keep its members in line with the common-sense traditions. In such rare cases the officialdom became a government—government as the institution of men who seek to control society in the name of all society. Normally the officialdom was not a government in this sense, as it claimed leadership rather than control, preached rather than punished, shamed rather than intimidated the people.

Confucius said, "If the people be led by laws, and uniformity sought to be given them by punishments, they will try to avoid the punishment, but have no sense of shame. If they be led by virtue, and uniformity sought to be given them by the rules of propriety, they will have the sense of shame, and moreover will become good."[6] In a governmental system which was avowedly Confucian, the officials were discouraged from trying to formulate rules, for such rules, if specific, could only duplicate the enactments of custom and, if general, might entangle the official in a web of words. If the officials were personally and individually worthless, there would be no hope for good government and the only remedy would consist in selecting good officials and placing them in high positions. If the officials were good, their integrity and common sense would show them the solutions to problems and they would have no need to solicit advice from some manual of commands. No lifeless paper and ink could guide a people unless there were upright officials to study the classics and put the judicious rules found in them into effect. The only safeguard against bad government was good government by good men; the only remedy for bad government was the effort of good men. The Chinese never set up an imaginary machinery and turned themselves into its cogs. To the simple, common-sense humanity of the Confucians, a government made up of rigid laws—a system having no reference to the personality or value of individuals, but embedded in a vast mechanism of numbers—would have seemed anathema and lunacy.

Government in China was an auxiliary activity, the reserve power of a hierarchy given to the pursuit of different ends. The officials were teachers first and magistrates afterward;

the emperor was a supreme model first and a ruler afterward; the people were shamed, and punished only when they were shameless. Such was the ideal theory upon which the Chinese built their world society. The facts were rarely as bright as they might have hoped; the reserve power never disappeared.

The necessity for government did not always proceed from the frailties of the governed. The Confucian system, although worthy of its great esteem, was marked by the difficulties which attend all human organization. Corruption and tyranny appeared, and were not by any means negligible. In many cases it may be supposed that a system of laws would have provided redress for individuals treated arbitrarily or unjustly; but, if one is to judge by experience in the West, even law brings with it other types of injustice peculiar to itself. In China some of the most benevolent and effective emperors advocated at times a government of rules and not of men, in order to check the caprice and the oppression of officials; yet the role of law in China, in contrast to the part it has played in the West, remained slight. The West affords instances of effective political work outside legal systems, while the Chinese have produced law codes of considerable breadth and significance. Nevertheless, the power of Chinese government aside from law is just as clear as the Western development of government within law.

The old Chinese system was based upon control through ideas, control exercised through the maintenance of clear notions of right and wrong, as founded in certain well-established commonsense traditions. The world of fact and the world of right and wrong were bound together, and the whole ideology was one of general and all-pervasive order. While the Western impact was felt cumulatively through the nineteenth century, the Chinese world of fact went down into the limbo of myth in a few disestablished generations, and with it went the compulsion which Confucian common sense had exerted.[7] The consequent development of new ways of acting, which had nothing to do with traditional control, upset the entire scheme. When the system of ideological guidance began breaking down, there was a stampede to get away from it. Men no longer trusted it, no longer trusted the tameness of their neighbors. A new wildness, a savagery armed with science, had come with the aliens from beyond the seas. It was the old hierarchy to which men turned, calling it *the state*.

As a state, as an all-embracing control institution, the old Chinese hierarchy was a pseudomorph—it looked like a state but was not really one. Now it had to develop those characteristics of regularity, impersonality, and machine effectiveness demanded of a state in the modern world. It had to restore the virtue of men by telling them how it was possible to be virtuous in a world in which all things turned and changed with the days and not with the centuries. It had to gather together the members of the old Chinese world-community, reorient them with respect to the new, divided world around them, and fight off the inroads of outsiders. Above everything else, it had to grow strong, so that it might institute order, so that it might someday grow weak again. On the other hand, if a governmental system were set up which tried to maintain the precarious supremacy that Western states have enjoyed, and which was subject to uncontrolled fluctuations in the thought of the people upon whom it rested, the Chinese might lose their character as Chinese. They might be absorbed into the Western world and become a group of yellow-skinned traditionless men, living according to the heritage of white men's laws and doomed to a perpetual inferiority because these laws were not their own. They might be aliens upon the earth, with no group to call their own. Such a nightmarish vision may have come to Sun Yat-sen when he pleaded with all his heart for the unification and defense of a China still Chinese.

The old system broke and collapsed in 1911–1912. This collapse was hastened by the fact that the imperial family was incapable of leadership. A succession of degenerates and children occupied the throne—the one intelligent emperor was imprisoned by a clique—and a fanatical old woman held enough power to keep anyone else from using it, but not enough to lead or to want to lead a revolution from above. When the old structure caved in, over four hundred million people were without effective government, and no one really knew how to create it.

## The Replacement of the Confucian Ideology

Only some of the movements which have occurred in China have had political significance. With the collapse of the old stable order, the Chinese fell into great confusion, devoting themselves to a variety of doctrines and crusades. Some of these movements may be regarded as subordinate to the day-to-day struggle for military or governmental power; others, though within the sphere of politics as far as their interests were concerned, never acquired sufficient importance to impress themselves upon the general political scene.

The only movements which need be here considered are constituent ones. It has been noted that the real basis for the stability and operation of the old Chinese society lay not in the power of an organized body of law-makers, law-enforcers, and law-interpreters but in the constitutionalism of common sense, in the deep harmony of agreement which the Confucian outlook on fact and value had created. Men were raised tame, and what tamed them was an ideology—a unified, coherent body of ideas—which related the knowledge of the world to the sphere of morals, which was applied by the intellectually dominant classes as a means of control, and which secured for the controlling classes hegemony over all groups in society.

The moment the old order weakened, it was inevitable that men would try to find substitutes which met four criteria: (1) a plausibly satisfactory explanation for the world of fact; (2) a persuasively related scheme of values (right, wrong; good, bad); (3) use of this explanation and the value scheme (both together forming an ideology) to control behavior; (4) authoritative status of the individuals promoting the ideology, whether or not organized as a group.

It will be recognized that these criteria fit the great religious movements of mankind; it is equally apparent that they lend themselves to the promotion of governance. Governing under conditions of ideological anarchy is at best a precarious effort—a makeshift, a pitiable building upon sand. The Western world faces today the same problem that the Chinese face: How are men to agree widely enough to live together in peace? But the Chinese approached this problem from an experience of deliberately fostered agreement. Confucianism had the effectiveness of the great religions and a sophistication and malleability superior, perhaps, to any of them. As a consequence, the modern Chinese were keenly aware of the necessity of the last two criteria. The problem of ideological guidance is only half solved with the presentation of a new scheme of facts and a new scheme of morals; propaganda and institutionalization remain.

Complaints are current in the West to the effect that art, science, and letters are becoming propaganda—that is, that they are being used to control men, or as attempts to control men. The Chinese of 1912 and after never had similar scruples. All human effort was propaganda, and whatever was not, was of only passing interest. There was no alternative while the Chinese tried to found a new common sense in the discredited ruins of their old world order. Their natural science had been impeached by the demonstrable superiority of Western science. Their code of ethics, whatever its aesthetic appeal, was ineffectual as a way of conduct among people who had different, more violent notions of right and wrong. Even the code of personal behavior—the elaborate courtesies, the leisureliness, the grace of life in old China—was worthless in an environment which put a high premium upon speed, impersonality, efficiency. As the Chinese turned to a revision of all aspects of their mode of life at once, different groups, trying to find some one key reform which would solve all difficulties, fell into discord. Economic advance, political reorganization, "realism" in outlook, educational reform—all these had their adherents. None was allowed, by either adherents or opponents, to stand simply as a group of separate reform measures to be considered on their own merits; the drive for a new ideology made all proposals important for their bent rather than their content. A simple thing like the desirability of using Latin letters in mass education immediately took on a vast significance when related to the *Kulturpolitik* of the time. The left-wingers once attacked the missionaries who had first tried to introduce it, on the ground that the missionaries were seeking to prostitute the Chinese mind and to make the Chinese betray the past. Later the Communists enthusiastically pushed the same scheme, stating that the Chinese ideographs were a stronghold of reactionary thought. The torments of the struggle inevitably caused the terms of conflict to resolve; gradually several more or less determinant movements emerged, around which all other reforms tended to cluster, because of sympathy or logical relationship.

*The Chief Movements in the Rebuilding of China*

Among the movements, Confucianism stands first. Even with its limpness and decadence, it still represents the greatest single intellectual force in the country. To the Chinese, this force may not even be apparent, and they take it as much for granted as the air they breathe. Nevertheless, the outside observer can see that even though Confucianism is inert as a movement, its inertia is more important than the pressures of other causes. Unconsciously, the Chinese accept whole tracts of Confucian thought. They accept, in other words, the guidance of Confucian ideology in much the same way that Americans who are not churchgoers still accept the major premises of Christianity, simply because their whole environment is charged with it. Just as in the West a universal and potent Christian revival in politics is not likely but is nevertheless conceivable, so in China it is not very probable but quite possible that there will be a successful resurrection of the orthodox Confucian philosophy. Whether a strict Confucianism could return without monarchy is doubtful; and Sun Yat-sen's blend of republicanism and Confucianism is so well established that it may prevent the successful promotion of uninterpreted Confucianism.

The Taoists and Buddhists are similarly inactive in politics. More strictly concerned with the supernatural than is Confucianism, they represent significant tangential forces upon the flow of political development, but do not express themselves in overt intervention. Among the leaders of all groups except the Communists there are important members of both sects. It is not uncommon for any of them, defeated in war or temporarily eliminated from politics, to turn to a monastery and study ancient texts, much in the way that an idle American politician goes to a farm, cultivating his health and his reputation.

Islam is a minor but living force in China. It has long prevailed in the border territories of the Northwest, and for generations has presented vital and effective opposition to the Chinese influence. The territory of the Mohammedans was consequently a hotbed of rebellion and separatism, until the ghastly religious wars of the past century drowned autonomous tendencies in an ocean of blood. At the present time the Islamic movement faces another equal to itself in ferocity and persuasiveness—Marxism—in Outer Mongolia, across the border in the U. S. S. R., and in the northwest controlled by the Chinese Red Army. Thus far Islam has given no promise of power.

Nationalism—the movement launched by Sun Yat-sen, which follows his doctrines of the *San Min Chu I*[8]—is the official movement of the National Government of China and of the Nationalist armies under Chiang K'ai-shek. It is consequently the chief power of positive action in the whole country. At various times, Sun's followers have been known as Progressives, Revolutionists, Republicans, and Nationalists—according to the phase of their program then uppermost.

Opportunism, rationalized by one or another ornamental philosophy, has been very common in modern China. It has accepted ideological materials the way they are used in superficial struggles of the West—making ideals fit the facts and using them for the sake of the facts. Opportunism has been characterized by the avid acceptance of wholly implausible doctrines, or by a disingenuous "realism." Proalien and defeatist movements have been opportunist in practical matters; "strong man" philosophies have served the causes of individual ambitions. Ideologically these currents were noteworthy only because they stirred up the mud, making genuine intellectual clarification all the more difficult.

Finally, three important movements have come from outside. These are Christianity, Marxism, and pro-Japanism.

Each sociopolitical movement in China has had economic connections. Some movements are avowedly bourgeois and capitalist and find their roots in Western tradition. Others are inspired by the challenge of the land problem, which is very acute. World production has upset Chinese farm prices; international trade has ruined many peasant craft industries; modern armies have imposed unprecedented tax burdens; opium and erosion ruin large portions of the people and the land. In some cases the chaos in the countryside can only be stilled by massacre. Despite the presence of capitalist, proletarian, and agrarian economic movements, it seems likely that economic questions will be settled by groups which do not concentrate upon them to the exclusion of all others. Meanwhile, each of the movements seeking to create a new China will have to provide for reform or replacement of the economic system, which is decrepit because of its internal decline and the appearance of economic devices from the West vastly more effective, but inconsistent with Chinese modes of existence.

*Confucianism in the Republic*

Confucianism as an official movement has been used to support other tendencies, to further the opportunist activities of particular cliques, and to bolster—by disguising—the Japanese occupation of Manchuria. It is incorrect, however, to limit the role of Confucianism in modern China to these facts. In serving as a foundation for other movements it possesses unmeasured potentialities.

Confucianism supposes that the truth and the socially desirable are identical; that both are identical with the Confucian tradition; and that an elite of scholars is required to propagate truth, clothing it with the language of tradition and morality. Confucianism is hostile to the very notion of sovereignty, leaves no room for a system of permanently separate nations, and is unable to accommodate the Western idea of an accidental growth in knowledge, dependent upon sporadic individual initiative. Confucianism is strong in so far as it promotes a society based upon knowledge, in which individuals can ascend or descend according to their personal virtue and competence. Such an ideal has a definite end in the physical universe by working toward a human immortality of the flesh and the spirit—flesh through the perpetuation of the family name in the male line, spirit through the transmission of records and knowledge. Its present-day defects are obvious. The world of fact in the Confucian ideology does not correspond with the beliefs accepted as fact by the dominant West. The intellectual insulation against the outside necessary to ideological control could not be achieved by any single modern nation without the use of tyranny. Moreover, Confucian ethics and politics, more than twenty-four centuries old, can scarcely be expected to conform to the changed minutiae of human life, dominated by technology. Nevertheless, while the Chinese may not turn again to the classics for guidance in concrete situations, or consult ancient authorities for solutions to simple practical problems, the moral and social doctrines of Confucianism, redefined or modified, could well play a definite role in the modern world. In China the chief rivals to Confucianism will be the new heterodox schools of reinterpreted Confucianism—such as the versions posed by Sun Yat-sen and Chiang K'ai-shek, or the watery Confucianism of Manchoukuo.

The nonformal unorganized power of Confucianism weighs more heavily. If Confucianism were to be considered alone on the strength of the movements featuring the password "Back to Confucius!" it would be so negligible as to merit no attention. Not the strength of its partisans but the concessions of its opponents and rivals make Confucianism important. Confucius can no more be eradicated from modern China than Plato, Aristotle, and Christ from the background of Western society. Every Chinese movement, starting with Confucianism as the status quo, will have to incorporate a large part of the traditional doctrines. It may well be that in the new breeds of thought the Confucian strain will prove dominant and most lasting.

Until the breakdown of the Empire, Confucian texts were studied appreciatively rather than critically. One does not criticize common sense unless one is anxious for the reputation of a crank. With the blinding dawn of Western knowledge, Confucianism went into the wastebasket. Two years in New York were worth a generation of study over the ancient authorities. From time to time, under the Republic, the various governments discussed plans for educational reform, or haphazardly encouraged the dying traditionalist schools; but nothing could restore the prestige of classicism. Strangely, the greatest impetus toward classical learning was provided by the challengers of the classics. Modern Chinese scholarship, using Western methods of critical study, and armed with new specializations undreamed of by the archaists, found that the traditional authorities were valuable not only for what they pretended to be—plain, direct, factual records—but also as source material for penetrating interpretations.

The Chinese have turned to this task since the opening of the various scientific agencies of the National Government at

Nanking and have already produced works of importance on their own past. They have pushed back their scientifically ascertainable history almost a thousand years. The modern Chinese students, who hated the classics when they were mouthed by sedate old scholars ignorant of the modern world, now devote themselves to the classics to criticize them; criticizing them, they study them; studying them, they love them. The "science of the country" (Sinology) has recently been added to the curriculum of the modern schools; it is causing a veritable renaissance. In fact, the Chinese are constantly becoming more anxious to find precedent for political growth and development in their own past rather than in the past of the West, which they could never appreciate as much as do Westerners.

The actual Confucian movements do not warrant attention. Militarists have sponsored little Confucian coteries, or have paid for the publication of sumptuous editions of the Confucian classics, with the expectation of acquiring a reputation for benevolence and intelligence. Wu P'ei-fu, the most accomplished scholar among the military leaders of his period, who owed part of his prestige to his scholarship, was diligent in promoting Confucianism. With his decline (1926) his example was no longer felt to be worth following; Confucianism as a practical political expedient passed from the scene. It gave too little sanction to the raising of local conscript armies, inflation of the currency, and the doubling of taxes. Its complete silence on such necessities could not be taken for consent.

In the Japanese-occupied territory in Manchuria, however, an interesting experiment in Confucianism has been made. The customs and organization of the last Chinese dynasty have been resurrected, touched up by a few classical scholars, given a somewhat more orthodox and unrealistic air, and proclaimed as the constitution of the Great Empire of Manchou (Manchoukuo). Since the effective government of the country is under strong Japanese influence, the venture is significant only as a political narcotic. The laws proclaimed are in Chinese; the officials' names are Chinese; the miranda of government, whatever the fact, are consistent with the grand traditions of Chinese history. The Japanese might have placed a handful of dreaming reactionaries in actual power and helped the growth of an anachronistic Chinese Empire in the northeast, but they seem to have spoiled their opportunity of creating a friendly and subservient state by acting too arbitrarily and making it impossible for the Confucian experiment to work.

Confucianism in modern China owes its position not so much to its prospects as to the fact that it has provided a frame of reference, however obsolescent, for the political struggle. Hence, through the tumultuous modern period, the Chinese have been strengthened by a philosophy which emphasized the separateness and stability of each institution in society, and which did not make them lose all with the fortunes of a single supreme organization. As a positive political force, Confucianism has done two things: It has kept the Chinese from depending too much on political control, and it has provided a rationale in the contest for power. It accomplished the first by making police a function of society as a whole, by stressing the appropriateness of behavior rather than its legality; and it has given the Chinese ethical values despite their sorry political condition. Confucianism has rationalized struggle by supplying each individual participant with a code to apply if he came to power, and by giving him a good pretense for seeking power. Confucius himself lived in a time when Chinese political organization was chaotic. He noted the need for righteous men in high places and pointed out the good which could be done, apart from general reform, by the furtherance of virtue through scattered efforts. Confucius supplied the ambitious men of his own time with a reason for aspiring to power—by making political responsibility a duty for the man of intelligence. The Confucian scholar was no saint contemplating eternity; he was a proud, correct, self-righteous, patient individual, obliged by his training to take public office wherein his talent could gain wide influence.

In modern China, the seekers of political office have been able to avoid the appearance of abject venality by professing respectability. Even though they may have been just as corrupt as the politicians of other nations, and more efficiently so, they nevertheless had the saving grace to eschew hard realism and cloak their ambition with a pleasantly virtuous tradition. A military leader could surround himself with a few scholars and give his efforts to reach power the air of a mild and well-mannered crusade. Whenever political strife in China has had no meaning but vanity and greed it has at least worn the decent cloak of the Confucian tradition.

NOTES

1. For a good general introduction to Far Eastern history and politics see G. Nye Steiger, *A History of the Far East*, Boston, 1936, the most complete of one-volume works; Harold M. Vinacke, *A History of the Far East in Modern Times*, New York, 1937, especially good for social, economic, and governmental developments; René Grousset, *Histoire de l'Extrême Orient*, Paris, 1929; and Richard Wilhelm, *Ostasien*, Potsdam and Zurich, 1928, a brilliant short outline. Diplomatic history is dealt with by H. B. Morse and H. F. MacNair, *Far Eastern International Relations*, Boston, 1931, the most detailed one-volume work; Paul H. Clyde, *A History of the Modern and Contemporary Far East*, New York, 1937, the most recent; and Payson J. Treat, *The Far East*, New York, 1935. The most useful one-volume history of China is Kenneth Scott Latourette, *The Chinese: Their History and Culture*, New York, 1934. All these works carry bibliographies; those of Steiger and Latourette are particularly informing.
2. Herrlee Glessner Creel, *Studies in Early Chinese Culture, First Series*, p. 254, Baltimore, 1937. Quoted by permission of the author.
3. H. G. Creel, *The Birth of China*, London, 1936, provides a brilliant popular account of the earliest known Chinese culture.
4. Creel, *Studies*, pp. 50 ff. For relevant information the writer is indebted to Professor H. H. Dubs, Duke University.
5. On Confucianism and its immediate background see Marcel Granet, *Chinese Civilization*, New York, 1930; Fung Yu-lan (Derk Bodde, translator), *A History of Chinese Philosophy: The Period of the Philosophers*, Peiping, 1937, an authoritative work; Liang Chi-chao, *A History of Chinese Political Thought*, New York, 1930; and Leonard Shihlien Hsü, *The Political Philosophy of Confucianism*, New York, 1932, brilliant but open to criticism. For a popular portrait of Confucius see Carl Crow, *Master Kung*, New York, 1938.
6. *Confucian Analects*, Book II, Chapter III.
7. For its loss of political support see below, pp. 34 ff.
8. See below, pp. 41 ff.

*Chapter* II

THE RISE OF NATIONALISM

Of the constituent movements of modern China, the most important has focused on the personality, principles, and following of Sun Yat-sen (1867–1925). Now known primarily as the Nationalist movement, it has at various times emphasized different aspects of its program. In its simplest and most fundamental points, the movement has fallen heir to early patriotism. It has assumed different names: the Society for the Regeneration of China (1894–1905), or *Hsing Chung Hui;* the League of Common Alliance (1905–1912), or *T'ung Mêng Hui;* the Nationalist Democratic Party or National People's Party (1912–1914), or *Kuomintang;* the *Chung Hua Kê Ming Tang* (1914–1920), or Chinese Revolutionary Party; and since 1920, again the *Kuomintang.* Kuomintang is the combination of three Chinese words meaning "country" or "realm," "people," and "party." The name of the party can be translated in innumerable ways: nationalist democratic, nationalist popular, national people's party, etc. The commonest rendering is "Nationalist," but it is to be remembered that the word "people" figures in the name. Furthermore, the Chinese version of patriotism has more cosmopolitan and fewer restrictive connotations than patriotism ever had in the West.

*Nationalism: Patriotic Anti-Manchu Phase*

Even in a world society that knew neither state nor nation the Chinese felt attached to their homes and their native land, which led them to repel invaders. They never personified this loyalty or tried to express it in specific institutions; nor did they admit outsiders to equality and concede that there was more of the civilized world outside, thus admitting the existence of nations. Their attitude rested on sentiment rather than theory. There was no elaborate bolstering of Chinese racial superiority, for—by and large—all the peoples in China, conquerors or conquered, seemed racially alike, fused under the pressure of great social homogeneity.

At the time of the Manchu conquest (about 1644) the Chinese developed a passionate hatred for the invaders from the northeast. In entrenching themselves the Manchus committed a fateful blunder which was to bring momentary strength but ultimate ruin: they enforced racial segregation in the political, social, and economic sphere. Legend has it that a Chinese statesman, forced into Manchu service, suggested this plan and thus laid the cornerstone for the eventual Chinese liberation. The Manchus prohibited miscegenation; they established Manchu garrisons throughout the Empire, keeping their troops from work (which might have led to intermingling with the Chinese) and thus ruining them by sloth. A fixed quota of Manchus was introduced into the government service, irrespective of the operation of the examination system. In time the Chinese scholars submitted willingly enough to the alien rule; two of the Manchu emperors were the most enlightened patrons which Chinese letters and arts had had in centuries, and the intellectual opposition dwindled away to a minimum.

Among the populace there was no such general reconciliation. Deprived for the first time of scholarly leadership, the common people, peasants and artisans, organized numerous secret societies. The societies flourished, coming to supersede the government in whole areas and marking many decades with insurrection and riot. Scholars fought the secret societies because of their uncouth rituals, their heterodoxy of ideas, their opposition to the existing system. The societies answered by building up political agencies which were able to act on the lower and more generally understood levels of ideology.

These groups kept patriotism afire. The greatest of their uprisings, the T'ai-p'ing rebellion of 1849–1865, was put down with the assistance of the Western Christian states, but it left a permanent mark on Chinese society. The rebels had shown that it was possible to wrest the greater part of China from Manchu rule. They were the first to welcome the invasion of Christianity, adopting a fantastically modified Christian faith. They awakened the Chinese to the immediate possibility of a war of liberation against the outsiders who held the throne of the Chinese world.

The T'ai-p'ing rebellion showed its strength as a patriotic movement. It was successful in shaking the established ideology with a rival compounded of the more vulgar parts of the old, combined with Christianity. And it indicated the weakest point of the dynasty—governmental inadequacy in dealing with the agrarian problem. The years of formal stability gave China a much increased population; the same years were years of political decline which raised the cost of government. A house-cleaning was in order. The T'ai-p'ing demonstrated the need for it; the Manchu dynasty refused to yield to the demand.

Sun Yat-sen was born in 1866 or 1867. An uncle of his had been one of the rebels. At Sun's parental home the countryside had known of the T'ai-p'ing rebellion; many in his native village had participated in it. He was as patriotic as any Chinese could be in the far south, where the Manchu conquest had penetrated least deeply, but his patriotism did not differ from the patriotism of his neighbors until he came to know life outside China. From the patriotism of the old Chinese realm to the nationalism required of China in the new Westernized world—this was a step to be traversed only by rich personal experience.

Sun took this step as a boy, when he went to Honolulu. He soon was converted to Christianity, learned English, and became acquainted with Western life. He was able to see the world in terms of nations, and he saw that from the Western point of view China was a large but weak nation. Already committed from childhood to the revolutionary cause, he was led by his knowledge of the West to change patriotism into nationalism. When he returned to China, after studying medicine in Hongkong, he arrived with the notion of transforming the old world community into an effective modern nation-state.

He did not seem at first to realize how necessary it was to dispose of the monarchy. For a while he petitioned the authorities, trusting that immediate reforms might be effected within the existing framework, pending an ultimate revolution of patriots. His success must be measured in terms of what he and his few fellow workers learned, rather than of what they accomplished. His technique of revolution was based upon the established traditions of Chinese history—the formation of a small nucleus, the gathering of affiliated groups, the permeation of a regional bureaucracy when possible, and the launching of terroristic attacks to shake the apparent stability of the government.

At the beginning of his work he came into contact with the secret groups. When he started organizing in earnest, the first major development was the admittance en bloc of a small secret society. In an unpublished autobiography Sun wrote: "After my graduation I practised medicine in Canton and Macao as a pretext for spreading my revolutionary ideas."[1]

*Nationalism: Revolutionary Modernist Phase*

The Sino-Japanese War of 1894-1895 was the cause of much disturbance in China and the first major event to shake the belief of the masses in their own ideology. Fantastic barbarians with deadly contrivances might harry the coasts and even allow themselves impertinences with the dynasty, but the situation became different when a small, inoffensive, ineffectual neighbor nation took over these same weapons and spoiled the internal arrangements of the Far Eastern universe. The peripheral countries could perhaps even demolish the central suzerainty; this was the *mene-tekel* of the Empire.

The revolutionary organization of Sun Yat-sen had by now become definitely modernist, nationalist, and antimonarchical, instead of merely patriotic and antidynastic. Under the name of *Hsing Chung Hui* there was established a confederacy of secret societies. After a short while the member societies were liquidated, and a modern revolutionary organization emerged, advocating overthrow of the Manchus. The intellectual elite of this group had no part in the ideological control which gripped the rest of China, in the form of the traditional mandarinate. As a new elite, with a new ideology, it broke the monopoly of leadership, the monopoly of thought. The consequences cannot be exaggerated. It was symptomatic that Sun's own family became estranged in part and that many members of the society had to die a civil death before working in the organization. They left their property to heirs and changed their names, lest—under the principle of group responsibility—terrible punishments be visited upon their native villages and their families. Furthermore, an important bloc of participants consisted of Chinese from overseas.

The Chinese overseas were for the most part men who had been kidnaped and sold in the coolie trade or who had stealthily deserted their native regions for adventure and wealth. With the increased foreign commerce it was possible for many Chinese to become wealthier outside their own country than within. But in leaving they left their custom and tradition and met peoples—especially Europeans and Americans—whose way of life, though utterly different, was effective in the practical, tangible terms of wealth and security. Chinese in increasing numbers bettered their condition outside. They did not amass wealth through family effort, nor did they broaden their learning through the classics. What they won, they won themselves; and they learned something for which the Confucian ideology had no place. When they returned home, they were greeted with contempt, though also with covert admiration. Those among them who had gathered knowledge of the West, of modern methods of business, of European languages, found that in the eyes of the traditional literati and officials they were lower than the lowest illiterates.

Such men came in great numbers to the revolutionary party. Among overseas Chinese merchants, workers, and students, there developed a group—possessing power in the form of money and family connections—which was determined to overthrow the existing order and bring China in line with the outside world. Their effort was idealistic, because the Chinese overseas felt that the economic and cultural advantages of the West should be secured for their countrymen at home; it was also realistic, since they were fighting in the only way they knew for a respectable, honorable return to their homes. They could not throw their lives away and admit that their ventures and dangers were of no profit. They felt that they had acquired something, and they wanted it recognized. It was Sun Yat-sen who showed them how they could do it.

In a sense, this feature of the Nationalist movement might be taken as the pivot of modern Chinese government and politics. Controlling men through controlling their minds and through making sure that every possible leader would lead from within the hierarchy—these devices of the past had failed. There were now Chinese to whom the Confucian rules were pleasant and homelike but not the real material of modern life. These Chinese possessed intellectually trained leaders who had nothing in common with the dominant elite—who were more interested in building railroads, improving water supplies, defending China's frontiers, and modernizing the country than in augmenting the virtue of mankind.

*Nationalism: Republican Phase*

Every year brought the Nationalists increased strength. The Manchu court yielded a series of constitutional reforms which by their promises disturbed the minds of those still content with the old order and by their nonfulfillment raised fresh storms of resentment against the Manchu rule. The court did not really seek to master the drift in the thought of the people; it tried to defeat change rather than direct it.[2] In a few short years before and after 1900 the Dragon Throne declined from the supreme office of mankind to an obsolete and picturesque ornament of a government so weak and disorganized as to render ornament artificial. While the Empire lost prestige, the Nationalists came to emphasize the republican part of their program more and more. As Nationalists, they differed little from the generations of patriots who had fought the alien rulers of China. As republicans, they were the Chinese vanguard of modernization. Some people accepted republican ideas as good in themselves; far more thought them better than the Manchu rule, especially since there was no Chinese pretender in sight—the heir of the Mings, the last native dynasty, was a pensioner in Peking. A large number probably thought little about the abstract issue one way or another but trusted the revolutionary leaders because they seemed to have a competence consonant with the times.

As the Nationalists advanced, they reorganized their party mechanism, and formed the T'ung Mêng Hui in 1905. At this time the principles which were later to become the *San Min Chu I*[3] were given public formulation. The Nationalists began to feel the necessity of an ideology with which to replace that of the Confucian monarchy. It had been possible to leave doubt unsettled so long as they were a small, conspiratorial group. As soon as they began to secure adherents among the masses it became necessary to provide their followers with a common set of ideas. In seeking agreement on fundamentals, they found disagreements within the party. Sun Yat-sen's role began to change from conspiracy to statesmanship. The future was to show that even a statesman was not enough—that a lawgiver, a state founder, was needed.

The T'ung Mêng Hui was one of the most effective revolutionary organizations which the modern world has seen, so far as achievement of immediate aims was concerned. In a series of activities which would rouse a mystery-story addict to startled incredulity, the revolutionaries tried to awaken the populace by spectacular revolts. They capitalized on the impotence of a government alien to China, one so ineffectual that it could not protect the Chinese from the other, newer aliens who had appeared. They realized that it was hopeless to attack the monarchy along its entire front, since the old ideological guidance, although waning, still held the broad masses in inertia. The revolutionaries accordingly attacked the Empire at its top level, its most obvious and conspicuous points of strength—the military and political headquarters of the viceroyalties and other significant positions. Knowing that they themselves could not monopolize the government of China, they looked forward to attaining a position of leadership among the various groups in the Chinese society and to keeping that leadership through parliamentary methods to be established under the Republic. Instead of regarding the Empire as a set of institutions, they considered it the mere decoration of the country. They had no reason to suppose, nor any way of telling, that in destroying the old regime they destroyed government and all possibility of government for a long time to come. They consequently tried to set in motion a snowball revolution—an initial conspiracy of terror which would intimidate the Manchus and cause the whole house of cards to collapse. It was their task only to start the movement, which could be counted upon to avalanche itself into history.

To the revolutionary group a republican scheme seemed possible. They felt that in the twentieth century men would disagree but amicably, and they regarded democracy as a form of government so excellent that its mere inauguration would guarantee success. Furthermore, republicanism and democracy were closely associated with nationalism; how could a nation be free unless it governed itself in the most direct manner—through the votes of its broad majorities?

In failing to provide a stopping point for the revolution before they started it, the Nationalists were scarcely guilty of rash action. No human being could have foretold the consequences of revolt against a civilization. The revolutionaries were men who had passed through the transition from the old Confucian ideology to that of the West with relative ease. They did not realize that what was obvious to them would be a mystery to the masses and that the political changes contemplated would rip asunder the very fabric of thought in China. It is evidence of the simplicity and usefulness of Confucian ideas that—even when admitted to be challenged by the new environment—they continued to operate without the sanction of intelligence, and operated well as empty habits.

With the old patriotic forces behind them, and an untested Utopia ahead, the Nationalists raced the Manchu Empire into revolution. The story of the revolution is not complex.[4] In a great part of China the people awoke to find no government. In the North the imperial officials and princes clamored for the assistance of a man whom they had once slighted: Yüan Shih-k'ai, the leader of the modernized armies of the Empire. He held the fate of China in his hands. But he betrayed the Empire so that he might betray the Republic; he joined the revolutionaries and thrust a settlement upon the ruling house. With his intervention the whole picture of Chinese politics changed. Yüan brought troops into the play of power, troops dependent upon himself, men no longer interested in ideas now that the all-compelling force of the old way of thought was gone.

*Nationalism: Constitutionalist Phase*

The Republic at Nanking enjoyed a brief Utopian existence, with Sun Yat-sen as its president. The revolutionaries were independent from October, 1911, to March, 1912, when the Republic became the instrument of Yüan Shih-k'ai. No substantial power accrued to the legislative.

During their bright heyday of power as a parliamentary party under the Republic—which they had founded only to give it away to the military—the Nationalists were known as the *Kuomintang*. At this time the Chinese name of the party was significantly translated "Democratic Party." Sun Yat-sen and the revolutionaries had expected that the Chinese people would accept the new ideology without understanding it and then would come to understand it very quickly. They could not hope to replace the old ideology before the revolution, because the presence of the imperial government made large-scale educational work impossible. After the establishment of the Republic, however, they found themselves hamstrung because they had not inculcated republicanism. It was a vicious circle. The governmental pattern set up at Nanking was replaced by another to make room for Yüan Shih-k'ai, who proposed a third, in which he should have more power, in order that he might create a fourth government, in which he should be emperor.[5] The armies of the revolutionaries, such as they were, became absorbed in the forces of Yüan. When, in a few months, the Republic had been won and lost, the Nationalists realized that the revolution of 1911–1912 was only the first step in their labors. They experimented with a minor revolution in 1913, and then turned to other measures for securing a return to constitutional government and the creation of a republic which should be as firmly rooted in men's minds as the majestic but irretrievable Confucian order had been. They had won the revolution by creating doubt and giving it tangible expression; they lost their revolution because doubt persisted, swallowed everything, leaving China in a turmoil beyond all systematic thought.

The first years of the nominal Republic, the beginning of the new order in China, were marked by a feverish pretense of changed forms. The outlook which superseded the ancient ideology was curious. It was a mixture of traditionalist acceptance of temporary disorder and resignation to a period of transformation into an unconceived and unproclaimed future. This outlook gave life no purpose, but it kept men from falling into complete anarchy. People were willing to accept illegal authorities, since local administrators had traditionally maintained a spotty cloak of public order. Modern Chinese were prepared to pay lip service to a preposterous parliamentary regime but soon found that it was comfortable to think in terms such as armies, foreign interference, and money—thus allowing their thinking to settle in the large framework of an accepted disorder.

The Nationalists tried to combat this anticonstitutional way of thought. For six years (1914–1920) they combined conspiratorial techniques with the role of a legally constituted power fighting for law. They assumed the name *Chinese Revolutionary Party* until they discovered that they could secure no ideological foothold upon which to base the order they proposed. Some of them went so far as to become anarchists, favoring a continuance of disorder until the world joined China in collapse. Others followed an unrealistic legalism; they held to the paper constitution, to the text of the president's oath of allegiance to the constitution, to the election laws, thinking that the magic of ink would conjure up a government. Sun Yat-sen, and the body of his followers with him, attempted to chart a middle course; in 1917 there was created a "lawful" administration in the South. With extraordinary good fortune the Republic might have succeeded, but the war in Europe, the Japanese interventions, and other adverse circumstances prevented this.

The Nationalists changed the name of their party back to *Kuomintang* after 1920 but did not discontinue their reformist policies until about two years later. Sun Yat-sen had spent years in study and propaganda; eventually his program became an ideology. No sharp line can be drawn between the two. In some respects the very first programs of the revolutionaries were ideological, in that they presupposed a change in man's outlook which would accommodate republican government. On the other hand, programmatic proposals may be distinguished from ideological theses by the fact that programs refer to things which should be done and ideologies to things in which men should believe in order to do anything at all. A program which is rooted in no ideology is one lacking context; unless a program refers to some accepted scheme of thought it is words in a vacuum. Similarly, an ideology without programs to put it into men's minds, to persuade men to believe in it and give it effect, is an airy prettiness for philosophers. The Nationalists had stood on the foundations of Confucian common sense and proposed a republic; they had destroyed the organization which made that common sense seem real and had cut the ground from under their own feet. They could not distinguish values because their critical attitude enveloped all moral notions or made them isolated points without coherent significance. The Nationalists themselves fell prey to day-dreaming when they appealed to worthless paper for their right to govern. The epoch is significant in the history of the movement in that it taught the Nationalists that men would not fight unless there was something to fight for and that there was nothing to fight for until men could find desirable elements embedded in some larger scheme of life. Politics had to have an end and an environment; without either it was a series of monologues in the wilderness, the soliloquies of logicians.

Sun Yat-sen during this time wrote the drafts of monumental treatises which were to relate the general body of his doctrines to the background of fact and thought from which they had emerged. He never finished them, but meanwhile he and his followers realized that if they were to have a grip over government they must grasp power within the brains of men. The revolutionary reformists had to supply some better medium of persuasion than the frivolity of military cynicism or the impudence of shadow government. They had to abandon legalism and bring forth an ideology capable of serving as the new foundation for a just and effective system of government in China. If their original importance was that of an effective counter-elite springing up in the intellectual borderlands between the Western and Chinese ideologies, their second period of significance begins with their realization that a new framework of thought would have to be set up before any of their programs could be effectuated.

*The Political Doctrines of Sun Yat-sen*

The ideology which the Nationalists were to teach was one which had lain dormant in the party for more than thirty years. It was the invention of Sun Yat-sen—his reinterpretation of Confucianism to suit the modern world. He did not settle down with books before him, pen in hand and notebooks all about, to formulate a Utopia; nor did he approach the subject as a historian, seeking scientific causes for the emotions and loyalties of men. He came to the subject as a political leader, modifying the given background only so far as was necessary. His doctrines grew with his personal growth and the development of his movement. They are scattered among a variety of writings and utterances, and are contradictory in many points although remarkably consistent as a whole.

Sun Yat-sen asked himself: What is China? China is a race, he said, a race which was once great and which held benevolent world leadership in the world it knew. It has declined because it has fallen upon evil days, under the rule of outsiders, barbarians, and has failed to develop in ways which the West discovered. This race should be a nation in the modern world; a great, powerful, united, effective nation in a world of nations. It should fight for its right of self-rule and should support justice in the international community. In order to achieve greatness, the Chinese will have to turn their nation into an effective state and add the devices of law to the devices of social control through ideology. They should rethink their ideology, keeping the old ethical philosophy and the old social knowledge (the technique of control through thought, as in Confucianism) but adding Western technics. They should then strive to make their nation the leader in progress toward world peace and eventual cosmopolitanism. China should turn to nationalism for the time—decades or centuries—that remained for the travail of nations, but the Chinese should never forget the world society whence they came. This is the first of Sun's three principles, *nationalism*.

The second principle referred to the problem of leadership and the organization of government. Obviously, the Chinese could not return to monarchy in the modern world. In the first place, it would not be modern; Sun lived at a time when the democratic tide was sweeping to its high point and when the world triumph of democracy seemed a foregone conclusion. Secondly, Sun thought it disloyal to China's past for the Chinese to evade the responsibility of democracy, as it was implicit in their most ancient traditions and thus an obligation laid upon them by their first great leaders. Thirdly, he thought that good administration was to be derived from democracy more readily than from any other system. Fourthly, because democracy was a modernizing force, it should be introduced; the people, participating in progress, would themselves become progressive. Fifthly and most necessarily, democracy was simply the self-control of a nation. If the nation was to be created and made free through nationalism it had to become democratic, since there was no other way for a whole people to express and rule itself. But the Chinese needed specific devices[6] in order to assure that the old system of selecting an intellectual leadership would not be compromised or destroyed by democracy. They should see to it that democracy did not become mob rule. The Chinese people should become self-indoctrinating and thus maintain ideological control along with political. But the Chinese should accommodate the concept of the state in their thinking, since the concentration of power in Western states made it necessary that there be in China an equivalent social device for canalizing and concentrating power, in order to meet Western and Japanese attacks. The egalitarian features of democracy should be congenial to the democracy of customs and manners which was indigenous to old China. This was the second principle, *democracy*.

The third principle was the restatement in modern political terms of the cardinal economic principles of the past, together with an infusion of newly invented doctrines. It protected the livelihood of the people, and may be summed up in a single sentence: No government deserves to exist unless it assures its people of the maximum of material welfare possible under prevailing physical conditions. Government was of no use if the people perished. The state was nothing if its substance was lost. Political leadership should aim at constant improvement of economic conditions, spread economic benefits, and make the nation healthy. In doing so it was not to be bound by any creed of capitalism or communism but was to experiment and seek the most efficient measures for the benefit of the whole community. This last principle involved the *life* of the nation, as nationalism did its *birth* and democracy its *freedom*. It was an ethical doctrine rather than a schematic principle, and cannot be properly translated. It should best be left in the Chinese, and expressed by two words which mean "people" and "generation": *min shêng*.

This ideology gave the Nationalists a faith to propagate. It was designed to achieve the revision of the old Confucian ideology; experience and the accepted ideology would supply this new skeleton with flesh. It differed radically from the Marxian doctrine in that it was traditionalistic and nationalistic; it resembled the Marxian doctrine in that it sought to create a whole new intellectual civilization before turning to the question of government.

The new ideology had to make headway against other propagandas, the partially adequate ways of thought which had grown up since the establishment of the Republic. It had to restore life to the vast corpse of Confucianism, and soon after its first general promulgation (1924) had to fight its temporary ally—communism—for power over Chinese minds.

*Opportunist Movements and their Anticonstitutional Effects*

The field which the Nationalists invaded to propagate their doctrines was already occupied. The slow evaporation of the Confucian moral, intellectual, and social system had given rise to various movements which, for lack of a better term, may be called *half-ideological*. These movements made no pretense of presenting a new order sufficient for Chinese thought and belief, but—in the opinion of those constituting them—they did afford an adequate frame of reference for immediate action. Some of the half-ideologies were: (1) military feudalism, (2) provincial *tuchünism* (3) China-wide militarism, (4) bureaucratism, and (5) capitalism. Although none of them succeeded in indoctrinating broad masses of the population, yet each was effective in a negative way. Each obstructed the development of any coherent system of social and political life. Each was anticonstitutional, since it proposed to constitute a scheme narrowly pragmatic or unattainable in fact.

The presence of these movements gave China an appearance of considerable freedom in the earlier years of the Republican era. Diversity of opinion based upon a fundamental concord in outlook—diversity circumscribed by one cohesive ideology—may be most wholesome in social and political life. When diversity penetrates so deep as to include all major aspects of human existence, it becomes insupportable, a hindrance and not a stimulant to action. When policy is predetermined by tradition, thought is easy, action relatively more difficult; when there is discord even on fundamentals, thought is difficult, action easy. Almost any scheme mitigating the evils of discord will be assured a hearing; if the world cannot be rationalized, the individual will be.

Yüan Shih-k'ai inaugurated, in his efforts to control China through military means, a way of thought which might be characterized as military feudalism of the twentieth century variety, an order based upon contract between commander and soldier, upon the payment of wages by the former and the performance of any task by the latter. This militarism never flowered in literature, never developed a political theory, never achieved governmental form. Even Yüan felt its inadequacy as a state philosophy, and by his attempt to establish a modern monarchy ruined what chances he might have had for anticipating Mussolini with a Fascist movement. As it was, the movement of military thought was derived from the facts rather than propagated to excuse the facts. The militarists themselves abandoned it whenever they found substitutes.

Nevertheless, the movement for a military ideology was at times the prevailing mode of thought among the men who held power in China. They were able to gain perspective on their own behavior by reference to the old traditions, regarding themselves as upright magistrates in a time of chaos. For working purposes they could claim from their subordinates and superiors a vague constitutionalism limited to army circles. Amid the cowardice, betrayal, and corruption in the military dictatorships, tendencies occasionally appeared leading toward an effective military spirit. Certain kinds of betrayal or cruelty were beyond the limits of good soldiering, but not many.

A more effective explanation for the condition of the armies in China from 1916 to about 1931 may be found in *tuchünism.* A *tuchün* was a military commandant ruling an area ranging from a few districts to a number of provinces.[7] The imperial regime maintained a military counterpart to the provincial governor. After the Republican Revolution provinces tended to become separate and autonomous under military leaders. The military man, who was prone to apologize for his position by admitting that he was not developing a permanent establishment, who held his troops together by a modern feudalism, could also rationalize his role by presenting himself to his province as a good son, by stressing the wickedness and strangeness of the soldiers in other provinces, and by suggesting the thought of federalism. The scheme was not convincing or edifying, but it could become temporarily popular. A great part of the news from China is still written in terms of *tuchünism*—since it is a simple pattern and requires no explanation involving Chinese peculiarities. Satrapies have become tyrannies in all ages. At the very best the *tuchünist* movement could not have served well as the constituent force of a new China. It would necessarily have ended in one-man government, almost unthinkable with modern Chinese conditions; or it would have implied a military federalism which is scarcely a solution to the problem of unity.

Military cliques at times had China-wide proportions, but despite the proclamations which were occasionally issued, there was no effective single movement for a general military regime. Such movements as there were developed within the framework of the shadow Republic. Moreover, the shifting alignments of Chinese wars within the nominal organization of the Republic were so confused as to make almost anything but order seem possible. Yet many Chinese thought in terms of a "realism" compounded of slogans and military exigencies.

If movements for military feudalism, provincial *tuchünism*, and (most nebulous of all) China-wide militarism failed to provide more than an explanation of immediate fact, there were counterparts in the civilian administration aspiring to political autonomy for particular cliques. Ministries tended at times to develop a spirit of independence. Finance was too close to the military, but the revenue collection services (with a large European and Japanese personnel) and the postal services behaved as *imperia in imperio*. The foreign office functioned frequently without effective superiors. Working without pay a great part of the time, in a period which offered no near solution for its disastrous troubles, bureaucrats saw in the increase of bureaucracy a possible inauguration of order. The ministries did function in a way, despite the chaos about them. They might have evolved a new bureaucratism to steal the *tuchüns'* power. Their spirit was helpful in particular and damaging in general, since it was bound to sabotage any government which might come to power. A few years of insecurity may weld a bureaucracy together more closely than would decades of spoils; this was the case between 1916 and 1928. Bureaucratism demonstrates the limitations of opportunist ideology as a foundation for government.

Capitalism flourished wherever economic conditions made it possible; such economic conditions did not last very long under the jurisdiction of the military. In treaty ports[3] the Chinese capitalists prospered, secure under governments which were international in effect, Chinese only in legal fiction. There Chinese soon amassed enough capital to compete with economic institutions erected by foreigners, and exercised an important indirect influence on the growth of Chinese government. Capitalism helped to thwart a peasant-labor alliance in China, for although the capitalists were an insignificant minority without country-wide influence, its form of control was mobile. No army, no surge of popular resentment, no propaganda, no conspirator can travel as fast as a telegraphic money order. The ideology of capitalism was content in China to remain subordinate as long as the political and legal conditions were favorable to it. Capitalist groups supported any sort of strong government which might protect property and increase opportunities for investment.

Among the most pitiful of the movements for the construction of a general agreement in China were the proalien movements. They were pitiful because they represented a prostitution of thought by men conscious of the nature of their action. The Anfu Party flourished in the first decade after the death of Yüan in 1916; together with its militarism and its meaningless "realism" it was pro-Japanese. The present "government" in North China[9] is another such movement. Manchoukuo bases little of her official ideology on such a dangerous outlook and prefers to propagate a Confucianist traditionalism in so far as she propagates anything. Pro-Japanese action may express a discontent with the competence of the Chinese for self-government, but more forcefully it relates to theories of Pan-Asianism or Pan-Mongolism.

The opportunist movements—militarism, *tuchünism*, military federalism, bureaucratic separatism, capitalism, and political puppetry—served to confuse the basic alternatives. Because they reflected a narrow and accidental scheme of power rather than long-range transformation, they possessed a specious realism which obfuscated real issues. They distracted attention without rewarding it and polarized opinion around conflicts which were beyond settlement. There is no possibility of agreement between men who think one another deluded in regard to fundamentals. Disorder in China was the more violent because of these different explanations. They delayed the creation of a framework in which men could find a common reasonableness, an ideology sufficient to rationalize all interests and to sublimate all frustrations.

## Christianity as a Political Force

Ever since the establishment of American and British Protestant missions in the nineteenth century, Christianity has been a conditioning force for a democratic ideology in Asia.[10] The Protestants were among the first to make a breach in the stronghold of Confucianism; they secured international action to assist them. Their role was that of counter-ideologues whose position was guaranteed by treaty (British Treaty of Tientsin, 1858; American Treaty of Tientsin, 1858). They possessed the power, under the legal sanction of the Chinese government, to preach against the moral foundations upon which that government rested. A missionary wrote in 1887:

> The foremost opposition to the introduction of Christianity comes from those who esteem themselves the followers of Confucius. They assent to our views about the "emptiness" of Buddhism, the deceptions of Taoism, the character of the priesthood, the mud and stone of the images, but when we gently allude to ancestral idolatry, the worship of heaven and earth, and the sacrifices of the mandarins, they are offended. Also, the Confucianists do the thinking for the people; they have the minds, the books, the schools, and the offices. Without a long residence in the country it is hard to imagine the influence of a penniless scholar in his neighbourhood, and the mental control he exercises over the minds of the peasantry. More than this, the graduates at the government examinations form a clique or "ring," and their voice is the unwritten law of China, their authority above that of His Excellency the Governor. The lamented Carstairs Douglas said at the Shanghai Missionary Conference of 1877, "Confucianism is the citadel; take it, and the war is ended."[11]

But for the presence of Christianity, a Chinese counter-elite with sufficient moral self-assurance and intellectual ability to attack the traditional institutions of the Empire might not have developed. Sun Yat-sen was a Christian, although in his case Christianity has been less of a modernizing force compared with the influence of his actual experience abroad. Large numbers of the reformist and republican leaders were Christian, some of them with missionary or Y. M. C. A. connections. These men were not bound by the moral tenets of Confucianism; those among them who had mission school educations had little in common with the long intellectual tradition of the Chinese. For a while Christianity spelled Westernization and provided an avenue of self-advancement hitherto unprecedented in China—one outside the archaic scheme of things.

With the coming of the Republic, Christian ethics appeared to have an open field. The emphasis which Christianity places upon the value of individual human life was favorable to the emergence of modern republican institutions. Even Yüan Shih-k'ai is said to have acknowledged the influence of Christianity in this respect; he is reported to have said, in an interview with a leading missionary educator, "You missionaries are responsible for this revolution. Now you must see us through."[12] The implication of doctrines of human brotherhood is obvious, despite the fact that such doctrines—in less forceful and spiritual form—were a familiar feature of certain Chinese philosophies.

In its more direct effects Christianity demonstrated a variety of new points to the Chinese. The intervention of the missionaries was not only moral; it was scientific, and the early mission leaders brought Western engineering and industrial methods with them. They published the first journal in Chinese to give regular accounts of practical mechanics. As the missions themselves developed, the physical presence of the Protestant missionaries and of Western ways of life—to which they adhered in contrast with the Catholics—became strong informational influences. Later the rise of churches and of Christian establishments gave the Chinese experience in the Western methods of social and business organization.

In practical administration the Christian impact has been striking. American missionaries were influential in developing popular education in China. They have led the way in public health. They have organized model orphanages and have assailed infanticide, footbinding, and concubinage. They have been the public opinion of the Western world, right on the spot, and have introduced the Chinese to a great many of the best features of Western life. Finally, the Christians have embellished and justified Western imperialism in China. The mission enterprises have been among the most expensive and elaborate philanthropic agencies ever set up by one state for the benefit of another. The advance of the West has been saved from seeming unrelieved imperialism. The West has taken, but it has also returned. Christianity has been the companion and the antagonist of Western exploitation in the East; it has suffered and benefited because of this position.

The total contribution of Christianity to Chinese politics cannot be assessed. The ways of Christian influence are frequently pervasive and incalculable. In the headquarters of the Chinese Red Army, Chinese Communist leaders have quietly gone away to pray. The Christians have breached the Confucian citadel and have weakened the ideological foundations of government. They have also torn the web of Chinese popular superstition and afforded a foothold for religion in a truer sense. There has been no genuine Christian party, no real Christian army, no government avowedly Christian in policy. Nevertheless, the first president of the Republic was a Christian, as was the outstanding founder of the National Government at Nanking, Chiang K'ai-shek. The Protestant Church counts among its members a large number of the highest government personnel; no other religion plays as active a part. Christianity, then, has been an indirect force, not a program or an immediate political challenge.

*Nationalism: Social-revolutionary Phase*

In 1912 the Nationalists had won their revolution, which was political in nature, but they found in the ensuing years that mere change in the form of government would not of itself bring about the needed regeneration of Chinese society. By 1922 Sun Yat-sen and his followers possessed a well-defined ideology and a definite new revolutionary program but they had neither a way of propagating the ideology nor a method of realizing the program. Sun himself thought in political and economic rather than agitational terms. He sought loans from abroad and schemed for power in the turbulent military politics of the time. His slogan was still that of the Confucians: "Hold office in order to teach." The Nationalists intended to gain a political rostrum from which to expound their teachings, since they no longer hoped to rule effectively without converting the masses to their way of thought. They had not yet realized that conversion scarcely required governing and that—given the appropriate technique—they might agitate more successfully as an opposition than as a government.

The means of systematically winning men's minds—wholesale and high-speed agitation—did not occur to the Nationalists because the Bolshevist revolution was the only successful demonstration of such methods, and Russia was not yet understood. China was just reaching that phase of revolution which the Communists had already traversed in Russia. Without the benefit of Russian advice, the Kuomintang might have become a political sect with long-range plans. Fortunately for their cause, the Kuomintang leaders were willing to learn and the Russians willing to teach. Mere physical contact served to inaugurate the process.

Contact was not afforded by way of the Communist Party of China, a small and largely academic group which developed after 1920, but through direct correspondence and negotiation between Sun Yat-sen and Moscow. Sun had communicated with persons of influence all over the world, trying to build up interest in the future of a united and powerful China. He had conceived a plan for the international development of China which envisaged the extension of Allied war budgets for one year after the war, and the lending of vast sums for the modernization of China. He believed that his project would appeal to imperialism and at the same time would serve to create in China a modern state-socialist industrialism. China would thereby become a customer for all the capitalist nations of the world and alleviate the depression which was bound to follow the war. Correspondence about other projects for ideological and political reconstruction elicited more replies from Russia than from anywhere else. Sun was not doctrinaire in the furtherance of immediate projects. He was willing to accept help from the Russians, just as he would have accepted help from the imperialist nations had they been prepared to risk their money. From 1920 onward he was in touch with the Bolsheviks.

In December, 1922, and January, 1923, the decisive turning point was reached. Adolf Joffe, the Soviet representative in China, had come to Shanghai and conferred with Sun Yat-sen. These two found that there were terms on which they could cooperate. The Communist ideology and that of the Nationalists coincided in their general opposition to imperialism. Resistance to the treaties which bound China[13] became more and more apparent to Sun as a necessity for further revolutionary progress. He had met polite regret or open ridicule in his solicitation of help for China from the imperialist powers, and his invitation to Western capital had not been taken seriously. The Communists seemed to have adequate idealistic and practical motives for joining the Chinese.

The Communists, moreover, conceded a point which they had not conceded to any other country up to that time. They willingly assumed a secondary position, agreed that the communist order of things was not suited to China, and in effect guaranteed their practical assistance to the Nationalists without demanding, as the price, the acceptance of Marxism. Sun and Joffe gave out a joint memorandum which made the issue perfectly plain. It was to be the constitutional compact between the Nationalists and the Communists for the period of their collaboration. The most significant paragraph read:

> Dr. Sun Yat-sen holds that the communistic order, or even the Soviet system, cannot actually be introduced into China because there do not exist the conditions for the successful establishment of either communism or Sovietism. This view is entirely shared by Mr. Joffe, who is further of the opinion that China's paramount and most pressing problem is to achieve national unification and attain full national independence; and regarding this great task he has assured Dr. Sun Yat-sen that China has the warmest sympathy of the Russian people and can count on the support of Russia.[14]

In the autumn of 1923 Chiang K'ai-shek was sent by Sun to Russia to study the Soviet military system. This was the first step in the formation of a non-mercenary Nationalist army. About the same time Michael Borodin arrived in Canton, where Sun had come to power for the third time. The ensuing period was marked by an intensive reorganization of the Nationalist Party and of its technique of revolution, to the end that it might become a movement depending upon mass conversion, not upon mass apathy, for power. The military mission was followed by other and more important grants of aid. The Bolsheviks not only trained Chinese sent to Russia but also supplied military instructors who reorganized the Nationalist forces on the spot.[15]

The assistance rendered by the Soviets in the application of tested propaganda methods to a revolutionary situation resulted in vast changes.  The Russians found that approximately the same devices could be used in China as in Russia without affecting the fundamentals of Nationalist philosophy.  Integration and regularization of the party machinery, formulation of immediate programs to bring large groups into the Nationalist fold, development of large-scale propaganda techniques, and other improvements designed to enlarge and speed up the Nationalist advance were effected within the Kuomintang.

Throughout, Sun Yat-sen worked in close collaboration with Borodin.  The details of Nationalist party reforms and of Nationalist participation in local politics are now part of the history of the modern Far East.  These details, while significant, tend to blur the cardinal change: the transformation of the Nationalist party from a revolutionary elite with long-range effectiveness into a mass organization designed for propaganda and immediate general measures.  The Russian Communists made it possible for the Kuomintang to perform in weeks what had been planned for the decades, or at least to reach the equivalent of the contemplated performance.

A new era had begun.  At first the Nationalists had proposed to develop a parliamentary government which would gradually foster a modernized ideology, and to govern China well in the meanwhile; when this hope vanished with the rise of Yüan Shih-k'ai's military power, in 1913, they had to reroute the revolution.  Had they relied upon the experience of the liberal nations, they might have resigned themselves to a policy of gradualism.  The Communist process of conversion was different from the Confucian.  The Confucians had gradually built up a body of the most public-spirited men and permeated the ruling intellectual class with Confucian ideas.  Their slow process of persuasion triumphed with the elevation of their main texts to the status of bibles in China and with their monopoly of advanced education.  The Communists proposed to take a few simple, obvious issues, to present them dramatically, to win as many people as possible to the support of immediate policies and to reach power through such support.  Once political and military authority had been established, they expected to go further in the "education" of the masses of the people.

To obtain tangible results quickly the Nationalists had to make extensive promises.  On the advice of the Communists, they led vigorous anti-imperialist movements which embittered both Chinese and foreigners and provided the whole country with issues more real than the personalities of war lords or the machinations of cliques. Communist-trained propagandists took the reforms which the Nationalists had proposed among themselves and carried them into the people. Sun's principle of *min shêng* appeared in practical programs as an immediate call for socio-economic revolution. Mass organizations grew, swelling their ranks by promises to all subordinate economic groups. These organizations were bound to cause difficulty as soon as it became apparent that the Nationalist-Communist promises could not be realized immediately and in full.

In the meantime, the Communists maintained their separate party organization within the Kuomintang. The Russians found China a fertile field for conversion, and while they assisted the Nationalists they fostered the growth of a Chinese Communist Party. From an academic group which meant nothing in 1921, the Communist Party grew in 1925–1926 to comprise the radical vanguard of the revolution. The Communists assumed the vanguard position because they were less bound by loyalty to the existing groups in Chinese society than were the Nationalists. The working alliance, in which the Nationalists received Communist help in money, technical political services, and arms, made the seizure of political power a reality. Sun Yat-sen died in March, 1925, before the great surge of the revolution came, but in 1926 and 1927 the Nationalist-Communist forces proceeded north, brushing the militarists aside as they went. The combination of a patriotic, foreign-trained, professionalized army, a powerful agitation department, and a party organization able to govern after conquest, came to prevail everywhere. Half of China was now under Kuomintang dominion, which operated through a council form of government.[16] Then came the schism. Conflict was inevitable between Communists and Nationalists when the Communists proved unwilling to look forward to the establishment of a republic according to Sun's principles, pushing on with the revolution as soon as the Nationalists slowed down or stopped.

Communist training helped the Nationalists to power, but under circumstances which made necessary either the institution of terror or the partial inhibition of the Nationalist programs.

The Nationalists had promised almost anything to almost everyone in order to secure power; this was a part of the propaganda methods which Communists taught. After seizing power in 1926–1927 the Nationalists could resort only to military dictatorship and party terrorism in order to achieve the fulfillment of their extravagant promises. But the Nationalists were Chinese, and as such cherished the old notions of moderation and humanity in government. They were not the master of any legalism or dialectic which would justify the slaughter of millions for the good of a system. Millions have died in China, but the Chinese never acknowledged the massacre. They could not face the program of class war which their promises inevitably implied. The Communists kept pressing forward, now giving pledges in their own name and in the name of the Nationalists, redeemable only by class warfare or involving the discredit of the Nationalists. The situation came to a head when the Communists began taking independent action. Indiscreet Communists informed Nationalist leaders that the Kuomintang was to be discarded so that the revolution could continue—along Communist lines. The breaks, first with the Kuomintang Right and then with the Kuomintang Left, occurred in 1927. The Russians went back to Russia. The Chinese Communists faced their future alone.

The Canton-Moscow Entente—as the Nationalist-Communist coalition has been called—changed the Nationalist movement profoundly in 1923–1927. It found the movement a small elite of opposition and left it a swollen party with a government and an army under its control, a vast schedule of promises to fulfill, a second revolution to vindicate.[17]

### Notes

1. Sun Yat-sen, *How China Was Made a Republic* (unpublished manuscript written in Shanghai in 1919, now in possession of the present author), p. 4.
2. On the Manchu reforms see H. M. Vinacke, *Modern Constitutional Development in China*, Princeton, 1920, and Meribeth E. Cameron, *The Reform Movement in China*, 1898–1912, Stanford, 1931. On the revolutionary group see T'ang Leang-li, *The Inner History of the Chinese Revolution*, New York, 1930.
3. See below, pp. 41 ff.
4. See below, pp. 145 ff.
5. See below, pp. 149 ff.

6. See below, p. 60. A description of other plans for democracy in China is given in M. J. Bau, *Modern Democracy in China*, Shanghai, 1923.
7. See below, pp. 102 ff.
8. See below, pp. 139 ff.
9. See below, pp. 185 ff.
10. See, among others, Tyler Dennett, *The Democratic Movement in Asia*, New York, 1918; R. Y. Lo, *China's Revolution from the Inside*, New York, 1930. The author wishes to thank J. J. Holmes, School of Religion, Duke University, for suggestions concerning this section.
11. Hampden C. DuBose, *The Dragon, Image, and Demon* . . . , pp. 48–49, New York, 1887.
12. Paul Hutchinson, *China's Real Revolution*, p. 155, New York, 1924.
13. See the literature cited above, p. 30, n. 1.
14. Lyon Sharman, *Sun Yat-sen: His Life and Its Meaning*, p. 248, New York, 1934. This is the most critical of the biographies of Sun Yat-sen. The one which Sun himself authorized and on which he collaborated to some extent is Paul M. W. Linebarger, *Sun Yat Sen and the Chinese Republic*, New York, 1924.
15. For the military development of this period see below, pp. 105 ff.
16. See below, pp. 163 ff.
17. For some of the ideological developments involved in the Moscow-Canton Entente see Tsui Shu-chin, "The Influence of the Canton-Moscow Entente upon Sun Yat-sen's Political Philosophy," *The Chinese Social and Political Science Review* (Peiping), vol. 18, pp. 177 ff., 1934. On the role of nationalism in education see Victor Purcell, *Problems of Chinese Education*, London, 1936.

*Chapter* III

BATTLING CREEDS

The right-wing Nationalists, establishing the National Government of China at Nanking in 1927, found themselves in the position of revolutionaries sitting at roll-top desks. After more than forty years of criticism and opposition, the movement had assumed the responsibilities of government. In breaking with the Communists the Nationalists lost the doctrinal edge of the extreme Left; thenceforth there were to be groups more radical than themselves. This disheartened some of the revolutionaries, who either lost interest in politics or continued revolutionary opposition to the regime their colleagues had formed.

*Nationalism: Governing Phase*

The Kuomintang was confronted with the issues of national unification, development toward democracy, and realization of the economic reforms and programs postulated by Sun's principle of *min shêng*. The instrument for their task was a brand-new form of government, fresh from the pages of Sun Yat-sen, which at its birth was beset with difficult military, administrative, economic, and diplomatic problems. But the Nationalists had one particular advantage which they shared only with the Communists—that of possessing a well-integrated ideology. It was possible for them to couch intra-Party struggles in a reasonably consistent set of terms. Even when respect for one of Sun Yat-sen's theories had been reduced to mere lip service another from the same source took its place. The intellectual outlook inherited from the humanistic political training of Confucianism kept the Chinese from a dogmatic political pseudo-theology, while the wide circulation of Sun's principles provided a moral and programmatic foundation for governmental routine.

The break with the Communists and the development of a Red military problem were continuing forces driving the Nationalists to the Right, where opportunists and reactionaries of all categories welcomed them. They were also drawn to the Left—by the social revolution which had carried them to power and by the need of agrarian and labor reform. Central to the very continuance of the government, however, was the military power of the Nationalist armies led by Chiang K'ai-shek. Without the armed force to implement their decisions the Nationalists would have been compelled to let their endeavors subside into subterranean defeat. To the considerations of Right, Left, and armed force were added responsibilities incident to government. The Kuomintang in its governing phase, therefore, plotted its course with reference to three points: doctrinal consistency, military necessity, governmental responsibility.[1] As an ideologically constituent movement, how did Nationalism use its power?

The Nationalists in power had to find their way through class alignments, inert and meaningless oppositions, the rancor of the Left, the contempt of the established monarchist Right. Personalities in conflict, cliques forming and disbanding, factions denied overt expression—these lay behind the pressure politics of the intra-Party contest for the control of policy conducted on a thin and novel constitutional plane. The written formulas guiding the struggle for power were supplemented by the bodies of unwritten practice which had developed in the years of the Republic. There were appropriate forms for extraconstitutional action, just as for constitutional. It was the outstanding contribution of the Kuomintang to modern Chinese government that it kept its internal conflicts within its own constitutional framework, and did so more successfully than any other movement in modern China.

The meandering and difficult course of Kuomintang policy flowed within the valley rather than the river bed of Sun Yat-sen's doctrine. The planning power of Sun's intellect bound the movement long after his death. In his plans for the regeneration of China are to be found the ideal requirements for the growth of modern government under the tutelage of a patriotic elite of overseas men, revolutionary veterans, and scholars. The Nanking government of the Kuomintang had to meet all the problems of government while keeping within the broad boundaries of Sun's demands. The movement as a whole, however, displayed certain broad shifts which are readily traceable.[2] Sun Yat-sen envisaged the establishment of authentic democracy by a course of action including three steps: (1) the military period, in which the movement should acquire power over the nation through the use of force; (2) the period of tutelage, in which the members of the movement should exercise a benevolent party dictatorship over the nation, while training the populace for democracy; (3) the period of constitutional democracy, in which the people should exercise actual self-government.

Shortly after its establishment, the National Government announced the ending of the period of military conquest and the opening of the period of tutelage, which was set for 1930–1935. The Japanese invasions caused the establishment of constitutional government to be postponed indefinitely, and it is to be feared that even if constitutional government were installed it would fall far short of Sun's programs, which called for truly effective training in the arts of democracy before Chinese government could be entrusted to the broad masses of the electorate. In the meantime, the arbitrariness, the political composition, and the outlook of the transitional Party dictatorship became subjects of hot controversy among the Kuomintang leaders.

The Party dictatorship demanded a rigor of discipline and a deflation of revolutionary enthusiasm which soon drove the militant Left out of the Kuomintang. Even Sun Yat-sen's brilliant young second wife remained outside the Party—a permanent and indefatigable opposition. Within the Party personalities came to dominate—Hu Han-min, the chief Rightist disciple and interpreter of Sun Yat-sen; Chiang K'ai-shek, Sun's outstanding military protege; and Wang Ch'ing-wei, the chief Leftist disciple of the Leader. There were also Sun Fo (Sun K'ê), the only son of Sun Yat-sen, and other ranking Party members whose opinions ranged from philosophic anarchism (as in the case of Wu Chih-hui) to a progressive business outlook not unlike Mr. Hoover's (as in the instance of T. V. Soong).

The National Government settled down with Chiang and Hu Han-min (military and Right) holding the leadership, which Wang Ch'ing-wei decried as reactionary. In 1931 Chiang ousted Hu, in the course of a conflict over a proposed American silver loan and over constitutional questions. Shortly thereafter Wang Ch'ing-wei assumed a place in the government, after participating in an unsuccessful armed rebellion (the "Nationalist Government" in Peking, 1930–1931).

This might seem to indicate a swing from the Right to the Left within the Party. Actually it was indicative of the growing practicality of the Nationalist movement and its preoccupation with problems of installing the form of government planned by Sun.[3] With the passage of time, the Nationalists adopted three main lines of endeavor: (1) the suppression of the Communists at all cost, even that of temporary nonresistance to Japan; (2) the tendency to abandon revolutionary fervor for administrative zeal, and to become governmental in spirit as well as form—a tendency illustrated most notably in the promotion of industry under H. H. Kung, railways under Sun Fo, and finance under T. V. Soong; (3) a policy of emphasizing military power, which meant the rise to effective personal leadership of Chiang K'ai-shek. The development of a United Front policy in 1937 and the war with Japan led to the reversal of the first two policies and an enormous emphasis on the third. The Nationalists again turned to patriotism on the mass level rather than government action in a patriotically bureaucratic sphere. This latter policy, although it may seem strangely nonrevolutionary, was actually a part of Sun's programs to which the Nationalists were bound.

The class theory held by Sun was based upon a distinction between power and competence. The people should have *power* to determine the range of government policy; they obviously did not have the *competence*. Competence was confined to the intellectual leaders and the thinking people of society (who were to form two classes) and could not be found in the vast majority of people untrained to contemplate political problems. Accordingly, Sun's scheme of government assumed the continuity of a bureaucracy made up of men of competence, but subject to the periodic check of the populace, which possessed the power.

Another of Sun's programs relates to the question: How can democracy be reconciled with ideological control? The Chinese had lived in a society so completely under the rule of common ideas that independent individual thinking had to be moderate, careful, and orthodox in appearance before it met with any welcome. The individual was not free to think freely; but since most did not think freely, sensing no need for it, they were unconscious of control. A problem larger than that of individual freedom is raised by the question of ideological control, since the controlled individual himself transmits control to his neighbors and his dependents. The ideology must be filtered, as it were, at some point. Sun believed that democracy would effectuate the filtering, allowing long-range revision from outside the bureaucracy. He expected that the bureaucracy of democratic China would rule well but would be subject to control from a people not completely under its thumb. The ideology was to be officially fostered, but it was to be subject to the check of the electorate. The Chinese were still to use orthodoxy as a tool of control and social pressure as the major instrument of constraint, but they were not to be allowed to fall into a blind traditionalism which would isolate them.

The old ideology was to be adjusted and supplemented with Western science, so that the new would be compounded of three things: old Chinese social and political experience, old Chinese ethical knowledge, and modern scientific truth. With respect to Western science, the Nationalists had to present few startling governmental innovations, since the need for a knowledge of the physical and technical sciences was widely recognized in China—not only by the Nationalists. That the Western technology should serve to build the new China was obvious; trade schools needed encouragement rather than initiation. As to the old Chinese social and political experience, the Kuomintang stressed study of China's past. They attempted to mend the gap between the generation born in the 1880's and that born in the 1910's by encouraging concentration on the classical texts, reverently, but critically as well. Archaeology has heightened interest of the Chinese in their past. As a consequence, their sense of national value has deepened.

For the restoration of the old Chinese moral and ethical system the New Life movement, which has been fostered personally by Generalissimo Chiang K'ai-shek, is of great importance. Its principles consist of a simple restatement of the cardinal Confucian personal virtues, interpreted to suit modern conditions. It has presumably been influenced by Protestant Christianity, and may be said to be a form of puritanism. Although the Nationalist movement has not been as successful in ten years as was the Confucian in two hundred, it has at least created a state pattern. A state in the full sense would require a type of organization so clear in its ideology that people would personify it willingly, would accord it existence whether leaders and governments fell or not, and would be loyal to it and to those who claimed to wield its power.

Among negative influences running against the Nationalist ideology, the Nationalist neo-militarism has stood forth. As in the other ideologically integrated states of the world (Russia, Germany, Italy), the army assumed especial importance because its type of law and order required no common understanding higher than the assent of idiots. An army is the one institution where complete harmony of thought is a luxury and not a necessity, where simple agreement on rewards, punishments, and organization morale will hold the structure together. The Nationalist armies, however, rose to a new position. Ideological control was introduced; the literate armies fought best. But despite the civilian and intellectual factors from outside, the mere force concentrated in weapons was so great as to amount to a constant temptation. Whenever the day's fortunes were inclement, the men in command tended to settle things with guns. In contrast with sheer ideals, the Nationalists were strongly military; in contrast with their predecessors, the Nationalist generals showed respect for civilian authority. The charge of Nationalist neo-militarism focused upon the personal popularity of army leaders, especially that of Chiang K'ai-shek. It can be adjudicated only by history.

The Nationalist movement neared its most drastic ordeal in 1936. The predetermined period of tutelage as decreed was passing, while the inauguration of constitutional government had to be deferred. With the approaching abolition of the Party dictatorship the Nationalist leaders were to demonstrate their consistency with their own ideals and programs. The programs of Sun Yat-sen called for the abdication of the patriotic elite, and the requirement—coupled as it had been with the proclamation of definite time limits—placed the issue squarely before the Kuomintang leadership. Were they to attempt the democratic experiment in a nation patently unripe for it, or were they to disavow the commands of their deceased and sainted Leader, and continue in power?

Before the Nationalist movement underwent this final test, however, other issues arose which swept all previous plans aside. The kidnaping of Chiang K'ai-shek at Sian, the reconciliation of the Communists and Nationalists, and the Japanese invasion in 1937 forced Nationalism into concord with all other patriotic movements and merged them all in a dramatic resurgence for national defense.

*Independent Marxism in China*

The proponents of Marxism were welcomed into China as trusted friends. In 1926 it was obvious to the whole world that China was definitely within the orbit of Marxism; in 1935 it was just as apparent that the Marxists faced a military doom, and that their forcible suppression might mean the end of their political effectiveness. Never ruined beyond all hope of recovery and triumph, never successful beyond all danger of disaster, the Marxists and their doctrines are the greatest uncertainty facing China.

Sinologues, judging from past experience and impressed with the deep continuities and repetitions of Chinese history, may well argue that Marxism is another religious distributive cult such as periods of turmoil always produce in China. They can point to the rise and fall of the Yellow Turbans in the third century A. D., when the two leaders—the Duke of Heaven and the Duke of Humanity—shook the great Han dynasty down into everlasting ruin. Or they can refer to the T'ai-p'ing rebellion, which held a territory infinitely greater than that ever occupied by the Marxists, which impressed a fantastic but politically operative Christianity upon its followers, and which promised to do in South China what Brigham Young and the Mormons had done with the United Order in Utah; but the T'ai-p'ing went down to an extinction so complete that no living advocate of the cult practiced by millions seventy years ago can be found today. Thus it would be no violation of the set patterns of Chinese history if the movement of Marxism were to rise to world-dazzling splendor and then pass into utter oblivion. Yet Chinese history is no longer the only kind of history which holds weight for precedent in China, and if the T'ai-p'ing rebellion is one example, the Russian Revolution is another. Bolshevism certainly has better chances of succeeding in China than it could have seemed to have—to anyone but a fanatic—in the Russia of 1915.

The Marxian doctrines had already eaten well into Chinese territory before entering upon the Chinese scene proper. One of the less savory bequests which the tsarist regime left the Communists was the question of Outer Mongolia, a vast stretch of land under the admitted suzerainty but beyond the real control of the Chinese. The area was used by White Russians as a base for operations, and—whether or not it accorded with their principles—the Red forces had to cross the frontier to pacify Siberia. Once in, they could not get out. It was essentially the sort of absent-minded conquest which has contributed so much to the British Empire: a strategic occupation leading inevitably to political domination. The Russians compromised as well as they might, setting up an Outer Mongolian People's Republic and administering the area in the way which the world was to observe on a much grander scale in the case of the Japanese in Manchuria—through advisers.

Marxism became a force in China through men and literature and money and arms reaching China by the sea route, as have most Western things. Its position reflected, however, the facts that Russia is China's greatest neighbor and that the Russo-Chinese land frontier is one of the longest in the world. China is much nearer to San Francisco, in terms of shipping costs and speed of connections, than it is to Leningrad, but the appearance of closer proximity to the latter played a considerable role. The Nationalist-Communist coalition[4] was the result of the impact of Marxism from Russia upon China proper. The Communists entered as allies, not as leaders. The period of Nationalist-Communist cooperation lasted because the practical projects of the two revolutionary parties lay in a common direction. The gradual shift in the role of the Communists from advisers and allies to teachers and masters led to the break between the two organizations.

How did this shift develop? From the Marxian standpoint it was the move of a party leadership which was bound by a true ideology, that of dialectic materialism. Whatever the ethics of broken individual pledges, there is no question that the Communists were justified according to their own beliefs in abandoning the Nationalists when the Nationalists ceased positive revolutionary action and began a Nationalist reconstitution. The Communists felt themselves bound to take up the standards of the revolution and proceed against Nationalists as against others. There was no room in the Marxian ideology for anything but the officially approved Communist Party; there was no ground for conceding that the Nationalists might be wise in calling a breathing spell.

The Kuomintang leaders, on the other hand, had every reason to feel aggrieved at the Communists. The Communists had come to help the Chinese revolutionaries in their struggle for national liberation and to bring about a common front against imperialism in the Far East. When the revolution of national liberation was more than half accomplished, the Communists had increased their following to such an extent that they regarded the Nationalist alliance as a mere episode in the growth of Marxian power in China. Marxists had come to help the cause of Sun Yat-sen; Marxism was spread to fight and undo it. The sobering shock of a grasp on power sent the Nationalists into relative conservatism. An eminent Chinese writer has suggested the change of mood:

> Our imagination was fired, our enthusiasm was kindled; thousands of young men have fled from home and school from the outermost provinces to join the Nationalist forces; they have toiled and they have sweated, and thousands have gladly laid down their lives on the altar of Nationalism that their dream of a regenerated and redeemed China might come true. But, alas! . . . The war has ended—so has all idealism.[5]

The Soviet Communists, deprived of their opportunity to broadcast propaganda on a large scale, and unable to ride the back of the Nationalist tiger any longer, found themselves on a defensive which seemed to be permanent. At the same time, the Marxists in China encountered difficulties in adjusting their ideology to the fact that their strength lay in elements which official Marxism discredited. They owed their existence to agrarian discontent and to their excellent army—the shock troops, in many cases, of the former coalition. The leader of Chinese Marxism, Ch'en Tu-hsiu, broke the party wide open with a schism; he believed in modernizing effort rather than orthodox Marxist symbols. Other schisms from the Left produced Marxisms intent on applying the European technique to China's small proletariat, indifferent to the land question and eager to make an Asiatic revolution from the textbooks of European labor conflict. Such deviations were as unrealistic and sterile as Blanquism, against which the nineteenth century Marxists inveighed so heavily. Even so the official Communist

Party withstood nine years of savage attack and persecution because necessity forced the Reds to pursue a simple line of policy—survival. Out of the test of deadly experience the Chinese Communists evolved means of allying themselves with the discontented peasantry, and found the point at which further social reform yielded diminishing returns in popular support. In relying on the people for practical help, instead of invoking theoretically popular appeals, the Chinese Communists attained a defensive strength which could easily be turned into an offensive.

The reorientation in attitude—the splitting off of both extremes, the iron necessity for an immediate and effectual popularization of the Party among the peasantry, and the lessons derived from responding to actual conditions—enabled the Communists to establish a state in Kiangsi in 1931: the Chinese Soviet Republic.[6] In 1935 and 1936 Chiang K'ai-shek began the most vigorous of his attacks, which led to the removal of the Chinese Red Army some two thousand miles from South Central to Northwest China—one of the most astonishing military feats of modern times. Some observers have suggested that Chiang had no intention of allowing the Communists to disappear altogether from the scene, as they provided his military power with a *raison d'être* in the eyes of the Japanese. Had he run them utterly to ground, the Japanese might have dispensed with him. Later events have made such an explanation seem less persuasive, after the *coup d'état* at Sian in December, 1936.

The personal factors and political events in this extraordinary drama are not yet known in their entirety, and it may be decades before the whole story is pieced together from the accounts of eyewitnesses and interpreters. Chiang K'ai-shek in his published diary mentions no formal agreement for the institution of a United Front policy, but the rumors from the Left persist in affirming the existence of a truce between the Nationalists and the Communists, the fruits of which were to be action against Japan. Certainly the military and political effects of Chiang's kidnaping were substantial,[7] and the ideological scarcely less. In brief, the kidnaping arose from action on the part of Chinese National Army troops under the command of Chang Hsüeh-liang, the ex-*tuchün* of Manchuria. His forces were mostly from the Manchurian provinces and had no stomach for fighting the Communists in the far west of China while the Japanese remained in undisturbed occupation of their homelands. They had inaugurated an informal understanding with the Communists, and fraternization had begun between the opposing armies. When Chiang came up to investigate conditions, he was promptly kidnaped (December, 1936). His bodyguard was slaughtered and he himself was injured in the spine. The kidnaping was nominally the act of the *Tungpei* (ex-Manchurian) troops. Even the Communist forces worked for the release of Chiang, since they felt that his death would mean national disaster. The release of Chiang was finally procured through the mediation of an Australian editor with a long experience in Chinese politics.[8]

The effect on popular thinking was twofold. In the first place, Chiang's popularity was made fully apparent by the vigor of the demonstrations in his favor all over China. It had long been asserted that even the most momentary relaxation of Chiang's despotism, as its opponents termed it, would be followed either by anarchy or a new revolutionary regime. Neither appeared. The strength of the National Government as a government was apparent, despite a strong odor of treason in widely separated quarters, and the people as a whole kept quiet. Students, workers, capitalists, officials, military men—all groups sought Chiang's release. Their anxiety for his personal safety was in some cases qualified by a hearty dislike of the man himself, but almost everyone admitted to an admiration, either grudging or whole-hearted, for the effectiveness of his work. The National Government and its chief military leader were indeed strongly entrenched in popular sympathy and thought—more so than even the most optimistic observers had dared to hope.

The second consequence of the *coup d'état* at Sian was even more important. The mere physical juxtaposition of the two leaderships, Marxian and Nationalist, and the probability that forced arbitration would be the result of the kidnaping, led to a wild stimulation of hopes. At the same time it was generally realized that failure to come to terms might end in the murder of Chiang and in fateful results for all groups in China. The kidnapers demanded a United Front; the Communists had issued a manifesto in behalf of it several months earlier (August 1, 1936). The problem was: could Chiang accede without ruining his prestige or impairing the ideological position he had so laboriously built up for himself?

A compromise was found, which amounted to a paper victory for Chiang, nominal punishment of Chang and the other perpetrators of the kidnaping, ceremonial apology to the nation by Chiang for having been kidnaped, and a series of formally unrelated but probably linked events—all of which brought the two ideologies and their adherents to a common ground. Throughout the following spring, progress was made in the negotiation of a truce, which broadened into an armistice and ended as an alliance. On April 30, 1937, for instance, the Young Communist Congress, composed of men whose brains Chiang would have cheerfully blown out a few months before, elected Chiang and other Nationalist leaders to honorary membership. On occasion, the Communists and the Nationalists exchanged classical Chinese poems; each side sought to excel in sincere courtesy. The armistice lasted through the period of the Japanese invasion in the summer of 1937; formal union was achieved in September.[9]

On the political surface, the course of Marxism in China has been one of the most startling developments in modern history. Alliance between Hitler and Stalin would seem more plausible than the reunion of Nationalist and Communist groups in China. To those in the service of the Nanking regime in 1936, such an eventuality was the one thing certain not to happen. The break between the Marxist and Nationalist leaderships and their subsequent reconciliation appeared, however, less improbable in consideration of the course steered by the Communist world movement during the decade 1927–1937. The United Front in China made it possible for the Chinese Communists to concede more than they would otherwise have dared to except at the suggestion of the Russian and international Communists.

The future role of Marxism in China is still undecided. Nothing can be regarded as beyond the limit of probability, except the immediate establishment of a permanent and unalterable regime. The challenges the Marxists raise are too important to be ignored—land and labor reform and the devising of workable techniques for distributive justice. If they do not take control of the country themselves, they will at least be a formidable factor for whoever does control the government. In the event of foreign conquest the Marxians could provide an underground resistance of spectacular value. If the Chinese, applying terror and espionage against the Marxians then regarded as traitors, were not able to root them out in ten years of ferocious warfare, what will aliens do—against Communists who have become patriots in the eyes of all the people and who are assured help from all sides?

*Japanese Efforts to Participate in Creating a New China*

China is Japan's greatest outside problem; she is only a secondary problem in the foreign policies of the other great powers. Japan owes much to China in the way of borrowed ideas and institutions. Japan and Siam are the only free nations in the modern world which share with China the background of a Chinese-dominated world society in the Far East.[10] The Japanese resisted the extension of Chinese suzerainty to their islands, and on only one occasion did they concede formally that the Chinese emperor was the head of all civilized society; this they bitterly regret. While the Siamese have maintained their independence, they are in no position to take an active part in the creation of a new Far East, and the issue is between China and Japan, with the other Pacific powers largely as spectators. The construction of a way of thinking to accommodate the men and territories no longer guided by the old order is a problem shared by Japan and China; the competition for imposing a feasible system is sharp. Japan wishes to create a new Far East in which the Japanese shall constitute the most cultured core; the Chinese take their ancient position for granted.

In addition to the ideational conflict for prestige between Chinese and Japanese, there is another realm wherein the two nations compete, using ideas not as ends but as means. The extension of Western industry and trade to the East produced acute dislocations both in China and in Japan, and in the case of Japan involved transforming the Japanese autarchy into a most dangerous dependence upon a share of the world economy. Japan is truly a commercial and capitalist power; hers is no mere affectation of modernity. It is conceivable, should the West go down to its Armageddon, that the Chinese might swing back to the ways of their past. The Japanese could not; their economic and political system has expanded too far. They are inextricably bound up with the rest of the industrial, capitalist modern world. In China the stock exchanges have a mere toehold on the country; in Japan they have become the spine of national life. The Japanese must either pay the price of modernization by accepting the lowly place of the latecomer or make up their tardiness in entering the imperialist scene by a veritable frenzy of expansion. Apart from the future of capitalism, there remains the question: Will Japan collapse before reaching imperial success in the world economy?

China and the unpredictable but colossal Chinese markets are Japan's goal, formulated after contact with the West. China and her unquestioned cultural prestige are the targets of the Japanese drive for the acquisition of standing, a campaign couched in indigenous Far Eastern terms. The conflict between the two countries weaves its way back and forth through elaborate and self-contradictory sets of terms. The Japanese have toyed with a multitude of policies for China. Some of these are: (1) simple conquest; (2) the establishment of a peculiar Far Eastern order under Japanese leadership—either in terms harmonious with Western concepts of international affairs (the "Japanese Monroe Doctrine") or in terms derived from a modification of the past ("Pan-Asia"); (3) a common cause of Japanese and Chinese against the white peril, without any special emphasis on the relative positions of the two countries; (4) a divine Japanese mission, not merely to save the yellow race but to rescue the whole world and put all nations under the protecting benevolence of Japanese overlordship; (5) a strict policy of day-to-day opportunism—binding those parts of China accessible for such procedure with treaties and agreements, and catching the Chinese as they come forth into the arena of modern economic life; (6) expediency couched in military terms, looking to absolute Japanese gains on the map, regardless of the erection of a social system to perpetuate the immediate military advances; (7) a pro-Chinese policy, to assure the Japanese a close ally (but in such a case a strong independent China would inevitably excel Japan, and the Japanese would have to yield to Chinese hegemony—however friendly—or else retreat from it into the isolation from which they emerged in the 1850's).

Direct military conquest has a considerable appeal to the Japanese, except for its limitations. All the armies of the modern world would not be enough to garrison and patrol a China desperately hostile through and through. The Chinese would not stop at suicide to embarrass their enemies, if there were complete ideological antagonism. The Japanese would have to persuade the Chinese whom they conquered to remain alive, to keep working, to grow wealthy so that the conquest might not be without value. It is not possible to consider a policy involving the outright murder of from one hundred and fifty to two hundred million persons; short of such extermination, there is no way for the Japanese to clear the field for colonization in Chinese territories. If the Japanese cannot replace the Chinese, they must make use of them; to make use of them, they must teach them to think in a way which will permit exploitation, for even the most inequitable exploitation involves some cooperation.

Ever since their peculiar Far Eastern order had been partially recognized the Japanese began building up theories of a zone of influence to be based not upon law but upon geographic and racial fact. The doctrines of Pan-Asia fitted their purpose. Writers in the different Asiatic countries had pointed out the desirability of a union of those Asiatic peoples which were not yet under colonial rule to prevent further occidental advance and to rescue their conquered neighbors. Sun Yat-sen himself thought well of the Pan-Asia idea and stressed it, along with the recommendation that all economically exploited powers confront the exploiting powers—a class war between nations. As soon as the Japanese began turning to Pan-Asia for furtherance of their own peculiar ends, these arguments lost much of their realism. The Japanese policies generated more disturbance in Asia than did the Western. Their call to prevent Western aggression, at a time when the Western powers were in retreat, sounded artificial. Nevertheless, the Pan-Asian movement forms a link between ideology-conscious leaders in China and Japan; Japan's ultra-patriotic Toyama had been friendly and helpful to Sun at the time when the former led the *Genyosha* and the latter the *Hsing Chung Hui*.[11] It was natural, however, that the Pan-Asian doctrine, although it never disappeared altogether in China, should be strongest in Japan. Pan-Asia or its restricted form—Far-Easternism (*Toa-shugi*)—played a significant part in the military indoctrination in Japan, even though attempts to propagate it in China ended in almost complete failure.

To the ideological conquest of China the Japanese have contributed very little. Their theories, summed up, amount to but a drop in the sea of doctrines. Only as the spokesman of China's ultra-reactionary monarchists—who flourished twenty-five years ago—has Japan presented an ideological program which is other than derisible. Rich in the ceremonial trappings of government, and in the personal elegance of its powerless ministers, the Great Manchou Empire makes a strong appeal to literary persons with archaic tastes. Even there, the blunt modernism of the Japanese military machine destroys the illusion.

*Patriotism: The United Front*

1937 was one of the most critical years of modern China. It marked a swift and startling grouping of the three active forces in China: Nationalism, Communism, and Japanese compulsion. For ten years the Nationalists and the Communists had waged a war of terror against each other; for six years a Chinese Soviet Republic had defied the National Government of China established at Nanking. Six years had passed since the Japanese invasion of Manchuria, five since the establishment of a Manchoukuo government. The Nationalists had hated the Japanese, but they hated the Communists more; at the humiliating price of non-resistance to Japan, Chiang K'ai-shek had brought the full military and agitational power of Nationalism to the suppression of the Marxians. The Japanese had no great attachment to Chiang and the Nationalists and regarded Nationalism itself as a force subversive to Japanese order in the Far East. But they had tolerated the Kuomintang because it seemed a buffer between themselves and the Communists, and because they did not have the power or the immediate inclination to destroy the Nationalist regime.

This triangular deadlock was first broken by the kidnaping at Sian. Nationalist and Communist leaderships were brought face to face, and preliminary terms were agreed upon. With each step toward a termination of the Nationalist-Communist wars the danger of a powerful China became more striking to Japan, while simultaneously the Nanking regime became less valuable to the Japanese as a bulwark against Communism. The spring of 1937 marked the settlement with the Communists in the Northwest, the continuance of a general armistice, and the sharp improvement of Nationalist prestige throughout the country. Circles which had been Rightist recognized the increased military and financial power of the Nationalists, now that the long and wasteful struggle with the Communists was ended, releasing men, weapons, and money for application in other quarters. Leftist groups again found the Nanking state philosophy palatable, and discovered in the official tenets of the Nationalist Party enough common principles to justify the re-coalition of revolutionary forces. The radical intellectuals and students, who had swung sharply to the Left as a result of continued Nationalist yielding to Japan, turned again to Nationalist leadership.

As practical solutions to the Nationalist-Communist conflict were found, the people in the larger cities were released from the governmental restrictions which the Nationalists—upon Japanese insistence and threat of force—had placed on the expression of patriotic sentiments. A vast and vigorous patriotic feeling came suddenly to life, having grown more intense under the cramping inhibitions of police prohibition. The patriotism was revolutionary in mood but not wholly different from Chinese patriotism of the past. The slogans all centered on national defense. Release of political prisoners, cessation of internal war, and democratization of the government were regarded as steps to union and defense.

When the Japanese decided to push forward in earnest and began fighting in North China in the summer of 1937, the patriotic movement became so powerful that for the time it supplanted all other separate movements. Only a number of aged or cynical opportunists remained outside. It was now possible, under the slogan of a United Front of all China against Japan, to disregard the fundamental differences between the Nationalists and the Communists. A Chinese Communist wrote:

> While we declare ourselves, despite the differences in principle that exist between communism and Sun-Yat-sen-ism, advocates of the basic revolutionary slogans of Sun Yat-sen, of the best revolutionary traditions of the Chinese people, we Communists never for an instant under any circumstances cease to be true followers of the Marxist-Leninist teachings.[12]

Such utterances were matched by similar ones from the Nationalist side.

In their haste the Japanese utilized an ideology which they had practiced in Manchuria—literary Confucianism colored by notions adopted from the Japanese cult of the emperor. They also appealed to the practical and immediate needs of the Chinese living in the areas which they conquered, setting up governments[13] to govern for them. But this was hardly more than an expedient. Of far greater importance than even the war itself is its long-range impact upon the Chinese mind.

The formulation of the present Chinese patriotic movement into a definite drive for the establishment of a new Chinese way of life may emerge as one of the lasting facts of the century. The various movements of the Republican era failed to disturb and arouse the masses sufficiently to make possible a replacement of the decrepit remnants of the old Chinese social and intellectual world, or a reinterpretation adding the ingredients needed in a modern civilization. If patriotism unites the Chinese permanently, Japanese invasion may have provoked what twenty-five years of Chinese effort could not bring about.

Furthermore, the Chinese have reacted to the emergencies of war in a manner almost unprecedented among modern nations. War has not meant the creation of a temporary despotism; it has brought democracy instead. The ideological concord, the supremacy of a common national purpose, which could not be achieved in a quarter century of peacetime agony, was brought forth in the ordeal of national resistance. Democracy and not tyranny was the unifying force. The Kuomintang Party Congress, meeting in Hankow from March 29 to April 2, 1938, reaffirmed the primacy of the *San Min Chu I*, but at the same time guaranteed the sanctity of private rights, even in wartime, of groups who had been liable to official suppression for years. The Communist press was flourishing openly in Hankow, a testimony to the curious tolerance with which the Chinese united for national defense. The governmental structure was increasingly democratized. Japan had provided a body of common assumptions strong enough to sustain democracy, despite the burden of mutually tolerated disagreements.

NOTES

1. For the military aspects see below, pp. 108 ff.; for the immediate governmental aspects see below, pp. 167 ff.

2. The best account of the internal politics of the Kuomintang between 1927 and 1933 is to be found in Gustav Amann, *Chiang Kaishek und die Regierung der Kuomintang in China,* Berlin and Heidelberg, 1936.
3. See below, pp. 172 ff.
4. See above, pp. 51 ff.
5. Lin Yutang, *Letters of a Chinese Amazon and War-Time Essays,* p. vi, Shanghai, 1930.
6. See below, pp. 182 ff.
7. See below, p. 184 ff.
8. On the Sian incident see General and Madame Chiang Kai-shek, *General Chiang Kai-shek,* Garden City, 1937; James M. Bertram, *First Act in China,* New York, 1938, an account by an Australian newspaperman in Sian at the time; and Edgar Snow, *Red Star over China,* New York, 1938—an extraordinarily valuable work on all phases of Chinese Communism, by an observer of great insight and acuteness.
9. See the references below, p. 190, n. 10.
10. See Yoshi S. Kuno, *Japanese Expansion on the Asiatic Continent,* vol. I, Berkeley, 1937, for an authoritative description of early Sino-Japanese relations. Chinese records of the time of Christ describe the payment of tribute by Japanese chieftains. The most explicit acknowledgment of Chinese suzerainty occurred in the time of Yoshemitsu, the third Ashikaga shogun (see Kuno, pp. 92–93).
11. The Japanese patriotic leagues are described in Kenneth Colegrove, *Militarism in Japan,* Boston, 1936.
12. Wang Ming, *China Can Win!* p. 44, New York, 1938. Wang Ming is a Chinese expert on Marxism residing in the U. S. S. R.
13. See below, pp. 184 ff.

# SECOND PART
## ARMIES

*Chapter* IV

## WARRIORS

From the outside, militarism seems to dominate the Chinese scene. China is frequently interpreted in terms of personalities instead of mass inclinations, wide-filtering habits, and extensive relocations of thought. The picturesqueness of the Chinese leaders has done nothing to prevent the notion of many romantic autocracies from appearing real: the Dog-Meat General, six feet tall, diabolically cruel and brazenly comic, with his veritable zoological garden of ladies from all over the world; the Christian General, burly, bluff, honest, Christian and Bolshevik, with the happy naïveté of a feudal politician; the Bandit General and his infatuation with fine arsenals; the Generalissimo, with his Christian wife, himself a Christian, rolling up a military machine against the third greatest naval power of the earth—such figures make Chinese news a confused but exciting serial story.

*Military Rule and Political Economy*

For long-range effects, the literary experiments of men like Hu Shih and the mass-education drive of Dr. James Yen and his associates are more significant than any one of hundreds of military leaders, but long-range trends are never news. The armies and their commanders have occupied the center of the stage, overshadowing the quest of the Chinese for civilian rule. Civilian rule, however, presupposes a sufficient area of common agreement on which to build laws and usages for government; armies require nothing but a nearly mechanical discipline and the crudest rule of thumb administration. The civilian government of Republican China has had to await the coming of at least a minimum of order out of the turmoil; armies, for lack of government, have dominated and continued that turmoil. China has been disunited in great part because she was impoverished by military rule; she has been ruled by arms partly because she was disunited. No unifier of the nation would have needed to maintain the armed hordes which were the greatest impediment to real national defense—hordes powerful enough to wreck governments but not powerful enough to build them. The war lords, as they are perhaps too flatteringly termed, do by no means measure up to the note of the intellectual and political leaders; but they have unqestionably held the greater bulk of day-to-day authority in China since 1912.

The most significant function of the armies is one which is quite frequently overlooked: their power as agencies of unsettlement. They have created disturbances more profound than mere public disorder; they have attacked institutions more vital than the public treasury; they have kept all parts of China from the dull apathy of conservatism. The arrogance and rapacity of the military rulers, their utter incompetence as administrators (with a number of honorable exceptions), and their ineffectiveness as propagandists have provided that loose and haphazard tyranny which some philosophers consider the prime requisite for social ferment. The military men have never been intelligent enough to impose truly totalitarian regimes, nor efficient enough to make the people of any one area content with a permanent separatism. The presence of the military rank and file has turned the Chinese social system upside down, reversing the accepted scale of ranks within the society and infringing upon the interests of every group—even the minimum interest of the very poor, their right not to starve to death. More conspicuously, the armies have given a picture of power which, in contrast with the scarcely traceable lines of influence and persuasion arising from ideological movements, is intelligible and reducible to concrete terms.

Without the militarists, there would have been no visible series of events to trace the change in China, no stereotypes at all by which to show the immediate alterations on the scene of power. Many men did rise and fall regardless of military considerations, but such occurrences were loosely and popularly ascribed to intrigue or else dismissed as beyond all rational understanding. The armies subsisted and roamed about, leaders and men both helpless on a sea of ignorance and doctrinal conflict; but the mere assent to unthinking discipline looked like order, and the most shadowy and insubstantial military hierarchy held out a promise of Caesarian peace. From 1915 to 1925 foreign comment stressed the movements of the war lords, singling out the man who might play the role of a Chinese Napoleon, and to the present this simple approach satisfies many. Meanwhile the foundations of social life shifted, falling away here, growing more solid there, behind the gloomy panorama of brutal, ineffectual warfare.

Closely related to the problem of armies was another category partially understandable in narrowly factual terms—political economy. The armies conditioned and set the pace, a slow one, for economic development. All financial projects were jeopardized by military rule, both by the exactions which the military might impose and by the constant threat that militarists, devaluating the currency or arbitrarily changing the political controls of economy, might alter the very economic system in which the project was being considered and fostered. Economic life in China could not continue through the traditional agricultural, guild, semicapitalist devices; Western trade and social dislocation prevented that. Yet no new economy could automatically replace the ruins of the old, since economic matters were part of a *political* economy subject to the extra-economic interferences which ideological change, military power, and halfway government could impose. One of the truly important achievements of the National Government at Nanking was the creation of a core for a twentieth century army. But all the military achievements in modern China pale before the staggering surprise of a managed currency, displacing a commodity and specie system which was older than all modern warfare.

One need not subscribe to either military or economic determinism to concede the relevance of military and economic matters in any society. In China there exists a peculiarly close correlation between the two. The absence of a class founded squarely on economic privilege and the subordination of the military to the bureaucratic elements in the imperial society were largely the result of the position occupied by the average nonacademic Chinese, who was typically a farmer capable of being a militiaman or a bandit. This duality of role strongly affected the development of government in China, and is a factor which still plays a great part. The Chinese owe many of their social and political peculiarities to the effectiveness of their mass action, which is able to take place with a minimum of formal leadership and coordination and with a maximum of secrecy and totality. In times when foreign conquest of China is no longer in the realm of the improbable, it is worth remembering that the Chinese are a people adamant in resistance to force and schooled in centuries of rebellion. Neither pacific nor military resistance could take place in the traditional Chinese way without the diffusion of military and economic power among broad masses of the population.

How, it may be asked, have the Chinese succeeded in being such a peaceful people, and yet a people so prone to popular uprising? How is it that, with their great talents for organization, they have let a shabby third-rate militarism sweep their land in modern times? The Chinese generals did not command the allegiance widely extended to even the meanest of South American despots; yet the people trembled before them. Not until the war lords lost power was there great popular enthusiasm for military ideals. If Chinese armies are considered solely as rough and primitive parallels to their European counterparts, paradox will follow paradox without rational explanation. To understand the Chinese military situation one must go back across the centuries and trace a system and a tradition which, at times obscure and frequently submerged, must come to the surface in the decisions upon which rest the question of national life or death for China.

*The Downfall of the Charioteers*

The Chinese have differed from other peoples not in being peaceful so much as in extolling peace. Not even in the Christian tradition of peace and love are there condemnations of war stronger than those of the Confucians. Yet, century to century, the Chinese have known war against the outside barbarians and with each other. Throughout historic times there are records of struggle and slaughter. H. G. Creel writes, "If we are to locate the traditional Chinese time of 'great peace' it must be far back in the Neolithic stage. Experts agree that in the earlier of the Neolithic sites known to us there is little evidence of warfare."[1]

At the very edge of history, about 1500 B. C., the Chinese appear as accomplished archers, using bows which were probably not dissimilar to those in use down to the twentieth century—heavy reflex bows, with a pull that was sometimes far greater than the longbow of the celebrated English yeomen of medieval times. The pellet bow, a form of slingshot, was also common in the earliest times. Armor was known in the earliest historic dynasty, the Shang, which by Chinese tradition is dated 1765–1123 B. C. The chariot, however, seems to have been less widely used than it later came to be.[2]

Under the Chou dynasty, in all Chinese history the most caste-bound, militaristic, and feudal (traditionally dated 1122–256 B. C.), the implements of warfare and the management of conflict fell into the hands of the ruling class. Previous to the Chou there was a relative military equality of all, despite the sharp lines between masters and men. After the Chou the great military states culminating in the warrior-bureaucrat tyranny of the Ch'in Shih Huang Ti (third century B. C.) tended to reduce war to mass movements, in which establishments, management, and broader considerations constantly increased. During this period the master class developed a scheme which was not as elaborately traced out in legal terms as Norman-English feudalism, nor as solidly grounded in outright military effectiveness as the Japanese system twenty-odd centuries later, but which amounted to a chivalric order within the limits of an ideology rooted in the family. The lords were the spiritual guardians and clan leaders as well as the earthly despots of their subjects. Standing above the law and invested with positions of high political dignity, their class nearly became a caste. Warfare—as apart from slaughter—was formalized and ritualized beyond all Western dreams of gallantry. According to Marcel Granet, who has brilliantly described public life of the period,

> The battle is a confused mêlée of boasts, generosities, homages, insults, devotions, curses, blessings and sorceries. Much more than a clash of arms, it is a duel of moral values, an encounter of competing honours. . . . The battle is the great moment in which each warrior proves his nobility, while in addition they prove to all present the nobility of their prince, their cause and their country.[3]

Our very word *chivalry* suggests horsemen; the Chinese nobles ruled their elaborate realm not from horseback but from chariots. The education of every patrician youth involved archery, music, writing, and reckoning, among other arts and virtues.[4] Archery was something which might be learned, after a fashion, by large numbers of common men; even peasants, with a bow and a lance or pike, might constitute light cavalry when provided, or providing themselves, with mounts. But the use of the four-horse chariot necessarily remained the exclusive privilege of the nobles. The chariot fighter had to have a driver and one or two others with him in his vehicle, which was itself costly, hard to obtain, and difficult to operate. A Chou noble driving forth to war thirty centuries ago was as technical a unit as an aviator in a combat plane today or a small group of men in a tank. Just as there is a democracy implicit in the light machine gun or the automatic rifle, so was there the potentiality of equality in vast masses of infantry, supported by light, cheaply armed cavalry. Aristocratic individualism meant something when wars were short and fought with elaborate equipment; but no noble could stand up against the mass forces which emerged and continued fighting until the feudal system lost any real significance and left the country open to the development of bureaucratic government and military power.

There was no overt attack on the feudal system. The system, however, possessed within itself contradictions which led to its doom. The central power was insufficient to keep the peace, and certain local groups were—by talent, economic factors, or geography—too strong to remain subordinate. The period known as the Spring and Autumn epoch (Ch'un Ch'iu; 770–473 B.C.) yielded to that known as the Age of Warring States (Chan Kuo; 473–221 B.C.). From feudal cores there grew states, which began to follow the course of development that led to the appearance of a system of sovereign nations in Europe; they increasingly interfered with the free operation of the feudal economy. By effecting the massing of power they eliminated the overawing charioteer from the field of decisive combat.[5] The chariots remained as the vehicles of the leaders or the focal points of battles, but they no longer implied a skill so great as to make up a monopoly of first-rate military force. While the most eminent thinker of the age, Confucius, lamented the decline of order, a new order was being shaped from the social, economic, and military realities laid bare by rapid development, Machiavellian intrigue, and the hard necessities of wartime economies.

The state of Ch'in, a Chinese Prussia, attained overwhelming hegemony in the third century before Christ. Its power rested on universal registration of the inhabitants, conscription, heavy policing, taxation involving constant intervention in economic matters, and legalistic administration. In its warfare there was little of the ritual which characterized the military period when chariots were dominant; codes did not amount to much. The immediate end of war was slaughter for political and economic purposes, not the hazardous parade of a feudal class. The Ch'in monarch who finally established a centralized empire took the vainglorious title of Shih Huang Ti (The First Emperor), and set himself the task of eradicating the regionalist ideologies of his conquered rivals by suppressing all political history but that of his native state. Proceeding from innovation to innovation, he ended by becoming one of the historic figures detested by later epochs. One of the practices which he extended throughout the Empire of China was the regularization of military service. He is also known as the originator of the grandiose project of the Great Wall; it is less well known that he forbade the erection of walls around cities within the Empire. His system of conscription involved three years of compulsory military service for all young men, and a corvee of three days' service each year at the frontier for every citizen; the former came to depend for its inclusiveness upon administrative integrity, while the latter was soon replaced by a money tax.

Although the First Empire established by the Ch'in did not last long, the Han dynasty (202 B. C. to A. D. 220) continued its military system[6] and kept standing armies at the northern frontier and at the imperial capital. The frontier forces were composed of militia augmented for special campaigns by volunteers and criminals. The Chinese fought the barbarians with the tactics of mounted archers, devices learned from the nomads. Away from the northern steppes, infantry seems to have gained constantly in importance. By the time of Christ the chivalry of the religious-social-military class of charioteers was ancient history, and mass armies had taken their place.

### Military Elements in Chinese Imperial History

Through the greater part of the past two thousand years, Chinese society has been governed by civilians. The scholastic bureaucracy secured and kept a position of primacy, and a common ranking of the social classes was: scholars, farmers, merchants, soldiers. The Confucians were antagonistic to war, and bureaucrats—if for governmental reasons alone—suspected the danger which lay in the broad dissemination of military knowledge. The Chinese consistently ranked the military man below the civilian; as a natural consequence most of the abler men went into scholarship and politics. Chinese history has its great military names and ample accounts of spectacular military exploits, but even here the elements of strategy, of diplomatic and cunning warfare, rate higher than in the corresponding European histories. Despite the fact that arms did not play as great a role in Chinese history as in Western, the difference is one of degree only; military considerations appeared and persisted which colored governmental action and social organization. Among these was the relation of the armed forces to the social order—in point of numbers and in point of force. When elections are lacking in a civilized society, fighting power demarcates an electorate of force, as it were; the distribution of power determines the center of political gravity as located in the society. In China there were, however, elements distinctly different from those in the West.

One of these was the correlation of mass power and military power. In epoch after epoch, armies seem to spring forth out of the very soil—armed groups radically unlike the Roman legion. For seasoned veterans marching forth with elaborately effective disciplines China substituted mass forces drawn directly from the populace, as need arose. In some dynasties the system was regularized in militia form. Of the Han, H. H. Dubs writes:

> Chinese armies were largely militia. Everyone was compelled to serve three years in the army or in forced labor; at the northern border, the whole male population had constantly to be ready to repel Hun forays. Hence all males seem to have been able to fight and to be required to do so. When the Emperor Wu [ca. 120 B. C.] wanted armies and none would volunteer, he merely had his officials sentence criminals to army service—and thus secured armies which seemed to be able to fight as successfully as his previous armies. Universal military con-

scription plus a registration of all able-bodied males seems to have been the Han method.[7]

The common people had crossbows for shooting birds or pronged hoes for digging which were efficient even in fighting standing armies; they were also frequently in possession of weapons because they were called up as militia against barbarians. Underlying such military conditions, with their highly important political consequences, there were several surprisingly concrete and simple mechanical considerations. The charioteers had come to an end partly because the chariots were drawn by horses yoked in such a fashion that when the horses pulled hard, they often choked themselves. Other factors are suggested by Dubs:

By the time that horses became plentiful, so that cavalry was employed, the crossbow had reached such a state of development that cavalry was shown to be inferior to infantry with crossbows. The medieval European crossbow was hampered by the mechanical weakness of its trigger mechanism—the crossbow was likely to be discharged prematurely by a jar; the Chinese Han crossbow had no such defect and was a powerful weapon. A group of crossbowmen with others in the rear to string crossbows and others to bring cocked bows to the marksmen in the front rank, could shoot down cavalry before they could come near enough to discharge the lighter bows cavalry necessarily carried. Cocked crossbows could be carried around safely and fired when needed. A bolt from a powerful crossbow could pierce any armor. Hence the strong-backed peasant with a crossbow had an advantage over the noble no matter how well the noble was armed or how good horses the latter possessed. The only advantage retained by the noble was that of leadership—tactical skill and command of large bodies of infantry. Cavalry became useful for scouting and pursuit chiefly.[8]

The character of military techniques caused Chinese politics to be qualified by rebellion or the fear of rebellion. The difference between a mob and an army became slight. In times of poor government there were rebellions almost yearly. Insurrectionary forces gained momentum overnight; from era to era huge mobs, tens and hundreds of thousands strong, swept away governmental armies and erased corrupt or oppressive dynasties. The process may be described as popular unrest made effective with arms, which professional armies could not resist. The low place of the soldier in society prevented men of genius from organizing a dominant military caste; the professional armies were insufficient to make military government effective. By a crude and brutal democracy of mob and murder the populace of China could destroy dynasties and governments whenever economic, social, or political conditions veered too far beyond the limits of the tolerable.

Trained fighters there were, but they had the function of frontier defense; when civil war broke out behind them, the imperial governments frequently called back the frontier forces together with the barbarians they had been fighting. At least two great dynasties, the T'ang and the Ming, were destroyed because they used the nomads of the northern wilds in order to put down domestic insurrections. Light cavalry supplemented enormous bodies of infantry. In fact, the Chinese were put down by foreign conquerors only when the foreigners had Chinese allies, or when a campaign of terror had broken the spirit of popular resistance. Chinese warfare showed the disadvantages as well as the advantages of being carried on by what were in effect militia forces. The cruelty was personal and direct, and not covered with fine disclaimers; restraint of armed forces was the distinguished exception rather than the rule. The line between soldier and peasant was one which could be crossed easily, and the line between soldiery and banditry a matter of intention. At its best, military technique was honest and robustly egalitarian; at its worst it led to abuse of force such as lynching, robbery, and fanatical turbulence. The formal records of Chinese dynasties show the use of trained armies in foreign expeditions, in some of which they achieved feats of military accomplishment which rank with any of world history. Domestic troops were also employed as guards and ornamental bodies attached to the throne and other great offices of the Empire.

The convenience of rebellion was such as to make revolt a part of the unwritten constitutional practice—that broad ideological framework upon which the Chinese world rested. It was sanctioned by the classics. It served as a barometer of popular opinion. An unsuccessful rebellion, one without the dimmest chance of success, might well be launched by intelligent and patriotic men because its very appearance could prompt the government to reform. In the words of one of the earliest Western writers on the subject:

A military and police is maintained sufficient to crush merely factious risings, but totally inadequate, both in numbers and in nature, to put down a disgusted and indignant people. But though no despotism, this same government is in form and machinery a pure autocracy. In his district the magistrate is absolute; in his province, the governor; in the empire, the Emperor. The Chinese people have no right of legislation, they have no right of self-taxation, they have not the power of voting out their rulers or of limiting or stopping supplies. *They have therefore the right of rebellion.* Rebellion is in China the old, often exercised, legitimate, and constitutional means of stopping arbitrary and vicious legislation and administration.[9]

Thomas Taylor Meadows, the author just quoted, also noted that "of all nations that have attained a certain degree of civilization, the Chinese are the least revolutionary and the most rebellious."[10] *Revolution* is a word broad enough to include principles; *rebellion*, more narrowly, suggests action against men. The same tight, enduring system of ideological control served to restrain the Chinese in their thinking even when they had the material power sufficient to shake off their past and build Utopia in its place. Rebels themselves obeyed the unwritten precepts. The triumph of the civilians was complete: with infantry prevailing on the battlefield, the peasants were the strongest; and with the total population saturated in compelling, uniform ideas of right and wrong, appropriate and inappropriate, the scholars had only to await the establishment of administration to assume the leadership. Against malgovernment, the populace retained the power of rebellion. Against misrule, the scholars held the power which came to them as interpreters of a vast and persuasive code of tradition. Whereas Western courts, citing the past, can negate the acts of the executive or legislative by interpretation or annulment, the Chinese scholars would do the same not merely for law, but for manners, morals, thoughts, and social activities as well. The great peasant armies, though able to destroy military dictatorship, were by their very nature too loosely organized to establish it.

*The Military Organization of the Manchu Dynasty*

Although the Manchus, who conquered China in the first half of the seventeenth century and ruled it until the opening of the twentieth, did not profoundly modify Chinese culture, they affected the military scheme. The general outline of Chinese war and its place in society remained largely the same; but there were two innovations: the establishment of a warrior caste and the introduction of military techniques from the West.

The Manchus were a non-Chinese people living in the northeastern peripheral zone of Chinese civilization. They had adopted the Chinese form of empire and bureaucracy in their capital at Mukden in the early seventeenth century, before advancing toward China proper. Invited by the Chinese to lend their aid in a civil war, the Manchus found themselves excelling in effectiveness and leadership, which soon led them to conquer the whole country. The numerical disproportion between Chinese and Manchus was such that the conquerors would never have taken over the Empire and founded a new dynasty (the Ch'ing) had they not been assisted by large numbers of Chinese. On the other hand, the spectacular terrorism of the Manchu cavalry was a potent weapon, and the Manchus did not feel that they owed their throne entirely to the Chinese. They were in the anomalous position of half-conquerors, a people coming into China partly as aliens and partly as the new leaders of the Chinese. At the very beginning of their rule (commonly dated 1644) they had to decide on a policy to determine their relations with the Chinese: Should they allow their people to mingle with and disappear into the vast Chinese masses, or should they attempt a policy of racial separateness to keep their blood clear of Chinese dilution? Underlying this question there was the even more practical one: Should the Manchus rule China simply as another imperial house, or should they attempt to maintain their status as a racially separate caste of conquerors?

There is a Chinese legend which tells of a high minister of state, a Chinese in the service of the Manchu conquerors, who saw no remedy from the oppression of China in his own generation, but who nevertheless worked with craftily concealed patriotism to sow the undoing of the house of the Ch'ing. He recommended to the Manchus that they keep their fighting men from demoralization by ordaining that no Manchu warrior should enter any trade or profession but those of warfare and public administration, and that they should guard the ancient heritage of their valiant blood by making miscegenation a crime. Thus he schemed to stiffen the Manchu monarchy in a position of unbounded arrogance, so that a few generations of peace would find its armies sloven, atrophied, and useless, and its people still alien to the Chinese. With neither military power to overawe the masses nor popular affection to uphold their foreign-rooted dynasty, they were bound to go down; all this, the legend tells, the Chinese adviser who lived and died with high Manchu honors clearly foresaw. Actually the Manchus did move in such a direction, and with the prophesied results.

They had conquered China with their own tribal-military system intact, organized into units termed *banners*. Unable to hold the country by their own force alone and, after putting down serious rebellions, unwilling to depend on the Chinese, they arranged a method of dual garrisoning. A Manchu military hierarchy paralleled the Chinese bureaucracy throughout the Empire, and Manchu bannermen were placed in every city of strategic importance. The Manchu garrisons were made up of men destined to arms, men who were the descendants of the wild horsemen of the northeastern plains, but who soon became tragic and useless idlers. Forbidden entrance into the vast and vital civilian society of the Chinese, by a decree of their own kinsman on the throne, they spent generation after generation in profound peace, forgetting war and losing their self-respect as warriors. Whatever the reason, they did not engage in practices such as the extended hunts, amounting in fact to great army maneuvers, by which Kublai Khan kept his Mongol troops hard and ready for war. An English writer, familiar with the state of the Manchu garrisons in their last years, thus described them:

But, unhappily, the inactive bannermen, both at Peking and in the provinces, had towards the end degenerated into idle, flabby, and too often opium-smoking parasites; they had long neglected to keep up their archery, which in any case had become useless in these days of magazine rifles, though it might have nourished a wholesome muscular habit of body if persisted in. . . . In the provinces these degenerate Manchus were often, practically, honourable prisoners, rigidly confined within the limits of the city walls, in the midst of a semi-hostile population speaking a dialect which the bannermen . . . had to learn, . . . if they wished even to buy a cabbage in the streets; and the Tartar General, who nominally outranked even the Chinese Viceroy, was really often a self-indulgent, ignorant incompetent.[11]

Politically, the Chinese found themselves face to face with a foreign group imbued with an arrogant racial pride and determined to maintain a separate existence. The Manchus did not bend to the superior numbers of the Chinese, nor yield to the attractions of Chinese culture. They maintained the Manchu language at the innermost citadel of Chinese civilization—the Forbidden City at Peking—and stamped their West Asiatic script on the money of the Empire. They worked out schemes by which the Manchus would retain a majority in the highest offices of the Empire, on the sole ground of race. Elementary rationalizations of two opposing racial attitudes were the result. The Manchu policy fortified and brought back from the past the racial pride of the Chinese. They were not merely the civilized heart of humanity; they were, civilization or no civilization, bound together by blood. If the Manchu garrisons served no other purpose, the presence of alien troops in the cities taught the Chinese the first lessons of resentment; it prepared them for the vigorous racial-nationalist appeal which the Nationalists were to put forth.

Governmentally, the effect of Manchu dual government was to force the Chinese to an increased consciousness of the implied presuppositions of their social and political system. The use of the garrisons constituted one of the four main causes of Manchu decline; the second cause was the violation of the strict merit system by racial preference in the bureaucracy; the other two were failure to maintain domestic tranquillity, and corruption in the hierarchy of scholar-officials.[12] Manchu rule by military power was unrealistic and a political affront. Their army of permanent occupation committed slow suicide in idleness and at the same time kept the Manchu dynasty from nativizing itself so that the Chinese might think of it as Chinese. Their creation of a hierarchy of bannermen, paralleling the older Chinese civilian institutions, brought to the surface of thought those prejudices and assumptions which had guided and controlled Chinese destiny for centuries. Government and society had been one to such a degree that the special features of a universal control did not require legalization or sharp tracing. The Manchus removed government from the rest of society by staining it with militarism and racial preference; it became ominously disparate and a conspicuous target for examination and consideration.

In the eighteenth and nineteenth centuries Manchu rule brought into a sharper focus the largely unformulated constitutional theory which had underlain the Chinese imperial society for nearly twenty centuries. With the sharper demarcation of rulers and ruled, the Manchus had to make frequent and overt use of legal authority over the ideology. The Chinese read of the sanction of rebellion in their own classics; they could turn to their histories for a description of the ignoble origins of their present masters. The dynasty turned therefore to literary censorship and ordered extensive excisions from all writings scholarly, artistic, or other, which might weaken the prestige of their house.[13] They ordained a most rigid and dogmatic interpretation of the classics so as to suit their purposes. This the Chinese met with sharp criticism. The literary struggle did much to weaken the scholastic class and to deprive the Manchus of academic supporters. At the same time it deprived the peasant Chinese of their natural leaders, with the consequence that secret and half-literate political associations faced an arbitrary government military in character. The old Chinese system remained, but it became more and more of a form with every generation. The theory of moral agency and ideological control was defamed by the very presence of the barbarian garrisons. The barbarians themselves weakened so much that in the later days of the Manchu Empire the military occupation became a myth instead of being a political fact. For the time being, however, Manchu military organization acted as a force-displaying agency until the scholars and the less favored classes of society were able to combine in a revolution.

Pacific government, government by moral agency, derives its greatest powers from assent and agreement; it thrives on symbolization and is never necessarily dependent upon the display of outright force. Government by force, on the other hand, remains effective almost in proportion to the exercise and vigor of that force; stereotyped and ritualized, it is essentially weak. Purely ceremonial administration and offices may be a burden on the body politic, yet their dignity may make up for their lack of efficiency. But an army that cannot fight is an object of ridicule, and its very presence a challenge to the resources of intelligence.

The Manchu garrisons in the key cities were under the command of Manchu military officers, whom Europeans dubbed with the picturesque title of *Tartar Generals*. The garrisons were made up of three racial elements: Manchu, Mongol, and Chinese. The Chinese in the banner armies were the descendants of soldiers in the renegade Han army (*han chün*), the Chinese section of the Manchu-Mongol-Chinese formations which conquered China for the Manchus in the seventeenth century. The military organization seems to have been a simplified copy of civilian bureaucracy, with examiners, censors, and other familiar devices of Chinese government appearing in quasi-military form. The principle of merit was violated, however, in that certain categories of men claimed special rank by hereditary right.[14] It was also possible for some of the bannermen to transfer between the civilian and the military branches of the government.

In the early nineteenth century the *han chün* possessed considerable artillery. There was a separate navy, comprising more than two thousand war vessels equipped from a score of dockyards. Even then, Chinese military technology was markedly inferior to European; the Chinese navy was no match even for Europe's wooden warships. When ironclads entered Far Eastern waters and breech-loading cannon were employed, the difference made Chinese naval and artillery establishments almost antiquarian in nature. With most of the banner forces of the Empire kept at Peking and the rest scattered over the country in the great cities, the Manchu force was widely diffused. In practice their armies hardly exceeded a quarter of a million men; whatever the exact total, the military were outnumbered far over a thousand to one by the Chinese, in the realm which the Manchus supposedly held by conquest.

The effective army in the later years of the Ch'ing dynasty was formed for the most part of the Green Standard (*lü ying*), provincial regulars, and the vast hordes of irregulars (*yung*, or "braves") who have traditionally done the greater share of the fighting in Chinese history. The Green Standard troops appear to have suffered, although to a lesser degree, from the long peace which ruined the banner armies, but their use in major police enterprises and troubles with primitive peoples kept them from the utter demoralization of the banners. The common practice under the Ch'ing was to recruit the local toughs, to appoint their leaders as probationary officers, and to use such emergency armies for real and immediate fighting. Although the Manchu dynasty had no system of organized reserves and little machinery for rapid mobilization, they were thus nevertheless able to swell their armies to astonishing numbers in a very short while. American military commentators said in 1900 that the peacetime size of the Chinese imperial army was about three hundred thousand men and its wartime strength about one million—minute figures for China's reserve of man power —and added:

> The total strength of the standing army of China can not be exactly ascertained, and if a statement of the number of men belonging to it could be given, it would be of little value, as many of the men who are carried on the rolls are neither armed nor equipped, and a great number of them are not even performing military service, but are following their usual vocations.[15]

This military regime bears the air of a vast preparation for some foreseen but remote emergency. The Manchus themselves seemed to sleep; armies drowsed through the centuries, weapons rusting, tactics forgotten in the mimicry of parade, while all about them the factual potency of military power passed to the Chinese. Even the Europeans at first shared the illusion of great although latent military power behind the Manchu throne. The easy defeat of the Manchu Chinese forces in the wars with England and France in the early and middle nineteenth century led writers such as Thomas De Quincey to cry out against the great fraud of Asia—the sleeping Manchu giant, who was not sleeping but dead.

The T'ai-p'ing rebellion[16] lasting from 1849 to 1865 provided an actual test of military power in the Manchu Empire, and demonstrated two remarkable new facts. First, the real forces were no longer the regular troops, whether banner or Green Standard, but the militia which might be organized and trained for immediate results by robust civilians like the viceroys Li Hung-chang and Tsêng Kuo-fan.[17] Second, the military technique of the Far East was obsolete; even a little Western equipment, leadership, and training made any Chinese army immediately more effective. The consequences were contradictory. If the military regime of the Manchus existed only in a formal sense, and actual power had passed to the Chinese masses, who had only to await a leadership to exhibit their power, then force had failed and government by moral agency would again be the need of the epoch. At the same time, the introduction of

Western technique showed the possibility of a new regime of force, another opportunity for a minority to overwhelm the vast majority by sheer technical military effectiveness, and government by moral agency could not be sufficient. The center of military gravity would not simply pass to the group possessing the largest army. A new form of government, making intelligent use of modern weapons, was called for.

Undoubtedly China was and is too large to be governed by mere military occupation—unless forces far larger than any which have heretofore operated in the Far East are employed. The very garrisoning of the country would absorb tremendous armies. At the same time, military force is sufficient to overawe and intimidate civilians in any given area, since the man with a rifle is superior to the man with the crossbow or spear. Conceivably, however, a rhythm may originate between the progress in introducing new weapons and the progress of the populace in learning new means of counteraction. In 1860 the British and French entered Peking and later burned the Summer Palace of the Manchu emperors as a lesson to the imperial government. The expedition, casual when measured by Western standards, showed that the Manchu bannermen and Chinese levies were equally powerless before the intrusion of a more advanced skill in warfare. As soon as peace was declared the Chinese began organizing some of their metropolitan forces after the Western manner, obtaining foreign instructors to put them through the Western manual of arms.

At the same time that the Manchu court was learning to its discomfort the importance of Western warfare, it was calling Westerners to its aid in putting down the T'ai-p'ings. The Manchus assembled a nineteenth century navy including steam vessels from British and other sources, which broke up without having accomplished much. With land forces there was much greater success; an American, Frederick Townsend Ward, and an Englishman, Major Charles George ("Chinese") Gordon, organized a small body of imperial regular troops along Western lines and with Western officers. This force was given the honorific title of "Ever Victorious Army" by the court, and together with the militia organized by Tsêng Kuo-fan and Li Hung-chang suppressed the T'ai-p'ing rebellion after the banner and Green Standard armies had failed.

The ensuing thirty years (1865–1895) witnessed the slow decline in Manchu foreign policy and military development and a gradual crumbling of Chinese society at large. Revolutionaries such as Sun Yat-sen received their first baptism of Westernization in the 1870's and 1880's, and foreign trade rose by great leaps. Occasionally the Empire's military regime seemed to rally. Between 1883 and 1885 the Chinese forces fighting the French in Indo-China were equipped with Mannlicher rifles far more up-to-date than the weapons of their enemies. In the preceding decade the Chinese destroyed a Mohammedan state set up in Chinese Turkestan in defiance of their suzerainty, and overawed the Russians into evacuating an area along the Ili seized under the pretence of maintaining order. The lack of coordination between the different agencies of government was as much to blame for China's weakness as were the specific defects of the central departments. When the army was winning, the diplomatic agencies yielded; when the army was unprepared, the diplomatic agencies, by some ill-timed impertinence, gave aliens the pretext for hostilities.

The first Sino-Japanese War (1894–1895) offered another test. Hitherto, the armed conflicts with Europeans, even including the entry of Westerners into Peking in 1860, had seemed remote from the actual problem of military power in China. The Europeans might possibly withdraw and leave the Empire in peace. But incalculable danger would arise to Chinese prestige should the *wo*, the sea dwarfs, defeat the Chinese and eat more deeply into the mainland. Chinese began to realize that in this war their status was at stake, not only in the dimly perceived wide universe of the Westerners but also in that of the Far East in which they had long held such comfortable hegemony. They entered the war relatively well equipped, so that even outside observers were doubtful of the outcome of the struggle. No one was more amazed than the Chinese themselves when they were whipped as no modern nation has been whipped, routed ignominiously in a sequence of slaughters, and ultimately forced to make important territorial and financial concessions to the Japanese.

This catastrophe was followed by a series of reforms, some designed to enable China to meet the West on its own ground. In January, 1896, a turning point was reached with the appointment of Yüan Shih-k'ai to command the one efficient brigade assembled in the course of the war.[18] Yüan was to find in modern arms the career which led to his dictatorship after the fall of the Empire, and was to perform notable work as a military and administrative reformer, although of restricted value. He joined the reactionaries and brought to an end the Hundred Days of Reform of 1898, a movement generated by the initiative of the idealistic young Emperor Kuang Hsü, who sought to direct China into the course already taken by Japan—modernization within the imperial system. In 1900 there occurred the wild upheaval of the Boxers. It began as a native racial uprising against the Manchus, but was deflected by the Manchus into the support of the court and hostility against the Western intruders. During the Boxer movement part of the fighting against the Westerners was done by regular banner and Green Standard troops, but the greater part by bands of desperadoes and fanatics. The imperial army suffered in the chaos following the international occupation of Peking.

Under the name of the *Wu Wei Chün* the first large-scale attempt was made to modernize the Chinese armed forces. After the military and naval experiments of the 1860's and later decades, this enterprise evoked great hopes. The new army was inaugurated in 1895 with foreign instruction and foreign arms. In 1901 one division was made the core of Yüan Shih-k'ai's new modern force. Rodney Gilbert, a British publicist, has summarized the military changes down to the end of the Manchu dynasty as follows:

In January 1901 the Yangtze Viceroys submitted a memorial to the Throne suggesting among other things the disbandment of the useless *Lü Ying* [Armies of the Green Standard], the employment of the Bannermen, almost as useless, in service other than military, and the creation of a modern army. This brought forth an Imperial decree ordering reorganization of the army, of which Yuan Shih-kai, then Viceroy of Chihli, took advantage to build up six new divisions, four of which were transferred to the Ministry of War in 1906. This was the real beginning of the *Lu Chun*, the Chinese National Army. In January, 1905, a comprehensive scheme was outlined designed to give China an army of 36 Divisions or 360,000 men, by the year 1911. Three years after this decision was made there were about 60,000 men, with 360 guns, in the North, and 40,000 men, with 174 guns, in the South. The army was developing along sound lines when Yuan Shih-kai was removed from office in 1908 after the death of his great patroness the Empress

Dowager, and the direction of military, as well as other affairs, fell into the hands of the Manchu princes, whose mismanagement contributed much to the downfall of their dynasty three years later.[19]

The beginning, although auspicious, did not mean that even the model sections of the modernized forces were comparable to those of other lands. The confusion of weapons was already evident. A member of the United States General Staff wrote in 1910:

> To arm these masses China has been obliged to use weapons that are considered somewhat out of date. There are four types of rifles, mostly Mausers and Japanese Murata rifles of old pattern. They are, however, breech-loading, small-caliber weapons, not to be despised, even if they do not reach the ideal which some nations set. In fact they are the weapons which have been used in the great wars of most recent date.
> It is so also with the artillery where even a greater difference of types is to be observed. This is, undoubtedly, a serious drawback, owing, of course, to the great difficulty of providing ammunition.[20]

It was during this period, from the decisive defeat of the dynasty by Japan in 1895 to the Republican Revolution of 1911–1912, that the Chinese revolutionaries most eagerly studied military manuals and sought to purchase Western arms to offset the great advantages gained by the modernized portions of the imperial army. Sun Yat-sen became almost as much a military authority as he was a political philosopher and leader; his chief military follower, General Huang Hsing, performed for the revolutionaries the services rendered for the regime by Yüan Shih-k'ai. On both sides there was the anxiety to master the mysteries of twentieth century warfare. The World War had not yet begun, nor had the staggering burdens of modern armament become evident. Great as were the improvements in fighting, prewar military organization seemed still primarily a matter of well-equipped infantry, properly led, properly drilled, and supported by adequate artillery and other auxiliary services. Wireless, gas, airplanes, tanks, submarines, torpedo launches, and mechanized or aerialized infantry were little more than a matter of speculation. The proportions of present-day military budgets no one could foresee.

## The Army and the Republican Revolution

The Republican Revolution of 1911–1912 was the last overt act in the collapse of the ideologically maintained social system; it brought armies into violently free play in the support of movements toward re-formation of the ideology and articulation and control of the society. On October 10, 1911, the troops of the Wuch'ang garrison rose in mutiny and sided with the revolution. A series of uprisings engineered by military and agitational leaders followed, province by province, all directed against the imperial power in the North. The use of violence in Chinese politics served to accentuate a condition which had affected China even in the earliest historic times—the unresolved contradictions between the North and the South. Differences of race, spoken language, and economy produced fundamental cleavages accentuated by temperament. Traditionally the North was more conservative and solidaristic, the South more rebellious and enterprising. Sun Yat-sen was a Southerner; militarism reached its sharpest effectiveness in the North.

Yüan Shih-k'ai, who had proved himself the evil genius of Emperor Kuang Hsü by betraying the monarch's reforms of 1898, was called to the aid of the Manchus only to betray them to the Republic; he then served the Republic with the intention of seizing complete power for himself. The Republicans set up their regime in Nanking on January 1, 1912, with Sun Yat-sen as president. They established contact with Yüan, who acted in the triple capacity of negotiator for the Manchus, representative of the modernized armies of the North (which were his), and leader in his own right and in his own interest. The Republicans realized that Yüan could not be dispossessed—indeed, it is fairly certain that he could have upheld the throne had he so wished. Their power was indefinite, and as Chinese they preferred compromise and order to ideals pushed to the bitter end. In the middle of February they yielded to Yüan, and Sun surrendered to him the presidency as a reward for his allegiance to the Republic. Yüan, for the Manchus, secured a settlement by which the Forbidden City (the residence of the emperor in Peking) was made into a second Vatican City; the emperor was allowed his formal and ritual titles (a status remarkably like that of the Pope) and a very substantial stipend. For the

Northern armies and himself Yüan obtained actual power over the country. A civilian, but a soldier as well, Yüan rose by both intrigue and the implied threat of force.

The Republic was launched by valedictory imperial edicts ordering the imperial officials throughout the realm to obey Yüan and the new form of government; by Republicans nominally headed by their greatest and coldest antagonist; and by a soldier of higher professional standing in the Western sense than any Chinese leader for centuries past undertaking the task of keeping order and ushering China through drastic reconstruction. For a few halcyon months it seemed as though the Republic might grow into reality from under the aegis of military dictatorship.[21] But soon it became apparent that the revolution was not a transfer of power and renovation of order but the dissolution of power and the erasure of order. What was left was ideological uncertainty, social turmoil, economic disorganization—with politics reduced to mere pageantry, and the armies, ominously growing under the care of President Yüan, maintaining what little order was left to maintain. In 1913 the Nationalist-Republicans rebelled in the Yangtze valley and were crushed by the armies of the government of the Republic of China.

From the military rule of Yüan Shih-k'ai there emerged an army system which was to bring China to almost complete political ruin in the decade after Yüan's death. Although he organized a model regiment as a sample of what could be done in China, inflation of numbers and deterioration of morale and *matériel* were the most obvious symptoms of the new role of the army—a role much more concerned with problems of domestic intrigue than with defense against the outsiders. For an army of national defense, high technical excellence and a commensurate smallness of numbers are desirable features; for an army of dictatorship or occupation, inferior equipment, poor supplies, and inefficient training are all trifling handicaps in comparison with the advantage of vast numbers which can be used to garrison large sections of the realm and meet the threat of civil war. The very shift from empire to republic involved the enlistment of additional thousands of revolutionary fighters; once in the army, they were hard to dislodge. The personal military interests of Yüan led him to expand the army, and his political ambitions nourished the thought that the country would be secure beneath him only through the medium of an extensive garrison system. Finally, there was a far-reaching shift in the Chinese social pyramid. Men of intelligence and of education flocked to the army, and Japan's military schools were crowded with young Chinese who saw in war their easiest avenue to fortune or to the service of their country.

A reconstituted army, soldiers who could command greater respect than ever before, numerical extension and qualitative deterioration of the national armed forces—these were the more patent military changes under the Republic. To them must be added the factors fusing the elements into a system that was to bring immediate fortune and ultimate ruin to practically all who ventured into its operations. Many of the provinces which turned to the cause of the revolutionaries in 1911 and 1912 became gradually militarized. When the Manchus were gone, the old distinction between the Tartar General and the civilian viceroy had lost its purpose; the new provincial executives combined both military and governmental powers. Provincial jealousies and the growing disorder favored a strong factual autonomy for the various provinces, even though there was no technical claim of provincial independence and very little even of confederation. The first Republic was in name a centralized parliamentary-presidential state with quasi-federal features; in fact it was the combination of an impotent, headless imperial bureaucracy and a presidential military dictatorship possessing physically limited and indefinable authority over a large group of provinces. Between China and the accomplishment of regular and orderly republican government there stood ignorance, turmoil, poverty, reaction, and despair. Between Yüan's regime and the *tuchün* system there stood only Yüan's might.

### NOTES

1. Herrlee G. Creel, *The Birth of China*, p. 141, London, 1936.
2. *Ibid.*, pp. 142–154.
3. Marcel Granet, *Chinese Civilization*, p. 270, New York, 1930. Quoted by permission of the American publishers, Alfred A. Knopf, Inc.
4. Henri Maspero, *La Chine antique*, p. 131, Paris, 1927. This is one of the most valuable surveys of ancient China.
5. An elementary discussion of this period is to be found in Paul M. A. Linebarger, *The Political Doctrines of Sun Yat-sen*, pp. 25–29, "Nation and State in Chinese Antiquity," Baltimore, 1937.
6. Pan Ku (H. H. Dubs, translator), *The History of the Former Han Dynasty*, *passim*, Baltimore, 1938.

7. In a memorandum prepared in response to a request by the present writer.
8. *Ibid.*
9. Thomas Taylor Meadows, *The Chinese and Their Rebellions*, p. 24, London, 1856. His accounts of the T'ai-p'ing rebellion even today possess great liveliness and interest and illuminate twentieth century Chinese problems.
10. *Ibid.*, p. 25.
11. E. H. Parker, *China . . .* , pp. 259–260, New York, 1917.
12. A. N. Holcombe, *The Chinese Revolution*, pp. 70–81, Cambridge, 1930.
13. See Luther Carrington Goodrich, *The Literary Inquisition of Ch'ien-lung*, Baltimore, 1935.
14. The most extensive source of information on Manchu military organization in China is T. F. Wade, "The Army of the Chinese Empire: Its Two Great Divisions, the Bannermen or National Guard, and the Green Standard or Provincial Troops; Their Organization, Pay, Condition &c.," *The Chinese Repository* (Canton), vol. 20, pp. 250–280, 300–340, 363–422, 1851, which is now unfortunately rare. William James Hail, *Tseng Kuo-fan and the Taiping Rebellion*, New Haven, 1927, presents an accessible and informative digest of this and other material in its opening pages. Two French works based on Wade are Jules Picard, *État générale des forces maritimes et militaires de la Chine . . .* , Paris, 1860, and P. Dabry, *Organisation militaire des Chinois, ou la Chine et ses armées*, Paris, 1859. William Frederick Mayers, *The Chinese Government*, Shanghai, 1897, is one of the most valuable references for the structure of the last imperial government of China; designed as a manual of titles, it presents a concise outline of all major civil and military offices. A more elaborate treatise is P. C. Hsieh, *The Chinese Government, 1644–1911*, Baltimore, 1925. See also Anatol M. Kotenev, *The Chinese Soldier*, Shanghai, 1937. The text refers to Wade, p. 391, and Hsieh, p. 260.
15. United States War Department, Adjutant-General's Office, no. 30, *Notes on China*, pp. 57–69, "The Chinese Army," Washington, 1900. Except for cursory references, this pamphlet is of no great value.
16. See above, pp. 32 ff.
17. See Hail, *op. cit.* in note 14.
18. See Meribeth E. Cameron, *The Reform Movement in China, 1898–1912*, p. 59, Stanford, 1931.
19. H. G. W. Woodhead (ed.), *The China Year Book*, 1921–2, Tientsin, 1921; chap. XIX, "Defense," by Rodney Gilbert, pp. 511–512. Gilbert's is a competent contemporary account of *tuchünism*, sketching the background very clearly.
20. George H. Blakeslee (ed.), *China and the Far East*, New York, 1910, Chapter X, "The Chinese Army—Its Development and Present Strength," by Major Eben Swift, p. 181. See also General H. Frey, *L'Armée chinoise: l'armée ancienne, l'armée nouvelle, l'armée chinoise dans l'avenir*, Paris, 1904.

21. For a discussion of the governmental changes of the period see below, pp. 145 ff. See also H. F. MacNair, *China in Revolution*, Chicago, 1931; A. N. Holcombe, *The Spirit of the Chinese Revolution*, New York, 1931. For a contemporary censure of Yüan Shih-k'ai see Paul Myron [Paul M. W. Linebarger], *Our Chinese Chances*, Chicago, 1915.

*Chapter* V

## CAUSES

Yüan's closing years might have resembled Napoleon's rise from the position of First Consul to that of emperor, had he not been checked at the very last moment by armed uprisings and expressions of deep popular contempt. Even so, he retained control of the country.¹ The humiliation of his defeat lacked even dramatic compensations, and he died in June, 1916, of disease, poison, or chagrin. With his death the Republic had a chance to stand by itself, but it could not.

*The Age of the War Lords*

Yüan had fastened the symbols of old on the scaffolding of a new order. With his death the momentum of administrative routine retained from the Manchu dynasty was lost; the Republican government in Peking degenerated from impotence to comedy. The process called government began to nauseate patriotic Chinese and foreigners alike; few were able to take a long view, to maintain their courage, and to keep on fighting against disgusting and disheartening realities. With the decomposition of the central government—except the modern bureaucracies such as posts and customs, which were kept intact by their foreign personnel and their special international status—the armies, though divided provincially, stepped into positions of unprecedented authority. There was a veritable epidemic of monarchical ambition, greed, and willfulness among the provincial military commanders; many Chinese expected a new Yüan to emerge from that group and become the "strong man of China." With such a stage to strut on, it is not surprising that the Chinese military lost constructive vision. A sober nucleus of idealistically hard-headed, patriotic men, each a George Washington, might have used military power to reunite the country, but order could not be expected to emerge from the unsystematized competition of armed forces.

Three broader factors affected the ascendancy of war lords, in addition to obvious motives and interests. The ideological ruin was bad enough; the consequent social disorder crippled China. But the armies now came to provide a refuge for the unemployed and dispossessed. A second factor, the mechanical mobilization of military forces through the railways, made warfare more expensive and ruinous than it would have been with the slow-moving infantry of the past. Thirdly, the war lords gave physical embodiment to the ideological and social disunity of China, inviting the constant intervention of the Western powers and of Japan in Chinese affairs.

Individually the war lords warrant no special attention. There was Chang Tso-lin in Manchuria; Tuan Chi-jui and Ts'ao Kun in North China; Yen Hsi-shan ("The Model Governor") and, to the west of him, Fêng Yü-hsiang ("The Christian General"); Chang Chung-chang in Shantung, significant more for his brutality than for his political and military position; the quaint, conservative scholar Wu P'ei-fu, in the Yangtze valley, minor figures in the South and West. It was not the generals who were important, but militarism.

Militarism machine-gunned the Confucian ethics out of politics; it taxed the land into ruin; it laid China wide open to imperialistic thrusts, and—by the same act—made her a poor market. Militarism built roads when they were strategically required, established a few railways and spoiled more, modernized China, but did so in the costliest way of all. Only in the intellectual world was military domination not outright destruction. The generals and their staffs were surprisingly ignorant of the power of ideas, ineffectual in their censorship, oblivious to the great leverage of undercover agitation. Trusting arms, they failed to see that the only opposition able to destroy them was not military but mental.

While the soldiery stirred the country with murder and oppression, their system progressed steadily toward self-destruction. Two great pressures forced constant further expansion of the armies. The first is obvious: military rivalry. The second was the growing abuse of army organization as a means of unemployment relief. Military taxation drove the peasants off the land, whereupon they had no recourse but to become bandits or soldiers. If they were bandits, consolidation under a chieftain transformed them into military irregulars and induced some ambitious general to include them in his forces. If they were soldiers, the bandit stage remained in reach. In either case, they added to the burden falling upon their commander, which in turn led to still greater impoverishment of the peasants, a further increase of dispossessed men, bandits, and soldiers. With the widening circulation of arms, Western guns and fighting methods became less and less a secret of small groups capable of establishing a firm military oligarchy and more and more the property of a cross section of the Chinese masses.

From an estimated total of 1,369,880 in 1921,[2] the number of men under arms rose to a figure estimated to be between 1,883,300 and 1,933,300 five years later.[3] This increase occurred in one of the poorest countries of the world, despite conditions of extreme misery:

> Recruiting goes on incessantly in every town in North China where there is a garrison. There are no statistics available, but it is known that the death rate from disease is very high because, even in garrison, sanitary precautions are crude and the medical service is inefficient and inadequate. In battle the care of the wounded is barbarously primitive, even in the best units, and death from infected wounds is rather the rule than the exception; while those who cannot walk from the field to the nearest hospital more often than not die of exposure or clumsy handling. One of a Chinese commander's major concerns is filling the gaps in the ranks, but at the same time these conditions have kept the proportions of the armies down to a fairly constant figure. Chinese officers have advanced the theory that if recruiting were everywhere abandoned, disease, desertions and losses in battle would account for ten per cent. per annum, so that the armies would automatically cease to exist in ten years.[4]

The use of the railways for military purposes unsettled large groups of Chinese geographically and caused meetings of extensive bodies of men from different areas. At first such contacts, especially under wartime conditions, would only intensify provincial sentiment and mistrust of strangers, but gradually this influence began to make for a new national consciousness. In the meantime, the troops learned the intricacies of modern transport. A coolie in a peaceful part of Asia might see trains for years, observing the Westerners riding in them, and remain impressed by the sight; a Chinese bandit sitting on a freight car in a commandeered train would become rapidly familiar with the fire vehicles.

The role of the militarists with respect to China's international status was ambiguous. In the first place, the weakness which they created reduced China to an international pawn. The discord into which she had fallen allowed for semipartitions—various foreign interests backing different war lords—although a genuine partition may thereby have been staved off. In China proper the influence of the Japanese seemed to be behind Chang Tso-lin and the Northern militarists; the British were regarded as friendly to Wu P'ei-fu in the Yangtze valley; and the French achieved something not far from domination in the province farthest southwest, Yünnan. Fêng Yü-hsiang was supposed to have veered picturesquely for foreign friends between the Protestant missions and the Bolshevik agents. A miniature replica of the European balance of power could be played in China, with outside groups friendly to one or the other war lord. An agreement between the chief participants in 1919 sought to prevent the shipping of arms to unauthorized military groups in China but proved largely ineffectual in the end.

Between 1922 and 1926 there was formed in South China a nexus of armies which were to provide the military edge to ideological revolution and establish the followers of Sun Yat-sen in power. These armies were built up with the assistance of Russian and German advisers and with American arms which had been left in Siberia and had fallen into the hands of the Bolsheviks; the troops were led by new-style Chinese officers under the leadership of Chiang K'ai-shek. The Whampoa Academy was the most obvious sign of the new school of military thought, coming forth as a consequence of the Nationalist-Communist coalition.[5] Armaments did not differ in any substantial degree from those of the war lords, but they were more carefully kept and more skillfully used. The military machine which arose in the South was better organized, better disciplined, better led, and better cared for than any army on the Chinese scene for a decade.

From 1926 to 1927 the ensuing campaign for the Nationalist conquest of China, as outlined in the principles of Sun Yat-sen,[6] drove forward with striking success. The Nationalist troops everywhere pushed their enemies before them with astonishing speed. The explanation is to be found in part in the efficiency and military honesty of officers and men, but even more in the nonmilitary factors which fortified the armies and the ideological weapons which cleared the ground before it. The new armies not only represented military might; they were also propaganda machines. To every regiment there was attached a political staff to keep up the morale of the troops and to win over the enemy and the civilian population. The troops themselves were propaganda brigades as well as military units. Literacy in the armies was made a point of great pride, and certain divisions made novel reputations for themselves on this ground. The Nationalists were known by many as the soldiers who did not harm the people. Without the troops the Nationalists would never have come to power; but without the supporting sweep of mass propaganda the Nationalist movement might have gone on for decades in the form of civilian conspirators fighting against overwhelming odds or else seeking to make venal mercenaries the prime instrument for the regeneration of Chinese civilization.

The military revolution of 1926–1927 brought new factors to the Chinese military scene. It indicated that a point of equilibrium had been reached between the military and the ideological modes of control and that it was no longer possible for sheer force and a minimum of intelligence to hold unchallenged power in the Chinese society. It was, furthermore, a threefold struggle: a patriotic and progressive uprising against domestic and foreign oppression and inefficiency; an agrarian revolt on a grand scale; and a proletarian uprising on the part of the relatively small but strategically placed Chinese proletariat. Only in the first of these aspects did the revolution meet with the approval of most Chinese—the victims and not the bearers of arms. Men of all shades of opinion were able to agree on a policy of attacking the system of *tuchüns*, which offered no planning for the future, no resurrection of the past, and little public order. The patriotic troops were enraged by the corruption and inadequacy all about them and by the fortresses of privilege reared by aliens on their coasts and in their greatest inland cities.

The campaign of 1926–1927 marked the identification of the coolie soldier with his own class and of the peasant fighter with his. The rank and file were given to understand that they were not fighting in some game beyond their understanding but for the security of people like themselves. Under the influence of the propaganda put forth by the Nationalists and the allied Communists, an incipient agrarian revolt was fanned into flame and proletarian uprisings in the cities were made possible for the first time. Whole sections of the countryside fell into a condition not far from anarchy as the revolutionary troops led the people in revolt. After 1927, however, the military forces developed along two antagonistic lines. The Nationalists, seizing the political instruments of the revolution but finding its ideological factors largely beyond their control, began to create a professionalized army with which to stabilize their regime. The Communists, and their agrarian allies, standing to the Left of the newborn Nanking government, were eager to fight on in the tested informal fashion. In the year of the establishment of the Nanking government, 1927, the Red Army could still demonstrate its effectiveness. Shortly afterward the precautionary arms embargo of the foreign powers, which had prevailed since 1919, was lifted, thereby opening up the means by which Chiang K'ai-shek could renovate and specialize the armies under his command.

The break with the war-lord tradition was much more obvious in the case of the Communists than in the case of the Nationalists. The Communists, lacking sufficient support to occupy any broad contiguous territory, fell back on guerrilla fighting of their own. The Nationalists, strong enough to hold a certain portion of the area, nevertheless compromised with the existing military system to seek mastery. For three years after the establishment of the Nanking government, it remained doubtful whether the whole government might not subside into inertia and neglect, leaving Chiang standing alone, distinguished from the other war lords only by his character.

Late in 1930 and early in 1931 a menacing alliance was organized between two of the most influential remaining Northern *tuchüns* and the "liberal" wing of the Nationalists. Operating from the north, after the proclamation of an insurgent "National Government" at Peking, the rebels at first seemed to have the military advantage. Chiang had learned many lessons, however, and in the most serious fighting which China had seen in years he broke the force of the Northern offensive. Airplanes appeared as a threat against the civilian population of Peking, although no actual deaths were reported. There were ugly rumors that gas was being used at the front. Small tanks from England, though giving a rather poor performance, symbolized a novel trend. More and better heavy artillery was used than ever before. Trenches came up to World War standards. The war ended with the intervention from Manchuria of Chang Hsüeh-liang, a strangely progressive and patriotic *tuchün;* but the fighting had been enough to show that of all the great armed forces in China the Nationalist armies of Chiang K'ai-shek and the Nanking government were the most effective.

The rehabilitation of men's thinking had not proceeded far enough to eliminate the dangers of an overemphasized military leadership, but the tide had turned. After 1931 the military situation in China had become subordinate to the problems of ideology and of government. The chief military factors were now the governmentalized armies, the guerrilla opposition of the Communists, and the problem of foreign war.

*The Age of Air Conquest*

The new military period which replaced the war-lord system was marked by (1) technical improvement of the armies, especially in the direction of air power; (2) supplementation of the armies by the quasi-military power of the civil government, so that Chinese wars ceased to be a question of armed bands drifting about the surface of the social system; (3) organization of the Nationalist armies into national units in fact as well as name; (4) increasing pressure of the disbandment problem; (5) development of guerrilla tactics by the Reds and of guerrilla-suppression tactics by the Nationalists; (6) problems arising from Japanese conquest, which overwhelmed Manchuria in one fierce onslaught and harassed China for six years of military aggressions before breaking forth anew in the catastrophic surge of 1937–1938.

Aviation was to leap to a sensational place. Aviation and national civilian government became almost natural complements of one another. Only by aviation could all parts of the country be brought under the jurisdiction of Nanking and the geographical handicaps of China be overcome, and only a national government could afford the long-term investments in machines and men necessary to effective air armament. The record of technical improvement in the Nationalist armies is clearly symbolized by the advancement of military aircraft. Military aviation in China previous to the establishing of the Nanking government demonstrated the weakness of the preceding regime. As early as 1909 a French aviator was giving demonstration flights over Shanghai.[7] The Ch'ing dynasty sought to establish an airplane factory but met with no success. Yüan Shih-k'ai purchased a few planes and set up a flying school. The first telling use of planes in Chinese politics and war occurred, however, with the bombardment of the imperial palace by a lone aviator in the course of an attempted monarchical restoration in 1917. In the period of the war lords there were many isolated efforts to build up flying services. The most promising of these, undertaken by the Peking Republic with British assistance after 1920, failed through neglect, mismanagement, and corruption. As late as 1928 there was no prospect of significant air fighting in China.

By 1931 the Nanking government had built up an air force of about seventy serviceable planes; a contemporary commentator observed, "Aeroplanes played a very considerable—some would even say a decisive—part in the civil war of 1930 . . . "[8] By 1932, when an American aviation mission arrived to help in the training of a Chinese military air force, the estimates ran into a total of 125 to 140 commercial and training planes.[9] In the ensuing five years the Chinese national air force developed rapidly. It played the leading role in suppressing the Fukien uprising of 1932–1933 and in driving the Communists into the Northwest. In 1937 the head of the American aviation mission, Colonel John Jouett, wrote, "Japan maintains that China has a thousand planes; my guess would be seven hundred and fifty of all types. But no one knows . . . "[10] Other experts would reduce the figure to one-third or less by the elimination of planes which would not be of first-class utility in actual combat. The preparations for foreign hostilities up to 1937 were accompanied by such a degree of secrecy that definite figures are not available. For domestic purposes, however, almost every plane would count, and the cardinal fact remains that domestically the National Government possesses a monopoly of air power in China. It is thereby in a better position to make its supreme will formidably known than was any emperor of any dynasty. The future may show that Chinese mastery of aircraft is psychologically as important as was mastery of the steamship for the Japanese —a visible demonstration to an Asiatic people of their own accomplishments with Western technology.

As for other improvements of the armies, only three factors need be mentioned. The armies were consolidated generally, and with their better status—in literacy, pay, means of subsistence, and regularity of control—there came a realization that the military force was the creature of the national state. The Chinese nation was taking form as an ideological and social entity of sufficient strength to command the direct allegiance of fighting men. A new respect arose for the officers and men of the armies. Under Yüan Shih-k'ai the armies had been able to evolve a respectability of their own making; under Chiang K'ai-shek this respectability began to be accepted at its face value by the rest of the society, so that a pilot was not only admired by the crowd but was recognized as an expert among experts, even in literary and civil-minded circles. Secondly, the armies affected the nation by road construction. In the course of the Nationalist-Communist wars of 1927-1937 the Nationalists built thousands of miles of highway in order to make full use of their new mobility gained from machine power. The military roads, supplemented by civilian roads built with an eye to military use, constituted a network of communications upon which a new political geography could be framed—with new strategic points and new avenues of commerce. Thirdly, the armies began to emphasize culture and comfort. The soldiers were given a taste of twentieth century life and standards; their civilian kin and friends who lived under less favorable conditions saw in the elite sections of the armies a mass demonstration of China's modernization.

In the age of air power in China the relation between the army, the government, and the economy was revolutionized. The new power of a state with actual authority[11] led to the creation of an army dependent on an intricate and sensitive financial and economic system, operating under a regular scheme of law. The strength of the government made modern armies possible; modern armies made corresponding political forms imperative. A resulting tendency was for the armies to take on national form. Even in those areas where *tuchünism* had left its imprint upon society, or where provincial autonomy provided a factual check upon the national authorities, the regional armies accepted organizational details and long-range plans set forth by the central government. Armies which had arisen as dumps for the unemployed or as resources for civil war were fitted together so as to make the Chinese forces resemble the other armies of the world—which exist for the preservation, defense, or aggrandizement of national states. Foreign military observers, equipped with the critical faculties of their profession, might look at the Chinese armies and state point-blank that China had not an army but merely armed men. They could not, however, deny that the Chinese armed forces in their latest phase were on the way to becoming an army nationally organized and fit to serve as the instrument of a great nation. The lessons of nearly a thousand years of European and American political experience may be epitomized in great part in the word *nation;* the Chinese armies helped to give this word true significance in China.

For the time being, the armies continued to serve their role of a refuge for the economically displaced. Armed paupers are a menace to the security and stability of any society; with the emergence of a higher degree of Chinese unity a great proportion of the armed forces lost their *raison d'être*. Nevertheless, the last great war-lord war, that of 1930–1931, was fought largely over the issue of army reduction. The National Government forces gradually increased in preparation for the disbandment of others—extensive bodies of irregulars were roughly systematized and placed under central supervision. They were used in moderately successful but insufficient colonization efforts in the Northwest, and as labor reserves in the construction of highways, airports, and similar projects. Even so, the size of the armies did not cease to interfere with their rapid improvement. Too much had to go into pay, even with the ridiculously low rates of compensation. As against the estimates of nearly 1,400,000 men for 1921 and about 1,900,000 for 1926, the size of the armies was unofficially estimated at 2,379,770 for 1936.[12] This figure did not include Communists, brigands, or the Manchurian garrisons in the service of the Japanese (the Manchoukuo army), which would bring the total to well over 2,500,000 men. Differences in definition of what made a coolie or peasant into a soldier caused violent discrepancies in the estimates. If training equal to that of a German Republican Reichswehr soldier were set

112     GOVERNMENT IN REPUBLICAN CHINA

as the criterion, the Chinese army could be measured in scores. If some more or less vague relation to a military payroll, or to the possession of arms, or both, were taken as the requirements, the number would run into millions. Japanese propagandists, in the light of these facts, made injudicious statements when commenting thus on the Chinese army of 1937:

> China had 198 divisions comprising 2,250,000 officers and men. This gigantic army has further been reinforced by 200,000 Communist soldiers whom Nanking worked hard to set against Japan.
>
> In comparison the Japanese Army is a puny affair, consisting of 17 divisions of 250,000 officers and men.[13]

The well-informed expert on Chinese famine relief, Walter H. Mallory, set the total for 1937 at 1,650,000, of which 150,000 were Communist and 350,000 the crack troops of Chiang K'ai-shek; arms would be available for less than 1,000,000.[14] All factors considered, the figure of 2,000,000 armed men with nonproductive occupations seems to be in rough accord with the facts. Two salient conclusions emerge from these figures: Firstly, the armies constituted an enormous burden, which could only be reduced by partial disbandment; this in turn would not be achieved until greater national prosperity had become a fact. Secondly, and in China's favor, the armed forces have spread some elementary notions of modern fighting throughout the rest of the population and have enhanced not merely the willingness of the Chinese masses to fight but also their capacity to do so.

Disbandment programs had not made enough progress by 1937 to alter the general position of the armies in Chinese society. Nevertheless, the counterpart of disbandment—selective recruiting—produced a central force which became the vocation, avocation, and passion of Generalissimo Chiang K'ai-shek. Though not marked in any recognizable way as apart from the rest of the armed forces, the central units were given special arms, special equipment, regular pay, mass education, and training in the patriotic and reform doctrines of the New Life movement. "Chiang's own" were to distinguish themselves; they seem to have profited by new *matériel*, modern military instruction (chiefly from Germans), and the excellent opportunities for practice which arose from the Communist wars of 1928–1937. They were a testimonial to the fact that, had the disbandment program fully materialized, a more effective and much smaller Chinese army might have appeared. Despite the failure of disbandment, alliance with the quondam enemies, the Chinese Red Army, gave the national forces of 1937 a great diversity and wealth of actual experience in all types of fighting. Although the Chinese have never had adequate training for aggressive, coordinated warfare, they possess a marvelous background in guerrilla methods. The Communist forces have been hunted for a decade; technical superiority they have learned to meet by tactics which force the enemy to meet them on their own terms. Ultimately they were driven by the Nationalists across China, but at most disproportionate cost. The Nationalists, on the other hand, learned to master the terrain of inland war and thus acquired the very knowledge which a foreign enemy would need most.

In time, the Chinese armies became increasingly less the free agencies of domestic tyrants and, after the Japanese invasion of Manchuria, more and more the protective force for the whole nation. The enemy began to force Chinese society into national form more sharply than could any pressure from within. Even the efforts of the National Government at Nanking to make a truce with the Japanese in order to continue the drive against the Communists failed to still the widespread clamor for unification. Whether or not Chiang, as a soldier, thought successful war with Japan conceivable, he found that destiny had cast him in the role of the defender—he had only the choice of accepting or rejecting the challenge.

*Governmental and Political Role of the Armies*

Broadly, the political role of the armies was that of giving a day-to-day index for the influence of ideological control, and of providing the framework to which government had to accommodate itself. The Republic was born with Sun Yat-sen as its father but with Yüan Shih-k'ai as its midwife. Yüan and his armies established the order in which the parliamentary Republic had its illusory success; with his death the military order broke into military anarchy, and the political order disappeared almost completely from the arena of actual power. The armies and the *tuchüns* expressed a certain provincial autonomy and a desire for a crude stability. They ruled the chaos but kept the society stirred by war until the Nationalist-Communist revolution in

1926–1927 brought ideology back to a conspicuous place in the play of events. The armies developed under Yüan into separate entities exercising the power derived from the monopoly of force. In time this monopoly of force was broken. The problem was one not of tyranny but of anarchy. Force was too broadly distributed, order too insufficiently achieved. The Chinese, said Sun Yat-sen, did not need liberty; they needed wealth, in the form of food for those starving and the necessities of life for impoverished millions.[15] When even soldiers were treacherous and tumultuous, order could not come from bayonets. It had to arise within men's minds, including the minds of the soldiers. This happened; the ideological revolution absorbed the military forces, but only to disgorge them, as it were, into opposing camps—the one identifying military power and the masses, the other seeking to build up a new military elite with which to impose government and law on the society. Each of the two incompatible ideals reached a considerable measure of fulfillment, and they were reconciled only by the very presence of alien invaders. From being the *de facto* rulers, the armies found themselves called upon to act as *de facto* defenders. Hitherto the forces unsettling ideological control, they became the instruments of ideologies reconciled on the minimal terms of national defense for national existence.

The armies had supplied the power necessary to government but not the order. The Peking Republic lost its claim to authority when it was made the tool of Yüan Shih-k'ai. The years after his death were a pitiful period wherein the civilian authorities in the central government constituted either the puppets of the war lords or their sycophants. The Peking Republic fell into the expedient of giving *de jure* status to every shift in the interplay of power. Military leaders of provincial importance easily captured the functions of *tuchüns;* regional leaders obtained correspondingly higher titles. The Peking Republic tried to govern on the Western pattern when the country was not ready for it, and it governed poorly. Soon it passed from nominal control into nonexistence.

The National Government established at Nanking in 1927[16] gained actual effectiveness partly because the armies under its command were in need of essentials not obtainable by merely military measures. The modernized Nationalist armies under

Chiang K'ai-shek were dependent upon a complementing state which would provide support behind the lines. Furthermore, the cry from the educated classes for civilian government was loud, and practical considerations prompted the acquiescence of the Nationalist generals in the development of civilian government. Although by 1938 a government primarily civilian was not yet in evidence, the auspices were favorable to the regularization and demilitarization of government.

Finally, the most significant role of the armies may be found in their destructive powers. Modern weapons coming into China pressed on her the mold of a modern state. By preventing any tranquil change from the Ch'ing dynasty to another form of government preserving the older controls of village and family, Western armament brought China into a condition of military anarchy in which a strong modern government became imperative. The armies and their irresponsible leaders goaded the masses into the revolution of 1926–1927, and the necessity of establishing military superiority for the sake of stability led the victorious Nationalists to create a modern defensive force, a working government, and the outline of operative statehood—to be partly Chinese, but modified by Western influences, according to the teachings of Sun Yat-sen. From 1931 on, the army and the government became more and more the integral parts of a single machine.

*War and the Agrarian Economy*

There is a close correlation between militarism and agricultural conditions in China. Distress among the Chinese farming masses is both a cause and an effect of war. Misery creates unrest, unrest brings war, war brings misery—until government stops the vicious circle. On the whole, the economic system of old China was probably more stable, and ensured greater distributive justice, than did the Western systems during the same centuries; but periods of famine, flood, and—worst of all— oppression were far from rare.[17]

At its best, the old economy rested on a vast body of farmers, associated in villages (*hui*) and families but tilling their own land in fairly small units. The farming class provided the nourishment for the bulk of society but did not hold a low status, since the compensations of interclass kinship and of free play in the hierarchy of politics and intellect made families (if not individuals) approximately equal. There were no families in old China to compare with the aristocracy which Europe inherited from the Middle Ages, nor castes to compare with those of India. When functioning well, the Chinese economic system resembled some Western ideals of freehold farming governed by a hierarchy of scholars.

But at its worst, when the government became sterile and unimaginative, or corrupt and demoralized, the taxes rose sharply, and usurers added to the burden. Lack of resources caused the loss of the land, and the peasant proprietor found himself a tenant farmer. When economic and political exploitation overreached itself, social upheaval followed, and peasant rebellions tore down the government and the economy together. Most Chinese dynasties met their end as a consequence of the land problem.[18]

Moreover, the Chinese farmer maintained very slight reserves of foodstuffs, so that flood or drought resulted in appalling famines, sometimes costing the lives of millions in one year. Governments established large granaries which, under good management, were filled in time of plenty and dispersed in time of need. R. H. Tawney says of drought and flood:

> Those directly affected by them cannot meet the blow, for they have no reserves. The individual cannot be rescued by his neighbors, since whole districts together are in the same position. The district cannot be rescued by the nation, because means of communication do not permit of food being moved in sufficient quantities. Famine is, in short, the last stage of a disease which, though not always conspicuous, is always present.[19]

Whether or not natural calamities struck in conjunction with specific extortions sanctioned by social injustice, the Chinese farmer has been faced with threefold oppression whenever times were bad. The tax collector, the usurer, and the landlord were able to lay their hands on the harvest, reduce the peasant to subsistence level or beneath it, and place him under a system of exploitation which was as severe as Western feudalism. The check which provided a stop to any indefinite decline into greater and greater horror was the fighting power of the peasants. Peasant revolts periodically followed agrarian oppression, and swept the land free for the time. The Han dynasty, in some ways the greatest in all Chinese history, went down in an uproar of peasant rebellions. Peasant bandits have provided the ancestry of many imperial houses. Politics or war might ease the economy, until the government again became weak and exploitation common.

It is one of the tragic coincidences of history that the Europeans should have appeared in China at a time when the Chinese were entering upon one of their most acute periods of agrarian decline and class exploitation. Roughly, from the middle of the eighteenth century down to the present day the lot of the Chinese farmers has become worse and worse. At periods the country as a whole seemed fairly prosperous, but the broad agricultural recession remained constant. The nineteenth century was one long record of rebellions, and the twentieth amplified the disturbances.

Government in modern China has fallen heir to a depression centuries old, arising from inequitable land distribution, overtaxation, insufficient public works for drainage and communications, and—in more recent generations—the evils attendant upon sharp economic change. Most economic writers agree that some of the difficulties of Chinese agriculture are caused by the smallness of individual holdings and by population pressure. Such factors are not subject to immediate remedy; the peasants have attributed their misfortune primarily to landlordism and political oppression. The Chinese Communists, on their economic front, may perform a valuable service if they are able to devise new methods of social organization which will provide relief for the organic difficulties of Chinese agriculture. Of all the important problems of China, the land problem shows government ineffectiveness at its worst.

Behind the T'ai-p'ing rebellion which flared up in unparalleled fanaticism in the 1850's and 1860's, there was the long provocation of a land system which made farming unprofitable and a government supine in the face of unreversed decline. The Boxer rebellion burst forth from the unrest of the peasants, although it could be deflected by the demagoguery of the Manchu officials and changed into wild xenophobia. When the fiercely discordant economics of imperialism and international industrialism intruded upon the old and already corrupted economy, farm existence became even less tolerable than it might have been if left to its native miseries. Dynastic decomposition was hastened by the collapse of handicraft economy and the fiscal disorganization caused by Western commercial activity.

In the earliest days of the Republican-Nationalist movement led by Sun Yat-sen, emphasis was on land reform. Sun Yat-sen's family had suffered from overtaxation when he was a boy.[20] Nationalization and equalization of the land were slogans used at the founding of the *Tung Mêng Hui;* the program seems at that time to have been derived from old Chinese distributism and from Henry George.[21] With the coming of the Republic, two years went by, however, before any agrarian legislation was passed, and the new laws had no perceptible consequence.[22] The problem of land reform had to be fought out on the ideological front and placed above the military before it could become a fit subject for competent government action.

The epoch of the *tuchüns* added to agricultural misfortune. Militarism had a direct effect on the deterioration of the land economy, and an indirect one in that it led to the cultivation of opium as the one money-making crop which could meet the excessive tax demands of the militarists. A Chinese writer has described the years which marked the ending of the *tuchün* system as follows:

> The . . . misery among the farming population in the decennial period 1920–1930 [must be] attributed to (1) internal warfare; (2) neglect of agriculture; (3) low stage of art; and (4) over-population. The civil wars during the last eighteen years have increased the cost of production, have added to the farmers' . . . burden of taxation, have raised the rate of interest on loan, and have caused endless suffering to [those] who form the basis of our social and economic life. Great many people have often wondered as to why a country like China with 75 per cent of her total population engaged in farming and with such a vast territory should suffer from the high cost of living; but to the student of social problems the question is comparatively simple, for the recurrence of civil war since the establishment of the Republic has [changed] conditions of supply and has driven millions of farmers out of cultivated areas, and this alone suffices to explain an unprecedented rise of prices of food and other necessities of life during the last few years, especially since 1926.[23]

These conditions led to farmers' movements, which became effective, however, only as they merged with the broader ideological tendencies in China.

The Farmers' Movement . . . may . . . be divided into four periods: (1) the period of reaction to bad conditions . . . (1921–1925); (2) the period of communistic activities and violence (1925–1927); (3) the period of retrenchment and preparation for reconstruction (from the spring of 1927–1928); and (4) the period of reconstruction (since 1928).[24]

The Kuomintang-Communist alliance struck severely at the *tuchün* armies by giving their own forces a sense of doctrine and by tying together the causes of patriotism and agricultural reform. The joint agrarian program was a failure in that it accentuated precisely those issues on which neither of the parties could compromise. When the Communists and the Nationalists parted, the Nationalists took one portion of Sun Yat-sen's economic program (industrialization and communications) for emphasis, and the Communists another (land reform). The agrarian issue was a source of strength to the Chinese Red Army, intent upon winning the peasantry. It was a military weakness to the new-style Nationalist armies officered largely by the relatives of landlords; they had little sympathy for the economic troubles of the farmers whose lands they occupied. The Nationalist Reconstruction aimed in great part at removing both the acute and the latent causes of peasant rebellion, thereby cutting the ground from under the feet of the Communists. Although it met with more success than any other project of its type in modern China, Western observers agree in regarding it as inadequate.[25]

*Imperialism and Chinese Wars*

A great part of the military disturbances in modern China can be regarded as both the cause and the effect of agrarian evils, and some of the struggles as peasant rebellions in modern guise, carrying on the immemorial farmer-infantry tradition. Another part is traceable to the impact of the Western economy on China. It was Western economic activity that gave most compelling proof of the fact that the Westerners had encircled China and were compressing it from a world in its own right into a nation. The military intervention of Western powers in China not only caused much of the ideological reaction and forced a reorganization of the government, but also provided deadly evidence of the superiority of Western fighting. Western economy helped to bring the confusion which meant war in China; and Western economy itself waged war.

Sun Yat-sen saw China's unfortunate position as a whole, and in his programs there may be discerned three separate demands, for (1) a national economic revolution, (2) an industrial revolution, and (3) a social revolution.[26] Since the Chinese could no longer function as a self-contained world economically, and scorn foreign trade as a magnanimous concession to the outer barbarians,[27] the Chinese would have to develop an economic system conforming to national patterns in the society and in thought. They must relate their economy to their independence and defense, if they were to survive. In the first place, they could not afford to remain the only free market of the world, subject to exploitation and haphazard development. It would be necessary for them to establish governmental controls over economic matters and protect their national livelihood. Secondly, they had to work toward a complete transformation of their technological system and meet Western productive practices, if they were to claim a competitive position; this involved an industrial revolution. Thirdly, they had to correct the abuses inherited from their forefathers. Simultaneously they would have to construct an economic system not only modern but equitable, if they wished to avoid the horrors of early capitalism and the tragedy of the industrialist class war. This would require a social revolution.

At the time that Sun Yat-sen formulated his ideas (1924), none of the three revolutions was making any progress. The Chinese did not constitute a nation in fact; they had even lost the old unity of the Confucian society. The *tuchüns* opposed Chinese nationalism by preventing the development of any one authority able to monopolize force, and by acting as agents of, or in alliance with, foreign powers. Thus they helped to make China something not far from a quasi colony under pooled control of all the industrial capitalist nations. The Nationalists and Communists were able to join forces on this issue of a class war of nations, both believing in the independence of China. The Nationalists, however, saw China's most direct approach toward national unity in the development of a national economic system, with a reasonable military independence of imports and the economic devices current throughout the world as instruments of national policy. The Communists did not agree that such an economy, national in form, would have much meaning unless it were grounded upon a peasant-proletarian regime. Nor did they feel that change from imperialist to native capitalism would constitute an advance in itself.

After the schism, the Nationalists devoted themselves to the national-economic and industrial revolutions, while the Communists stressed the social revolution, particularly the land problem. The Nationalists were able to secure tariff autonomy for China, and thereupon entered upon a policy of protective tariffs and other mechanisms designed to make China a reasonably self-sufficient nation. At the same time they pushed hard toward the industrial revolution, in developing highways, railroads, airways, and radio, and in creating the economic controls required for modern government—standard weights, measures, currency, civil law, and fiscal uniformity.

T. V. Soong (Sung Tzŭ-wên), a veteran minister of finance, stands out as the organizer of the modern Chinese economy. Veritable miracles were performed in the development of national credit; after 1928 the National Government adopted the policy— as remote as a mirage to its predecessors—of floating all government loans within the country and making the Chinese government independent of Japanese and Western financiers. The only loans of any importance contracted abroad were taken up with other governments. Financial independence was a great step toward the realization of the Nationalist ideals, but it may be questioned whether the loss of financial allies was a price to be paid without hesitation in a capitalist world. Had the Chinese had more bonds in the Western capital markets, or larger debts to the American or British governments, they might have elicited greater international support in repelling the Japanese invasion in 1931.

The crowning point in the economic achievements of the National Government at Nanking was the successful institution of a managed currency. China had dealt with currency merely as a convenient form for specie, and the Chinese were accustomed to regard a dollar as worth only the amount of metal in it. When the National Government placed the currency on a national basis, it drew together the whole financial structure of China by one gigantic move, and placed finance in a position of greater unity and dependence upon government than ever before. Together with the financial reforms, the Nationalists organized a legal system providing a minimum foundation of law and order. The codification of laws, the revamping of the judiciary, the clarification of policies by legal formulation—all these contributed to China's emergent nationhood.

The economic program accorded with considerations partly Hamiltonian, partly state-socialist. The economy had first of all to be organized and integrated in national terms, and later to be revised so as to ensure social justice. The Nationalists were convinced that a policy of immediate land reform would lead to internal disharmony and frustrate the very purposes for which the revolution of 1926-1927 had been launched. The Communists, on the other hand, succeeded in keeping the agrarian issue from being forgotten and forced the Nationalists to better the lot of the peasant. In the meantime, China's boom in physical development and the unification of the commercial, financial, productive, and legal systems began to startle observers.

As a result, China was able to build national armies in direct ratio with the invigoration of her national economic system. The war machine of the National Government, under the care and leadership of Generalissimo Chiang K'ai-shek, became the most powerful in China. The central government's military power in turn speeded up the pace of general unification. There was thus a remarkable interaction of forces tending toward national integration. From 1932 to 1937, between the first and second major phases of the Japanese invasion, progress was rapid—stimulated, perhaps, by the external menace.

The two greatest dangers to the Nationalist policy of military and economic unification were (1) the dismal condition of the Chinese proletariat, as yet small but constantly growing, and (2) the vested interests of the industrial powers. Had China's growth been less rapid, the foreigners might have withdrawn slowly and found compensation in Chinese commerce for their losses in direct ownership in China. There was one power, however, to which Chinese unification was a living and increasing threat. The rising military-economic power of the Chinese was incompatible with the position which Japanese leaders visualized as part of the manifest destiny of their country. The Japanese might have tolerated the *tuchün* system for decades had the *tuchüns* been able to establish orderly regional governments; or they might have aided a reactionary Chinese regime which asked for survival only. The appearance of a genuine republic in the Far East was a menace to Japan; if that republic was bound by sheer physical proportions to overshadow Japan, the unification and modernization of China had to be averted at all costs.

Nevertheless, China's development, even apart from the hindrances of war, cannot be regarded as possessing the same potentialities as did American growth during the past century. China, from all indications available to date, is an area much poorer in natural resources than is the United States; she does not offer comparable opportunities for the heavy industries. The steel, coal, oil, and water power necessary for large-scale industrialization are by no means negligible, but not sufficient to make possible the rise of another America. The far future may change man's dependence upon currently utilized resources and facilitate greater strides in China's technological advancement. Meanwhile, she can look forward to decades of measurable development through exploiting raw materials already available, if political conditions permit.

The conflict with Japan has thrown Chinese economic development back to conditions not too far from the pre-Nanking stage. China not only faces the handicaps of social dislocations but also the ruin of her factories and her industrial centers. The Japanese have destroyed much of the Chinese manufacturing equipment and are placing what remains under Japanese control. Significantly, the deadliest enemy of Japanese business—in the unlikely event of a complete Japanese success—will be Japanese-owned factories in China. Chinese labor will deeply affect Japan's domestic production, unless the Japanese succeed in rationalizing their economic system to an extent not yet contemplated. Hence, Japan's losing the war may well be brought about by bankruptcy from sheer military indebtedness; her winning the war, however, may lead to more remote but no less certain ruin—through the competition of Chinese output with Japanese home industries disadvantaged by the cheaper labor markets of China. But Japan's loss is not inevitably China's gain, and the Chinese may find themselves, at some point in the future, controlling an industrial system which has been wrecked, looted, and bankrupted.

Whatever the ultimate outcome, loans will again play a part in Chinese development. The placing of large foreign loans has been a key part of Chinese development, and the task of reconstruction in China—no matter who undertakes to do it—will require large amounts of capital. Consequently, the loan policies of the wealthier nations may return to the importance which they enjoyed in 1913, and the dictates of the Western states may again direct the lines of Chinese economic progress. The effects of the Japanese conquest, if it is partial and then lapses into a stalemate, may well be determined by the extension of loans to the Chinese or to the Japanese in China. The effect of the war has already complicated the picture of China's economic future to the extent of making even cautious prophecy hazardous.[28]

In the military sphere, the Chinese have come of age, although their fighting strength will be determined by the importance of infantry. If later wars continue to depend upon man power, China will become more and more significant in world politics. Internally, the armies provided (1) a transitional administration from the Empire to the Republic; (2) a physical expression of the ideological confusion and the regional disunity of China from 1916 to 1931 (the period of *tuchüns*); (3) the armed edge of the ideological revolution of 1926–1927; (4) decisive instruments in the conflict between the Communists and Nationalists from 1927 to 1937; and (5) one of the most powerful unifying agencies at the command of the National Government at Nanking. The Chinese military system spread the knowledge of Western warfare and, with it, of modern techniques throughout the country; it shaped the ideological and governmental experience of modern China.

### NOTES

1. See below, pp. 154 ff.
2. Rodney Gilbert in *The China Year Book*, 1921–2, p. 519, Tientsin, 1921.
3. *Ibid.*, 1926, p. 1065.
4. *Ibid.*, p. 1062.
5. See above, pp. 51 ff.
6. See above, pp. 58 ff.
7. Gilbert, *loc. cit.*, 1928, pp. 1283–1285.
8. *Ibid.*, 1931, pp. 251 ff.
9. Source confidential.
10. John H. Jouett, "War Planes over China," *Asia*, vol. 37, pp. 827–830, 1937.

11. See below, pp. 167 ff.
12. *The China Year Book*, 1936, p. 427.
13. Japanese Chamber of Commerce of New York, *The Sino-Japanese Crisis*, 1937, p. 18, New York, 1937.
14. Walter H. Mallory, "Japan Attacks, China Resists," *Foreign Affairs*, vol. 16, pp. 135-136, 1937.
15. Paschal M. d'Elia, S. J., *The Triple Demism of Sun Yat-sen*, pp. 252-273, Wuchang, 1931. This is one of the most useful translations of Sun Yat-sen's lectures on the *San Min Chu I*. Others are Frank Price, *San Min Chu I, The Three Principles of the People*, Shanghai, 1930; and L. S. Hsü, *Sun Yat-sen, His Political and Social Ideals*, Los Angeles, 1933.
16. See below, pp. 167 ff. It is to be noted that the Nanking government did not secure international recognition until 1928—the year following its establishment.
17. Among the more recent discussions of economics in Chinese history is Chi Chao-ting, *Key Areas in Chinese Economic History*, New York, 1936.
18. See Karl August Wittfogel, *Wirtschaft und Gesellschaft Chinas*, Leipzig, 1931, and the same author's outline of one of the boldest programs of Chinese studies, "A Large-Scale Investigation of China's Socio-Economic Structure," *Pacific Affairs*, vol. 11, pp. 81-94, 1938.
19. R. H. Tawney, *Land and Labour in China*, p. 77, New York, 1932.
20. Paul M. W. Linebarger, *Sun Yat Sen and the Chinese Republic*, pp. 67-71, New York, 1924.
21. See Lyon Sharman, *Sun Yat-sen: His Life and Its Meaning*, New York, 1934; and Paul M. A. Linebarger, *The Political Doctrines of Sun Yat-sen*, pp. 132-156, Baltimore, 1937, for discussion of the development of Sun's economic programs.
22. Jefferson D. H. Lamb (Lin Tung-hai), *The Development of the Agrarian Movement and Agrarian Legislation in China*, p. 134, Shanghai, 1934.
23. *Ibid.*, p. 221.
24. *Ibid.*, p. 77.
25. See *Pacific Affairs* for 1934 and 1935, for articles by George Taylor and others dealing with reconstruction.
26. Linebarger, *op. cit.* in note 21, chap. VII, "The Programs of Min Shêng," discusses these points at greater length.
27. See P. H. B. Kent, *The Twentieth Century in the Far East*, p. 364, London, 1937, for an extract from the mandate sent by the Chinese-Manchu Emperor Ch'ien-lung to England's George III.
28. See G. E. Hubbard, *Eastern Industrialization and Its Effect on the West*, London, 1935, for a very illuminating survey. J. E. Orchard, *Japan's Economic Position*, New York, 1930, is equally informative. Much current information will be found in *Far Eastern Survey* (semimonthly, New York), and *Amerasia* (monthly, New York) on economic matters. *Pacific Affairs* (quarterly, New York) and *International Affairs* (bimonthly, London) possess book review sections which are useful guides to the literature. The *Bulletin of Far Eastern Bibliography* (quarterly, Washington, D. C.) is the most complete guide of its kind, but has just completed its initial volumes.

# THIRD PART
## GOVERNMENTS

*Chapter* VI

## THE EMPIRE

The governing of China is not and has not been confined to governments. In many instances the working of specific institutions called *governments* has been of less importance than that of other establishments and organizations. The problems of government in Republican China are affected but not determined by the fate of individual governments. Movements and armies have predetermined action; governments have reflected it. Government in China may be divided into three chief periods. The first extends from prehistory to 221 B. C. The second is the imperial period.[1] The third—the Republican epoch—did not begin until 1912, although it was foreshadowed in the nineteenth century.

*Government to the End of the Warring States*

In the semihistoric Shang dynasty, which ruled China during the second millennium B. C., there was a central overlordship which might well have claimed primacy over all offices of the world. In its own territory, Shang rule seems to have been based not upon a feudal system such as developed later in the time of the charioteering lords but upon the reduction of defeated princes to positions of vassaldom. History cannot yet tell of the exact relations between the Shang overlord and his vassal princes, nor of other monarchs who, in the shadowy bypaths of present knowledge, stand forth vaguely from complete obscurity as rivals to the hegemony of Shang. The rulers of twenty-five or twenty-six centuries ago are recognized by modern Chinese as the direct predecessors of the Ch'ing emperor who in turn yielded to the Republic. This is no case of a Mussolini seeking to weave together the long-broken threads between Augustan and modern Rome; in China the succession is as direct as that from St. Pius I to Pius XI. The central monarchy comes over the edge of history as an identifiable institution.

In rudimentary form this monarchy already suggests the features of bureaucracy. Like the Prussian kings thousands of years later, the Shang monarchs seem to have relied upon commoners as their royal officials, and for the same reasons. A commoner strengthened the position of the monarch: "He could not easily usurp the place of his master, even if he had the power. And if he was disobedient he could be executed on the spot, with complete impunity; he had no powerful clan to exact vengeance."[2] Whether or not the system of loose overlordship be termed *feudalism*, social forms not too unlike European feudalism originated under the next dynasty, the Chou (traditionally dated 1122–256 B. C.). Conquering the great city of the Shang, the Chou turned to feudalism for means of internal control and defense. Powerful vassals arose, however, so that after the eighth century B. C. the original Chou dynasty was no longer in actual command. From the eighth to the third century B. C., when China was consolidated under the Ch'in Shih Huang Ti, a rapid spread of feudal organization brought about a state system resembling that of early modern Europe.

Before the Chou rulers lost their power and became the faraway analogues of the late Holy Roman emperors or the Tennos of shogunal Japan, there emerged from their house one of the most remarkable of all Chinese political leaders. The Duke of Chou, who lived in the eleventh century B. C., seems to have done most in founding the system which later ages called *Confucian*—after Confucius had reformed it, clarified it, and given it ethical stature. He is also regarded as the father of the Constitution of Chou, a plan for a bureaucratic monarchy with an emperor, three Great Dukes, and six ministers (in charge of administrative, educational and economic, religious and historiographic, military, judicial, and engineering matters, respectively) ruling over nine large provinces.[3] The Duke of Chou is finally credited with the authorship of several important treatises. He has served as the archetype of intellectual statesmanship in Chinese legend. His work may have contributed in great part to the long life of the Chou dynasty, as a *de jure* ruling house, since a family which had produced such an eminent member was not to be set aside lightly.

In the earlier part of this period the feudal order seems to have ensured relative stability, but in the later part a system of states arose. The greatest Chinese philosophers, Confucius (Kung Fu-tzŭ) and Lao Tzŭ, lived in interstate turmoil. They saw all about them the displacement of virtues which had long been recognized, the advance of states which substituted greed for morality, the centralization of power, the destruction of the feudal economy, the transformation of ceremonial warfare into outright slaughter, and the rising disrespect of the advancing kings for the Chou overlord. Lao Tzŭ preached a philosophy devoid of constructive politics; he had little use for the state and for the organization of society. Not quite an anarchist, his programs are probably closer to those of Herbert Spencer than of any other Western thinker. But the spiritual and psychological background from which he wrote is roughly identical with that of the world's great mystical intuitionists. Confucius (551–479 B. C.) preached a system of ethics and education which was to rationalize and systematize preceding Chinese thought and lead to the system of ideological control known as Confucian.

Chinese historians themselves term the closing period of the Chou the Age of Warring States. Diplomacy lubricated the machinery of conflict, smoothing struggle without eliminating it. The regional governments fought each other for centuries, though at times venturing into collective security pacts entrusting authority to a preeminent king for defense against the outer barbarians. The last years of interstate wars, however, were marked by an ever increasing awareness of the meaningless character of a struggle which had enveloped the Chinese world. Legalism and militarism, twin media of centralized monarchy, blossomed forth. While the Western political system, molded by geography and conditioned by language, has frozen into a pattern of theoretically sovereign and theoretically eternal states—the "mortal Gods" of Hobbes's imagination—without promise of workable universal government, China's states were swept aside by the conqueror Ch'in Shih Huang Ti, who established imperial unity for Chinese government. With the rise to domination of the state of Ch'in, its king took the title of

*Shih* (First) *Huang Ti* (Emperor), and the Chinese Empire was established.

*The Chinese Imperial Government*

The Shih Huang Ti was not revered by succeeding ages for the great mission which he performed. His methods were those not of a cautious reformer but of a bullying conqueror. With the aid and advice of a legalist philosopher, he organized all of China (covering the area of much of modern China) into a strongly centralized and despotic military monarchy. He destroyed all books not of obvious practical use, completely eradicating the histories of rival states and the works of philosophers whose opinions might undermine his regime. His tyranny brought his house to a rapid end; his heirs held the throne only a short while. But the work he had done was done. He had persecuted the worship of the past. He had extirpated a large part of the literature which might have survived as a source of dissent. He had cleared China of all military power but his own. He had brought operative law into being and had spread the institution of private ownership of land. Feudalism might remain as a form, but its economic and political realities were lost.

In 206 B. C. there began the reign of the Han dynasty. They effected a compromise between the past and the governmental, military, and political system created by the Shih Huang Ti. They retained legalism in practice but turned more and more to Confucianism. Under them the cult of Confucius grew into the major influence on the state.[4] The Han allowed the imperial system to grow, whereas the Shih Huang Ti had sought to build it. In consequence, Han rule—although interrupted in the time of Christ by a Utopian usurper—lasted from the third century B. C. to the third century A. D. There followed the turbulent Chinese middle ages, extending until the reinstitution of organized government with the Chin and the Sui.[5]

Out of the earliest tradition attributed to the Duke of Chou and put in definite shape by Confucius, out of the arbitrary military despotism of the conqueror of the Chinese world, Shih Huang Ti, and out of the actual practices of the Han, there evolved a governmental system which, though altered dynasty by dynasty and epoch by epoch, nevertheless retained its general form down into the days of men now living. It never became, however, the prime agency of government, even of the men governing. Ritual and scholarship were more significant functions of the dominant hierarchy than was administration itself. The emperor was the head of the country's family structure, the focal point in the social sphere, the outstanding member of the community at large, the chief examiner and model of the scholars, the pontiff of the quasi-religious hierarchy, the moral scapegoat and intermediary between destiny and mankind, and the autocrat of a despotism constitutionalized, as it were, by the power of traditional practices.

The imperial system of China was thus a monarchy in the proper sense of the word, with none of the parvenu features suggested by the etymology of the word *imperial*. As the pre-eminent leader in an organic society, the emperor held a position comparable with that of other family heads. His authority could rival that of a father but not excel it; among all the families of the Chinese Empire the imperial stood forth as a family. Second, the emperor was the chief dignitary in the social life of the Chinese world. He was not unlike the British monarchs, providing a model of formal propriety and elegance in setting the fashions of the decade. The physical isolation of most of the emperors prevented them from playing this role with widespread effectiveness, but it was a part of their function. Third, the emperor bore the relation to the Empire which the outstanding villager bore to the village. It was he of whom men talked; his behavior commanded greatest interest; his future conduct was a constant source of speculation. Apart from his role as a formal dignitary, he occupied the more immediate position of most conspicuous person, of the first member of society. He had the human accountability of a leader and was to be praised or blamed for his actions in the histories and by his subjects. In the normal routine, the emperor himself was not to govern; but he selected and supervised his ministers, who did and who consequently bore the odium for evil deeds.

Fourth, the emperor himself was the ultimate examiner of scholars. He thus had contact with the most successful of the civil service candidates and completed their examination. These examinations served the emperor as a means of selecting advisers who upon further testing became ministers. The Forest of Pencils (*Han Lin*, the Imperial Academy) was within his jurisdiction, and the emperor was supposed to be enough of a scholar to check the most important of the documents of state. The myth of intellectual supremacy is suggested by the fact that the chief implement of the imperial office was a red pencil. The imperial symbolism did not stop here. Fifth, the quasi-religious hierarchy of the Chinese, competing with Buddhism and the superstitions of popular Taoism for the support of the people, centered on the performance of certain rites in the propitiation of fortune and the honoring of the dead. To this were added the cult rituals of Confucianism. The Confucian temples, with tablets bearing the names of worthies, served as the visible demonstration of the ideological power wielded by the scholars over the populace, and of the emperor over the scholars.

Sixth, the emperor had the more definitely religious status referred to in his title *Son of Heaven*. He was the intermediate figure between the will of Heaven and mankind. In him were summarized and epitomized the virtues or the evils of the generation; he had to represent mankind in its best light to all supernatural forces or agencies. Upon his conduct of worship depended the good or ill will of the deities and hence weather, crops, life and death. Conversely, he was responsible to mankind for the misbehavior of nature, and an earthquake, a two-headed calf, or any other monstrous occurrence was blamed on his disturbance of the routine of things. The order which enveloped the Confucian society was conceived not merely as a set of traditional and moral man-made customs but as a type of behavior which fitted in with the life of the natural world. In the eyes of the Chinese, perturbations in the world of men soon produced consequent natural calamities. Lastly, the Chinese emperor was the autocrat of the administration. His action, however, was limited by various customary devices; for example, while the countersignature of a minister was not needed on an edict, the emperor was supposed not to take the initiative but to secure the wisest suggestions and adopt them. Practical considerations rendered a stable bureaucracy impervious to constant intermeddling of the emperor, although the effect of imperial action was not negligible.

The administrative outline of Chinese government from the establishment of the Empire by the Ch'in Shih Huang Ti in 221 B. C. to its overthrow by Sun Yat-sen and his followers in 1911 varied from dynasty to dynasty and ruler to ruler. Nevertheless, certain general characteristics were common to the whole period. The government operated as the chief implementation of the emperor's power over the people. The people maintained its social organizations, but none of these developed office hierarchies comparable to that of the government. The government alone served as the connecting link between the ideologically unified Chinese world as a whole and its many separate parts. The T'ang dynasty (A. D. 620-906) provided an exceptionally clear articulation of the Empire, which not only compelled the admiration and imitation of later ages but even served as a model for state governments on the periphery of the Chinese world. In the great Taikwa Reforms of 645, the Japanese made a heroic attempt to adapt the T'ang form of government to dissimilar conditions; the scheme worked on paper but failed to recast the fundamental mold of Japanese society, which remained feudal.

The three most striking features of the Chinese bureaucracy were: (1) the central administrative organization; (2) the operation of civil service examinations and the use of administrative supervision; (3) the integration of government operation on the imperial, regional, and local levels. The metropolitan administrative organization under the T'ang dynasty was headed by the emperor. But the intricate regularity of the hierarchy beneath him was such as to preclude imperial autocratic caprice. The outline of the hierarchical organization was as follows:[6]

THE THRONE
THE GRAND COUNCIL
The Departments:
a. Department of Ministerial Coordination
1. Ministry of Administrators
2. Ministry of Finance
3. Ministry of Rites
4. Ministry of War
5. Ministry of Justice
6. Ministry of Public Works
b. The Imperial Chancery
c. The Grand Secretariat

The Tribunal of Censors

Imperial Commissioners
Provinces (10) and *Governments-General* (at the frontiers)
Prefectures
Subprefectures
Townships
Villages

The general structure of Chinese administration differed little from that of preceding ages, and has not changed markedly during the following centuries. Later developments strengthened the provinces, at the expense of both the central government and the local areas; earlier conditions had tolerated a much greater extent of feudal establishments. Nevertheless, the six ministries may have been established as early as about 1000 B. C., and remained a feature of Chinese government until 1906.

The Grand Council met daily. It was composed of grand ministers, who—in the phrase of Baron des Rotours—"under the T'ang held in their hands the government of the Empire."[7] The emperor's chief power lay in appointing the council members, to whom fell the greater share of governing in fact. Directly under the Grand Council there were the three departments. The Department of Ministerial Coordination served as an administrative center and clearinghouse for the work of the separate ministries under it. The names of the ministries are self-explanatory. The Ministry of Administrators was in charge of the examination system and the arrangement of the offices in the bureaucracy. The Ministry of Rites, by an extension of its protocol features, was in charge of the reception of foreign ("barbarian") princes and ambassadors, and emissaries. The other two departments provided one of the most ingenious systems of checks and balances to be found in any constitutional scheme. The Imperial Chancery received all communications from the various parts of the Empire. Since most of the governing was carried out by means of written orders, instructions, and requests for reports, the Chancery occupied an important place. But the function of drafting replies to such communications, preparing manifestoes, or issuing ordinances was in the hands of the Grand Secretariat. Thus the Chancery was prevented from exerting an outside influence, while it was impossible for the Secretariat to receive any communication directly. As a final check, all outgoing documents of state had to pass through the Chancery to receive the official seal, without which they were invalid. Thus any item of government business was routed first through the Chancery for registration and classification, then to the Secretariat for reply, and back to the Chancery for what amounted to countersignature (by seal).[8] Yet the Secretariat was no mere drafting agency for the Chancery.

The Tribunal of Censors occupied a position not unlike that of the great independent establishments of the United States government. It was directed by a president and two vice-presidents, and concerned itself with ferreting out and exposing irregularities and abuses in the administration. The morale of the censorate varied from time to time, but at its optimum efficiency it was a formidable and significant institution. Han Confucianism provided the general background from which the organization rose to effectiveness.

This sophisticated and rationally designed central bureaucracy was supplemented by regional administrations. Under the T'ang the regional establishments were a source of trouble to the government. The Empire was divided into provinces, but the provincial administrations were superseded by Imperial Commissioners whenever an emergency arose. Later dynasties placed the provincial system on a more stable basis, which resulted in genuine and geographically sound regionalism. The provincial governments were replicas in miniature of the central; their heads might be regarded as appointive and removable satraps whose authority was a smaller reproduction of the power of the emperor. It was not until the Ming dynasty (A. D. 1368–1643) that the provinces took on their modern form. The provincial governments were a source of great strength to China in that they made possible a quasi-federal government. In the Ch'ing period no officer was eligible to a post in his native province;[9] this custom had considerable centripetal effect and offset the danger that populace and officials, united by common sympathies, might revolt or secede.[10]

Another feature to be noted about the Chinese government under the Empire was the examination and civil service system. The T'ang dynasty provided for three major types of examination: (1) The *chü* corresponded most closely to a modern academic degree, and allowed the candidate to qualify in any one of a number of subjects, including the classics, law, and mathematics. (2) The *hsüan* was the special examination necessary for appointment to a post in the bureaucracy; it was both written and oral and included the personal history of the candidate. (3) The *k'ao*, an in-service examination, consisted of annual reports on the performance of all officers in the Empire. They were transmitted to the Bureau for Examination of Merits in the

Ministry of Administrators on a schedule varying with the distance of the office from the capital. There were five points on which to report: virtue and justice; integrity and circumspection; equity and impartiality; diligence and activity; and one of twenty-seven special talents suitable to the particular office in question. The grades received on these reports determined the advancement or demotion of the officer, in accordance with an elaborate and exact schedule.[11] All three examinations provided the administrative form for the close relation between the government and the scholastic elite. The *chü*, with its emphasis on the classics, framed the content of all curriculums. The *hsüan*, with its oral examination and personal record, made the prospective candidate careful in observing the customs. The *k'ao* kept up the morale and efficiency of the bureaucracy, while the ominous Tribunal of Censors was present to guard against abuse of the system. Every detail was precise, well ordered, explicit, to a degree that would delight present-day industrial personnel managers. Formulation was refined and impressive. In fact the T'ang laws, although their part in Chinese life was less than a Westerner might expect, were a code of such force and appeal that the Japanese and the Annamese used them as a model for their juridical systems.[12]

The decline of particular dynasties in China—caused by poor economic policy, demoralization of the court, corruption of the bureaucracy, laxity in the examinations, oppression of the farmers —did not effect great alterations in the structure of government. With the centuries the Chinese government settled into more and more definitive form. Unfortunately, the Manchu government (1644–1911)[13] had sunk into administrative demoralization when the full force of the Western impact was felt. In the early nineteenth century a British observer wrote of an imperial official:

The late *tungling* [gendarmerie commander] Wanking, degraded last year for connecting himself with a magician whose confessions went to implicate a large number of nobles and public servants, was a Reader at the Classical Feasts, Manchu President of the Board of Civil Office, Revisor-General of the Veritable Records of the Reign, a Superior of the Academy, Supervisor of the Household, t'utung of a Banner [military division], superintendent of the Gymnasium in the Ning-shan Palace, and of the Treasuries of the Board of Revenue, and Visitor of the 17 Granaries in the City, and at Tungchau.[14]

When such conditions of indifference toward sharply defined hierarchic ethics began to be common among the bureaucracy, the end of the dynasty was near. The Chinese Empire had remained intact even when it had fallen into the hands of Tartars, Mongols, and Manchus. It had returned to the bases of its former greatness, and the administrative machinery created since the day of the Shih Huang Ti continued for twenty centuries. With the decrepitude of the Manchu dynasty, and the simultaneous collision with the Western world, the old political system broke and had to be reshaped into new forms. Nevertheless, even in the Republican era techniques of the T'ang have reappeared in the administration of government services.

Underneath all shifts there remained a series of social groupings which were affected far less than were the broad and conspicuous central regimes. They have existed since the times before organized government, and may well be sufficiently strong to set the conditions under which any government or any race of rulers will succeed or fail in China.

*Family, Village, and Hui*

The ideological control in old China operated through those groups most closely attached to the individual. The government was not one of them. The fundamental strength of Chinese society rests upon the cohesion and power of three outstanding quasi-political agencies: the family system, the village and district, and the *hui* (associations, leagues, societies or guilds.)[15]

The family was an intricate structure, "composed of a plurality of kin alignments into four families: the natural family, the economic family, the religious family, and the sib."[16] The natural family corresponded to the family of the West. The economic family commonly extended through several degrees of kinship, and may have included from thirty to one hundred individuals, who formed a single economic unit, living collectively. The religious family was an aggregate of economic families; it would be difficult to give any specified number of constituent families as an average. This unit provided the organization for the proper commemoration and reverence of ancestors and maintained an ancestral shrine where the genealogical records were kept; the cult feature has largely disappeared in modern times. The sib resembled the clan as found in the

West; its role was determined by the immediate environment. In some cases, especially in the South, the sib was powerful enough to engage in feuds; at times one or more sibs dominated whole communities. In the greater part of China it was a loose organization, holding meetings from time to time to unite the various local religious families which constituted it.

Family consciousness played its part in sustaining certain elements of the Confucian ideology. It stressed the idea of the carnal immortality of the human race. It oriented the individual not only philosophically but socially as well. The size of each family determined his position spatially, and family continuity fixed a definite location in time for him. With its many-handed grasp upon the individual, the family system held him securely in place and prevented his aspiring to the arrogant heights of nobility or falling into the degradation of a slavery in which he might become a mere commodity. A Chinese surrounded by his kinsmen was shielded against humiliations inflicted upon him by outsiders and against the menace of his own potential follies. It was largely through the family system, with its religious as well as economic and social foundation, that the Chinese counteracted undesirable mobility of individuals in a society stable as a whole. Stability thus obtained a clear and undeniable purpose—the continued generation of the human race through the continuity of innumerable families, each determined upon survival. A materialistic interpretation would point out the need for cheap and plentiful human labor in maintaining the agrarian economy of China, and reduce the rationale of the system to a mere web of justifications.

The family was equaled if not excelled in importance by the village.[17] Had the family been the only vital social grouping, it might have been impossible for democratic processes to develop in China. The family pattern provided, indeed, the model for the government, but the influence of villages in Chinese life mitigated the familistic tendencies of government. It would have been heresy to revolt against an unrighteous father; but there was nothing to prevent the deposition of an evil village elder. In times of contentment, the emperor was the father of the society; at other times he might be looked upon as a fellow villager subject to the criticism of the people. The village was the largest working unit of local self-government; it, and the groups within it, such as the sib, was almost completely autonomous and subject to outside interference only in very rare cases. At the same time, the village was the smallest unit of district organization. The District Magistrate, as the government officer in charge of a district containing from one to twenty villages, relied on the village leaders in performing the duties imposed upon him. Village government was at times very democratic.[18]

Next in importance was the *hui*. It was in all probability the last to appear. Neither ordained, as the family seemed to be, by the eternal physical and biological order of things, nor made to seem natural, as was the village, by the geographic and economic environment, this association emerged from the Chinese propensity toward cooperation. Paralleling and supplementing family and village, the *hui* won for itself an unchallenged place in the Chinese social structure. The *hui* may be classified into six categories[19]: (1) fraternal societies; (2) insurance groups; (3) economic guilds; (4) religious societies; (5) political societies; and (6) militia and vigilante organizations. The *hui* made up the greater part of the economic organization of old China, and offered vocational education to men not destined for literature and administration. Under such names as the Triad and the Lotus the *hui* provided the party organizations of old China and challenged the dynasties whenever resentment was ripe.

The old Chinese society, made up of innumerable families, villages, and *hui*, comprised the whole "known world." Its strength was inexhaustible. Having no one nerve center, the world society could not be destroyed by the inroads of barbarians or the ravages of famine, pestilence, and insurrection. The Confucian ideology continued. At no one time were conditions so bad as to break the many threads of Chinese culture and to release a new generation from tradition. Throughout the centuries education and government continued side by side, even though dynasties fell and the country was overrun by conquerors. The absence of any rigid organization of legal authority facilitated survival, while a certain minimum of order could be maintained even in the absence of an emperor or, as more commonly occurred, in the presence of several.

The governmental superstructure kept the Chinese world together in a formal manner; it did not give it vitality. The family, the village, and the *hui* were fit subjects for imperial attention, but the emperor could not remove his sanction from their existence and thereby annihilate them. No precarious legal personality was attributed to the family, the village, and the *hui*, which could be extirpated by a mere edict. It was possible for the English kings to destroy the Highland clan of the MacGregor—"the proscribed name"—without liquidating the members of the clan *in toto*. In China the emperor could wipe out a family by massacre, but it was practically impossible for him to destroy an organization without destroying all its members. On the whole, however, the government of China pursued its three main ends—the maintenance of the ideology (education), the defense of the realm against barbarians (military affairs) and against adverse forces of nature (public works), and the collection of funds for the fulfilment of these functions (revenue).

*Governmental Changes Foreshadowing the Republic*

The pressure of the West compelled the Chinese government to define more clearly than ever before its own boundaries, its relations with the vassal states, and its lines of contact with the Chinese people. By the Treaty of Nerchinsk, negotiated in 1689 with Russia, the Chinese tried to demarcate their land frontier. The vassal nations presented a crucial problem. The Chinese failed to make explicit their quasi suzerainty in terms comprehensible to Western jurisprudence. At the same time they followed a policy of brisk exaggeration of territorial rights alternating with outright disclaimer of responsibility. The scope of government itself was affected by new functions which arose with the coming of the Westerners. The tax system was expanded. The development of an imperial customs service with Western personnel and Western methods of accounting provided the government with a source of large revenue. The demands that Western states be given adequate consideration in the transaction of business led to the establishment in 1860 of the Foreign Office (*Tsung-li Yamên*), a new institution which modified the traditional administrative pattern.

In addition, the Western states introduced their own type of government into China through the demand that their citizens be subject only to the law with which they were familiar at home.

In dealing with Westerners the Chinese had at first employed a code far more Draconic than the provisions of Chinese penal practice. After many years of irritation the Western powers, under the leadership of Great Britain, secured extraterritorial privileges for their citizens. Extraterritoriality placed Westerners in China solely under the jurisdiction of their respective national representatives. If an American today were to shoot down the Dalai Lama in Tibet, he could be tried legally only in the United States Court in Shanghai—although it is improbable that the Tibetans would insist upon juridical niceties. Apart from the guarantee of personal immunity from Chinese law for their citizens, wherever they might be in China, the Western powers, through a long series of special arrangements and actual usage, obtained certain footholds on Chinese soil where even Chinese were under Western rule. These areas were known as *concessions* and *settlements*, and the cities of their location as the *treaty ports*. Both the presence of Westerners subject only to Western law throughout the Empire, and of areas where Western governance was paramount, taught the Chinese the lesson of strong government.

Nor was this all. The British-Chinese treaty of Nanking (1842) and that with the United States (1844) both contained provisions relating to the protection of the life and property of foreigners. The imperial government found itself pledged to the fulfillment of a policy which collided directly with the xenophobia engendered by ideological control. The enforcement of these provisions, half-hearted as it was, involved constantly increasing imperial intervention in regional affairs, although the issues arising between the central government and the provincial authorities were settled through negotiation rather than enforceable commands.

Toward the end of the nineteenth century the gradual transformation in China gave rise to a reform movement carried forward by a group of constitutional monarchists. One of their leaders, K'ang Yu-wei, became in 1898 the tutor of the young Emperor Kuang Hsü. The summer of that year witnessed a steady stream of edicts which ultimately might have made China under the leadership of the throne as progressive as Japan. The reforms aimed primarily at efficiency and modernization, and partially at the parliamentarization of the regime. The young Emperor, however, was soon checked by Yüan Shih-k'ai, his leading military adviser, and outmaneuvered by the reactionary Empress Dowager. He spent the rest of his life in actual imprisonment, and the Six Geniuses—as the reformers behind his policy were called—were exiled or executed. One of those who were put to death was the poet Tan Shih-tung, a man of great skill in the classical literature and of ambitious visions for the future, who might, had the Hundred Days succeeded, have lived to be a guardian of the throne in a modern Chinese Empire. Just before his execution he wrote the following poem, calling forth the memory of Chiang-ch'ing and Tou-keng, upright men of the past, and comparing his faith with the mountain range of Kuang-lêng:

LAST SONG FROM PRISON
*Prison door facing me—thoughts of Chiang-ch'ing—*
*I could die easily, if like Tou-keng . . .*
*Laughing and alone, I lift the knife to heaven:*
*I die but leave behind hopes higher than Kuang-lêng!*[20]

Reform, indeed, could not be downed. The Manchu dynasty itself began to tread cautiously in the footsteps of Japan. In 1905 an agency was set up for the purpose of studying various foreign forms of government and of making recommendations for the modernization of the imperial government. In 1908 a draft constitution, very similar to the constitution of the Japanese Empire, was approved. A nine-year program, from 1908 to 1916 inclusive, was to lead to constitutional, parliamentary monarchy—if parliamentary monarchy be regarded merely as a monarchy with a parliament appended. The principle of cabinet responsibility to parliament was not established, and from the very beginning the Manchus, less wise than the ruling house in Japan, not only failed to grant sufficient powers on paper but began packing the quasi-parliamentary institutions before they were set up. Hand-picked, the preliminary National Assembly which met in 1909 began wrangling with the Throne.[21] The old Empress Dowager had died in the preceding year; so had the imprisoned Emperor Kuang Hsü. The new Emperor was an infant, and the court was little more than a gathering of bewildered Manchu princes listening to the advice of the eunuchs and palace officials.[22] Reform from above, had there been a single man of will and courage to take charge of it, might have had considerable chances of success. But while the Manchus tinkered with the superstructure of government, the foundations of society were washing away beneath their feet. More was involved than the improvement of administrative technique and the illusion of popular representation. A political and social revolution was in the making. Sun Yat-sen was the man who, more than any other single person, shaped its course.

In 1893 Sun had gone north to advocate reform and present a petition to Li Hung-chang, an eminent imperial statesman.[23] The mission failed. In 1897 Sun was willing to speak openly of revolution. He refrained, however, from advocating a republic before Western audiences, even though his party was committed to it. He wrote in his book *Kidnapped in London:*

> The prime essence of the movement was the establishment of a form of constitutional government to supplement the old-fashioned, corrupt, and worn-out system under which China is groaning.
>
> It is unnecessary to enter into details as to what form of rule obtains in China at present. It may be summed up, however, in a few words. The people have no say whatever in the management of Imperial, National, or even Municipal affairs. The mandarins, or local magistrates, have full power of adjudication, from which there is no appeal. Their word is law, and they have full scope to practice their machinations with irresponsibility, and every officer may fatten himself with impunity. Extortion by officials is an institution; it is the condition on which they take office; and it is only when the bleeder is a bungler that the government steps in with pretended benevolence to ameliorate but more often to complete the depletion. . . .
>
> This official thief, with his mind warped by his mode of life, is the ultimate authority in all matters of social, political, and criminal life. . . .[24]

In 1905 Sun Yat-sen lashed out at the monarchical reformers, subjecting their motives to vigorous criticism:

> Since the Boxer war many have been led to believe that the Tartar [Manchu or Ch'ing government] is beginning to see the sign of time and to reform itself for the betterment of the country, just from the occasional . . . edicts . . . not knowing that they are mere dead letters made for the express purpose of pacifying popular agitations. It is absolutely impossible for the Manchus to reform the country because reformation means detriment to them. By reformation they would be absorbed by the Chinese people and would lose the special rights and

privileges which they are enjoying. The still darker side of the government can be seen when the ignorance and corruptness of the official class are brought to light. These fossilized, rotten, good-for-nothing officials know only how to flatter and bribe the Manchus, whereby their position may be strengthened to carry on the trade of squeezing [graft].[25]

He also insisted that China's difficulties could be solved only by the establishment of a republic, which he envisaged with great optimism:

A new, enlightened and progressive government must be substituted in place of the old one; in such a case China would not only be able to support herself but would also relieve the other countries of the trouble of maintaining her independence and integrity. There are many highly educated and able men among the people who would be competent to take up the task of forming a new government, and carefully thought-out plans have long been drawn up for the transformation of this . . . Tartar monarchy into a Republic of China. The . . . masses of the people are also ready to accept the new order of things and are longing for a change for better to uplift them from their . . . deplorable condition of life. China is now on the eve of a great national movement, for just a spark of light would set the whole political forest on fire to drive out the Tartar from our land. Our task is indeed great but it will not be an impossible one. . . . [26]

Sun's diagnosis of the situation was remarkably correct; he clearly sensed the coming Republic whose first president he was to become seven years later. The ideological revolution was already under way, and the Empire about to dissolve into the past. What neither Sun nor anyone else realized was that ahead of China there lay government problems more serious than misrule. The ideological shift had terminated the reality of the old regime, and the military conditions were favorable; but would men be ready to invest their faith durably in a new order?

### NOTES

1. See above, pp. 17 ff., 83 ff.
2. Herrlee G. Creel, *The Birth of China*, p. 138, London, 1936.
3. Leon Wieger, S. J., *La Chine à travers les âges: hommes et choses*, pp. 22–25, Hsien-hsien, 1920. This is among the most useful handbooks of Chinese history and bibliography. It is written on a popular level and designed for the rapid and easy information of Catholic missionaries in China. H. F. MacNair, *Modern Chinese History, Selected Readings*, Shanghai, 1923, will be found entertaining as well as highly informative.

4. See John K. Shryock, *The Origin and Development of the State Cult of Confucius*, New York, 1932, for a description of the rise of Confucianism.
5. For a list of the Chinese dynasties see below, p. 197.
6. T'ang government is outlined on the basis of Baron Robert des Rotours, *Le Traité des examens*, Paris, 1932, a lucid and detailed translation of a section of the T'ang dynastic history dealing with the civil service. The book includes a valuable account of the organization of T'ang government and may well be cited as a model of Sinological achievement. The rendering *Department of Ministerial Coordination* was suggested by the usage of Professor C. S. Gardner, Harvard-Yenching Institute.
7. Rotours, *op. cit.*, p. 10. See also *ibid.*, p. 3.
8. Cf. Hans Wist, *Das Chinesische Zensorat*, Hamburg, 1932.
9. For a Western parallel see Fritz Morstein Marx, *Civil Service in Germany*, in: *Civil Service Abroad*, p. 181 n. 31, New York and London, 1935.
10. For further detail on local home rule see below, pp. 177 ff.
11. Rotours, *op. cit.*, pp. 26–55, "Les examens sous la dynastie des T'ang."
12. Jean Escarra, *Le droit chinois*, p. 97, Peiping and Paris, 1936. This is the outstanding work on Chinese law, by a French scholar long in the service of Chinese governments. The exhaustive bibliography of Escarra may be supplemented by Cyrus H. Peake, "Recent Studies in Chinese Law," *Political Science Quarterly*, vol. 52, pp. 117–138, 1937.
13. P. C. Hsieh, *The Chinese Government*, 1644–1911, Baltimore, 1925; William F. Mayers, *The Chinese Government*, Shanghai, 1897.
14. T. F. Wade, "The Army of the Chinese Empire," *The Chinese Repository* (Canton), vol. 20, p. 300 n., 1851.
15. The following discussion has been taken from the author's *The Political Doctrines of Sun Yat-sen*, pp. 38–43, Baltimore, 1937.
16. D. H. Kulp, *Family Life in South China*, p. xxiv, New York, 1925.
17. See H. G. Creel, *Sinism*, Chicago, 1929.
18. See Arthur H. Smith, *Village Life in China*, p. 228, New York, 1899.
19. See J. S. Burgess, *The Guilds of Peking*, New York, 1928. The present classification is a modification of that of Burgess.
20. Translation by the present author.
21. See Hsieh, *op. cit*, in note 13; Meribeth E. Cameron, *The Reform Movement in China*, 1898–1912, Stanford, 1931; Harold M. Vinacke, *Modern Constitutional Development in China*, Princeton, 1920.
22. Reginald Johnston, *Twlight in the Forbidden City*, London, 1934, presents an interesting narrative of court life before and after the revolution of 1911–1912.
23. Lyon Sharman, *Sun Yat-sen: His Life and Its Meaning*, pp. 30–32, New York, 1934.
24. Sun Yat-sen, *Kidnapped in London*, pp. 13–15, Bristol and London, 1897. This is a most engrossing work, whether considered as a political revelation, a personal narrative, or a story of adventure.
25. Sun Yat-sen (Hu Han-min, editor), *Tsung-li Ch'üan-chi (The Complete Works of the Leader)*, vol. IV, p. 357, Shanghai, 1930; from "The True Solution to the Chinese Question," pp. 347–368, an article written by Sun himself in English.
26. *Ibid.*, p. 366.

*Chapter* VII

## THE REVOLUTION

On October 9, 1911, a follower of Sun Yat-sen, one of the heroic and desperate "Dare-to-dies" who had harassed the imperial government for years, was working over a bomb in the Russian concession in the upriver port of Hankow. The bomb exploded accidentally; the secret storage of munitions was discovered; the next day, in the ensuing turmoil, the Republic of China was born. Double Ten Day (October 10, 1911) has since been celebrated as the Chinese Fourth of July. When the imperial officials sought to suppress the insurrection, they uncovered a conspiracy in the ranks of their own troops; in self-protection the troops revolted. In the next two months the Manchu Empire crumbled away. Sun Yat-sen, who was in Chicago at the time of the outbreak,[1] could trust his organization. Sure that destiny was working with him, he took his leisure in returning to China and stopped in London to forestall financial aid to the collapsing Empire.

*The Presidency of Sun Yat-sen and the Republican Revolution*

The fall of the Empire was not the result of a great mass movement agitating the whole population; it developed from the revolutionary nucleus which Sun and his followers had built up to secure power. They had hammered away at the imperial regime by instigating mutiny and terror for many years, since they realized that the incompetence of the government was matched only by its impotence. The revolution itself was a chain of rebellions, occurring province by province under the leadership of revolutionaries or officials joining the revolution. Except for the massacre of Manchus in some of the cities, it was a nearly bloodless revolution. However, the various groups pushed in different directions, and different men tried to seize power. The constitutional monarchists compelled the throne to issue a very liberal constitution, which might be accepted by the populace in place of the Republican programs. Military men began to come to the fore, as the army units alone were in a position of unchallengeable power. Men who had no thought of revolution might join it in time to become leaders of the revolutionary-military juntas. Li Yüan-hung, an officer of the Empire, hid under his bed when revolutionary soldiers sought him out; given the choice between death and adherence to the revolutionaries, he sided with the new powers, and in a short while became the commanding officer of the revolutionary forces in the Wu-han cities. Similar instances were not uncommon.

The revolutionaries managed to call together representatives of their party and of the troops to a National Convention at Nanking. They were seriously handicaped by the absence of Sun Yat-sen, who now hastened back to China from London. Few of the members of the revolutionary group—heretofore forced to operate as a secret society—were well enough known to have the prestige needed to form a new government. Huang Hsing, Sun's chief military follower, sought to manage in the interim, but not until the arrival of Sun Yat-sen in Shanghai on December 24, 1911, was there a prospect of consolidation. Five days later the National Convention elected him president of the Provisional Government of the United Provinces. On January 1, 1912, he took office; with the adoption of the Gregorian calendar now in use, this date became the first day of the Year I of the Chinese Republic. With the presidency there was created a cabinet, whose ministers did not yet hold any specific portfolios. The portions of the country under revolutionary control were ruled for the time being by a temporary system which combined the military and civilian governments in each province.

Meanwhile, the Empire was still the internationally recognized government of China and continued to function in Peking. Thoroughly frightened, the imperial court saw no alternative to calling into its service the one man who could be expected to master the situation—Yüan Shih-k'ai, who had ruthlessly terminated the experiment of the Hundred Days in 1898 and whipped up the first effective modern army of the Empire. Yüan, who had fallen into disfavor as a result of court machinations a few years before, waited his time, receiving offers from both sides. Finally he went to Peking, on October 27, 1911.

The negotiations which ensued over the establishment of a new government and the pacification of the country brought into the spotlight two of the outstanding personalities of modern China—men whose characters were to mold the institutions in a highly plastic society and whose influences were to last beyond their deaths. Sun Yat-sen, a Cantonese with many overseas connections, stood outside the old-style elite—a constitutionalist and an idealist. Yüan was a soldier and diplomat from the North, narrow in outlook, altogether a tradition-bound official despite his up-to-date military ideas—an opportunist and a realist in politics. Rarely have two leaders represented such opposite extremes.

In the conclusion of the negotiations Yüan played a part which would have filled Machiavelli with admiration. The imperial family was cajoled into taking the baby Emperor off the throne but was at the same time wheedled into refusing outright abdication. The edicts of February 12, 1912, are among the most curious state papers of modern times. They turned over "the power of government" to Yüan, admitted the faults of the dynasty, and ordered him to negotiate with the revolutionists and establish a Republic of China. Nothing was said about any eventual resumption of power by the dynasty, although provision was to be made for the comfort and dignity of the court. The Manchu house was to retain the Forbidden City (imperial palace) in Peking, where the monarch could continue to exercise his functions, freed from the cares of government.

Sun Yat-sen indignantly repudiated any idea that the Republic derived from a formal authorization extended by the hated Manchus—the Republic for which he and his revolutionists had struggled for decades. But he held his peace, unwilling to upset the chances of national unification on a point of form. Yüan was recognized as an able man, although he lacked trustworthiness and intellectual ability; it seemed possible to make use of him and simultaneously to satisfy him by giving him a position within the Republican framework. After the edicts of abdication, the issue became one of ultra-idealist constitutionalism versus brutal military realism.

It was agreed that Sun should keep the provisional presidency until Yüan could be inaugurated as president. Under the circumstances it was the only possible course. Yüan possessed decisive military power, and there could have been no hope of bending him. Furthermore, Sun actually did not wish the office of president. He realized that his own strength was that of ideologue and leader and felt that by enforcing his principle of *min shêng*[2] he could serve China best.

Yüan, it was arranged, was to come south to the new capital at Nanking. This was something which he had no desire to do, as the city was in the hands of the revolutionists and his army was in the north. When he was pressed to take office, he engineered a military mutiny in the Peking area, which did enormous property damage and gave him an adequate excuse for remaining where he was. By thus forcing the government to establish itself at Peking, he followed out the spirit of the imperial abdication edict and brought the Republican regime to the very city in which the Emperor still lived, and in which the imperial bureaucracy awaited its new Republican garments—socially and ideologically the stronghold of resourceful reaction. There was thus no problem of creating a new modern administration. The old Peking mandarinate continued, and the revolutionary Republicans came into the government offices as strangers intruding into a closed system. For the initial months of the Republican experiment Peking's novel status was merely the evidence of Yüan's prestige; thereafter, Peking was to become the embodiment of archaism, blind pragmatism, and corruption.

On March 10, 1912, Yüan Shih-k'ai took a solemn oath to preserve and defend the Republic and assumed office as president. On the same day a Provisional Constitution went into effect, whereby the National Convention placed the greater share of government power in the hands of a National Council, to serve until the promulgation of election laws for the choice of a national parliament. Republican mistrust of Yüan was evident in this action. Yet Sun Yat-sen was satisfied that his first principle, nationalism, had been realized in great part by the expulsion of the Manchus, and that his second, democracy, was in the process of fulfillment. He turned to the realization of the third, *min shêng*.[2] Yüan placed him in charge of all railway development in China, and Sun cherished the freedom to carry out the practical aspect of the revolution. He had passed beyond the stage of agitation and conspiracy, of wandering about in the world, his life in year-long daily jeopardy, seeking men and funds for a revolution which seemed Utopian to most. Now he could do his work quietly, without inducing simple merchants and workers to risk sudden death or the torture racks of the Board of Punishments. He had no way of realizing that his miraculous success was to be followed by defeat and that the revolution for which he had fought was not over but had only begun.

The presidency of Sun Yat-sen in Nanking, terminated by Yüan Shih-k'ai's assumption of office, was little more than a military and revolutionary junta linking together the various provincial revolutionary groups. It had to face no serious problems of administration, and the collection of taxes was the last thing that a brand-new revolutionary government would dare to stress in China. Its principles were republican, but it inaugurated no formal institutions and resorted to no elections, referenda, or plebiscites. The task of constituting democracy in China was placed under the stewardship of the most versatile military opportunist of the age: Yüan Shih-k'ai.

*The Parliamentary Republic*

After Sun Yat-sen relinquished the presidency to Yüan Shih-k'ai and the Republican regime settled down in the citadel of the old regime, a form of government was set up which did not immediately reveal itself as patently unworkable but which in retrospect seems a curiously ill-conceived experiment in transplanting institutions. Sun and his followers assumed that democratic, parliamentary institutions were adaptable, that the existing grouping would soon lend itself to the purpose of effective multi-party government, and that parties would arise organically from honest differences of opinion. They considered the republicanization of the provincial and local governments of less immediate importance than the establishment of a national democratic order. They expected to have a constitutional government with the five "races" of China—Chinese, Mongol, Manchu, Tibetan, and Turkic (Mohammedan)—united under the new five-barred banner. At the time, these assumptions seemed practicable.

The Provisional Constitution of March, 1912, established a relatively weak presidency though with somewhat greater powers than the French. Article 45 required the counter-signature of all presidential orders by the appropriate cabinet minister; the ministers were to be appointed by the president with the concurrence of the legislative. Unfortunately, the principle of ministerial responsibility to parliament was not explicitly stated, although it might have been expected that the far-reaching powers of the legislative body would have led to actual parliamentarism very shortly. It was obviously the intention of the Republicans to promote Yüan to a position of ineffectiveness. The premier and the cabinet selected by the president with legislative concurrence were to be subject to interpellation. On the other hand, they were granted the privilege of speaking in the legislative body (Articles 43–47). The unicameral National Council (*ts'an-i-yüan*)—to continue only until the election of the legislative body—was to be constituted in the following manner, under Article 18:

> The Provinces, Inner and Outer Mongolia, and Tibet shall each elect and depute five members to the National Council, and Ch'inghai [Kokonor] shall elect one member.
> The electoral districts and methods of election shall be decided by the localities concerned.[3]

As a result of this procedural latitude, the delegates to the National Council were either elected by the provincial assemblies or appointed by the military governors or came with no formal credentials whatever. All officials were ordered to continue in their posts. The revolutionists still exerted control over large military bodies in the South and held many of the provinces under their military leaders or juntas, so that Yüan proceeded cautiously in the creation of his first administration. He chose personalities acceptable to the revolutionists, but appointed no outstanding men of Sun's Tung Mêng Hui.

The parliamentary system looked well enough on the surface, but the basis of government had disappeared and the problem of mass democracy was more fundamental than anyone then imagined. Many groups in the country began organizing as parties; Yüan himself appeared to further the new way. But he had his own thoughts. He ordered his followers to enter the revolutionary units to undermine them, and simultaneously pushed for the establishment of a party of his own. There was on all sides a pathetic eagerness to live up to the formal expectations of the Western world. Tragically, this government was comic opera. Yüan began having skirmishes with the Council within a few months. The Republicans allowed the actual power to slip away from them while seeking to exercise the authority derived from a constitution which most citizens of the new Republic could not understand at all. In the summer of 1912 Sun Yat-sen's followers began to face a definitely hostile executive. The Council looked for redress but found that parliamentary tricks turned easily against it. The conservative members, supporting Yüan, walked out, and the Council lacked a quorum.

In August, 1912, the old revolutionary organization of Sun Yat-sen, founded by his coordination of earlier secret societies, was transformed into a regular party, the Kuomintang. The Kuomintang devoted themselves to the development of genuine party government; looking upon the Republic as their own creation, they were less ready for compromise than Chinese usage might have required. This did not improve the position of Sun's adherents. Yüan countered by forming the Progressive Party (*Chinputang*). While both sides lost control over the people, the party system was not even important enough to amount to carpetbagging. The only power in the country, as doctrine and administration melted away, was the military.[4]

Under the terms of the Provisional Constitution the Council was to yield to a bicameral National Assembly, for which it should provide by law within ten months. It was to be the duty of the National Assembly to prepare a permanent constitution (Articles 53 and 54). In the summer of 1912 the Council passed the required law, providing for the indirect election of a Senate and the direct election, by a limited electorate and under a very complicated electoral scheme,[5] of a House of Representatives. About $\frac{1}{35}$ of 1 per cent of the total population voted. The Kuomintang came out far ahead of any other party, with a definite plurality but one insufficient to give it absolute control of the Assembly, which met early in 1913. Inexperienced even in the elementary requirements of parliamentary practice, let alone the conduct of government, the legislative branch was destined to be sheer ornament. The Kuomintang had relegated themselves to the occupancy of the least important branch of the government. The new parliament met amid great theatricals and placed heavy emphasis on form but was unable to make its will felt. The quarrels with the President over foreign loans, democratic policy and party rule were not settled by a showdown, but by resort to technicalities on both sides.

Yüan, however, had his finger on the trigger. March, 1913, was marked by the murder of Sung Chiao-jên, one of the ablest of Sun's followers. It was the first political act to indicate that Yüan was embarking upon a program of assassinations. Even upon this occasion, Sun Yat-sen held his hand, ready to let the new regime prove its character. Yüan used the waiting spell to replace Kuomintang men in the provincial armies and governments with his own adherents. In July, 1913, a second revolution broke out. It was a move of self-defense on the part of the Republicans, followers of Sun. The revolution was suppressed by Yüan.

Undisturbed, the work of constitution drafting proceeded apace in the North. Again, the trend, paradoxically, was toward French precedent. The paradox became patent when Yüan forced the advance adoption of the provisions relating to the presidency; on October 10, 1913, the Assembly elected him president of the Republic. This gave him full *de jure* status as head of the Chinese state in the eyes of the foreign powers. On November 4 Yüan suppressed the party which had created the Republic, the Kuomintang. This not only eliminated serious opposition to him but paralyzed the Assembly as well. It was left without a quorum and without a constitution under which a new Assembly could be elected—one of the most surprising constitutional cul-de-sacs in modern times. The dictatorship began.

*The Presidential Dictatorship of Yüan Shih-k'ai*

Not content with having immobilized the National Assembly, Yüan proceeded to kill it. He called together an extraconstitutional body of his supporters, known as the Political Council. It recommended two measures: the dissolution of the National Assembly and the calling of a Constitutional Council to frame a permanent constitution. On January 10, 1914, Yüan suspended the Assembly by presidential decree. With that day the Chinese Republic ceased to have a government consonant with its laws. Technically the whole Republic lapsed into unconstitutionality and illegality, until it was swept out of existence by the National

Government in 1928.⁶ Nevertheless, the military leaders had sufficient belief in the political value of twentieth century formalities to preserve the appearance of constitutional procedure. During the following months Yüan's Constitutional Council, which succeeded the Political Council and was, similarly, made up of persons favorable to his rule, labored over another constitutional document. On May 1, 1914, the document was promulgated under the name *Constitutional Compact*. The Compact changed the style of Yüan's rule from a nominal parliamentarism to presidential government, and legitimatized the dictatorship.

Two and a half years after the establishment of the Republic, the country had grown accustomed to the rule of Yüan. His government had the advantage of carrying on from the seat of the former imperial administration. Yüan's peculiar faculties of old-school diplomacy and his grasp of modern militarism stood him in good stead. The Republic was generally admitted to be not much of a democracy, but even democratic Westerners applauded the hard-headed competence of the "strong man of China." Government was more efficient and more despotic than it had been in the last days of the Manchu dynasty; resistance and defiance did not take open forms, except for the activities of Sun Yat-sen and his followers, who had reverted to revolutionary tactics since the outlawry of their party. Their agitation was spreading with rapidity. Yüan made the same mistake the Republicans had made before: he failed to sink the roots of government into the minds of the people and to provide a coherent explanation for his own existence. Underestimating the change which had taken place, Yüan sustained the illusion that the Chinese society in which he was reared still existed. While he failed to evolve a symbolism emphasizing the rise of a new order with him as the head, the realization that the old Empire was gone was allowed to spread slowly across China. There was no more throne; the child Emperor dwelt quietly in his museum.

In 1915 Yüan embarked upon one of the strangest exploits in modern Chinese politics. After prostituting the democratic formulas in accordance with which he professed to govern, he began to use the same formulas for a cautious approach to the creation of a new monarchy. He was partly encouraged by a memorandum presented to him on August 9, 1915, by his constitutional adviser, Professor Frank Goodnow. The memorandum suggested, as a sane political theorem, the desirability of establishing a constitutional monarchy *if* there was general demand for it rather than of maintaining the trappings of Republicanism without operative democracy. But Yüan's scheming met with strong opposition. Both sides to the ensuing monarchical controversy misconstrued Professor Goodnow's memorandum; Yüan's foes denounced it even as a recommendation for autocracy. Seen from a purely institutional point of view, there was no harm in the proposal. A disadvantage might lie in the fact that other military leaders would be jealous of Yüan's obtaining the throne on which so many of them speculated. If the state of mind of the Chinese and the new doctrines of the Republicans are considered, the proposal becomes less feasible. Having gone through the terrific mental and moral jolt of a fundamental shift of living forms, and having realized that the Empire was irrecoverable, substantial sections of the population were in no mood to allow an untried Republic to be superseded by an even less tried modern military monarchy.

Yüan used Japan's Twenty-one Demands of 1915, which might have made China a quasi protectorate of Japan, as an argument for the immediate necessity of strengthening the central government. In sponsoring the movement for monarchy he virtually copied the procedure of Napoleon III in establishing the Second Empire. The whole technique of modern usurpation was brought into play, and no one stopped to consider who might be impressed by it. The only audience which might have taken at their face value Yüan's carefully staged "popular demonstrations" and his recommendations for "representative" public bodies was the Western public outside. Chinese familiar enough with elections to understand their meaning were for a Republic; the Chinese who did not understand them were not impressed.

Had China possessed a man with the administrative and military talents of George Washington, a genuine republic might have developed from beneath the tutelage of a strong military ruler. Sun Yat-sen, because of his Southern birth, his thoroughly revolutionary tenets, and his impatience with the jobbery of petty politics, was not prepared for the presidential office in

Peking. He might have headed a revolutionary government elsewhere in China but not a carry-over administration in Peking. Yüan misjudged his own opportunities and went back to the ritual of the Empire in an endeavor to place himself on a widely coveted throne. In December, 1915, after a circus of plebiscites and constitutional councils had been provided, the constitutional monarchy was proclaimed. In the same month Yüan performed the ancient ceremonials of the Imperial Sacrifice to Heaven, clad in the traditional gowns of the emperor. On Christmas Day, 1915, the province of Yünnan—in the extreme southwest of China—revolted against Yüan. The revolt spread, and in March, 1916, Yüan renounced the throne. His dream had come to a dismal end; he died on June 6, 1916. In the same month Vice-President Li Yüan-hung—the imperial officer whose political career began when he was dragged from beneath his bed in 1911—assumed the title of president. The National Assembly was convoked. The Provisional Constitution was put into effect again. And, as a sign of the times, the provincial military commanders took the new title *tuchün* in place of the older version *tutu*.

*The Phantom Republic in Peking*

When the Manchu Empire fell in 1911–1912, it left the military power to Yüan Shih-k'ai, who cloaked it with the Republic which he appropriated. When Yüan died, control of the armies passed to the provincial military commandants whom he had installed as a prime feature of his "strong man" regime. With the passing of the Empire, civilian bureaucracy fell into disuse yet retained just enough cohesion to serve the purposes of Yüan, so far as they were to be served by government. After Yüan's death, the governments in the provinces followed the flow of power—to the provincial commanders. The Indian summer of the parliamentary Republic was founded upon its toleration of the army system which Yüan had left standing in its fragments. The weight of power was now to go into these fragments and not into the Republic, which fell heir merely to Yüan's naive and almost contemptuously conceived "constitutional" show.

Sun Yat-sen was favorable to the newly restored Republic but did not participate in it, since it was made up largely of second-string revolutionists—men who had joined when the cause was winning in 1911—with a sprinkling of his own followers, together with a substantial cohort of the new-style military. Sun had been in exile in Japan during Yüan's regime, sounding out the possibility of Japanese assistance in furthering his movement. Without the participation of any group competent to attract ideological support to civilian government, and without any one military leader able to serve or master its cause, the Republic had to rest upon the administrative structure. Its power was virtually nil. The legislative, as in the early days of the Republic, was dominated by Sun's revolutionary Republicans, the executive by a conservative cabal of soldiers. The situation differed from the earlier one in that the military leader from the North, Tüan Chi-jui, occupied the post of premier instead of that of president. Within a year the fundamental contradictions in the regime displayed themselves. Tüan quarreled with the President and the Assembly, demanding dissolution of the latter. Not obtaining what he wished, he joined in 1917 other military chieftains in forming a provisional military junta in Tientsin. The President called in for his support the most reactionary army man of all, Chang Hsün. Chang forced the dissolution of the Assembly, the very contingency he was supposed to prevent. He capped this act by restoring the Manchu dynasty and putting the boy ex-Emperor Hsüan T'ung back on the throne (July 1, 1917).

While the country was startled to learn of the restoration of the dynasty, and to receive edicts by telegraph issued in the name of Hsüan T'ung, forces of opposition began to gather. The restoration lasted until the Northern military leaders could catch their breaths; on July 12 Tüan Chi-jui marched back into Peking to prevent Chang Hsün from stealing a march on him. The unfortunate ex-Emperor was promptly deposed for the second time. He was not to be put on a throne again until he became the Emperor of Manchoukuo in 1934.

At this juncture the arena was to broaden. In October, 1917, Sun Yat-sen was elected Generalissimo of the South by the remnants of the parliament which had gathered in Canton. Their action was provoked largely by China's declaration of war on Germany—a step which Sun bitterly opposed as serving no Chinese interest. From now on there were to be *two* Republican traditions in China, each one of them with theoretical claims to the legitimate succession from the 1912–1913 Republic. The government established by Sun Yat-sen in the South did not secure any international recognition, nor did it contain remnants of the imperial bureaucracy, or win the respect of the soldiery. But it did fall heir to the ideological revolution. The people were still skeptically indulgent toward Sun the idealist and his ramshackle governments, although they conceived of government in China largely as the problem of fattening the Peking phantom and raising it to husky manhood. The Northern Republic survived until 1928, increasingly a puzzle and an illusion.[7]

The details of its slow death are intricate. The military did not ignore the Republic altogether. They requested its sanction for their manipulation of the balance of power. The Republic legitimized the gradations of military strength which grew out of conspiracy, tax exploitation, opium farming, and ineffectual war. The Republic and its presidency were the chief pawns in the pointless game of Chinese militarism. The Republic lent a color of unity to the country and preserved those proprieties dominant in the Chinese mind. Even banditry becomes respectable if it observes "political" formalities, and at times the line between banditry and generalship became a matter of day-to-day intentions or of the size of the armed forces at hand. The government in Peking struggled to provide a suitable organizational form for the status quo, though never quite catching up with the new *faits accomplis* of each week.

In three connections the Republic of China at Peking is worthy of consideration: in its constitutional development, which in a dreamlike and ineffectual way mirrored the political ideals of the nonrevolutionary elite;[8] in its international role, which was of genuine importance and value to China; and in its administrative accomplishments, which—for a government—were negligible to the point of absurdity, but admirable indeed for bureaucracy working in chaos.

The Peking government was technically based on the Provisional Constitution of 1912. At the earliest period of the restored Republic (1917) it fell into the hands of the Anfu clique, which administered to China a dose of Reconstruction on the American model. The treasury was literally looted, and the politicos who attached themselves to the government and to the military dominating it fell over each other in their haste to sell the nation out to Japan. A peace conference with the representatives of the South met in 1919 but accomplished nothing. A new parliament was chosen from the areas claimed by Peking; when this passed out of existence another parliament stemming from the National Assembly dissolved by Yüan in 1913 assembled in 1922—a rare modern instance of a legislative body succeeding its successors. This so-called Old Parliament returned to the task which had been interrupted ten years before and in 1923 gave birth to a constitution.

The 1923 constitution—China's third Republican constitution, after the Provisional Constitution of 1912 and the Constitutional Compact of 1914—was adopted by a body revoltingly corrupt. The constitution itself was the work of political scientists; it was as admirable a document as John Locke's constitution for the colony of Carolina, although the parliament elected Ts'ao Kun president under conditions which set a record for indefensible practices. The constitution itself was federalist, but with many adaptations of French institutions in so far as the central government was concerned. As a theoretical device for government, it would stand high among the constitutions of the world, but if not stillborn it was never brought to life. Within a year it was set aside, and another provisional system of government was established. A committee was set to work on a fourth constitution more strongly federal.[9] The provisional government lasted from 1924 to 1926. In 1926 Chang Tso-lin, the *tuchün* of Manchuria, took over the city of Peking and the government. In doing so he did not bother to appoint a constitutional committee or to bribe a parliament. He appointed himself dictator (*ta yüan shuai*) and let the legalistic logicians construe it as they might. On June 5, 1928, Sun Yat-sen's armies from the South occupied Peking, and the Peking Republic was at an end. A ghost of a ghost, it was to reappear as a Japanese device in 1937, at a time when constitutional debate was at a minimum.

From the metamorphoses of the Peking Republic the Chinese learned most bitterly the lessons of political reality. It dawned upon them that government would have to rest upon foundations reaching deep into society and could not be superimposed upon the existing disorder. Their constitutional experience also satiated the Chinese with Western formalism. Yet the phantom governments at Peking enjoyed the full recognition of the Great

Powers, and the Waichiaopu (Foreign Office) maintained an impeccable diplomatic front. Although the Chinese scored no triumph at the Paris peace conference, they came off much better than they would have done without any representation. Three years later, at the Washington Conference, the Chinese, favored by the jealousies prevailing between the other powers, won a notable diplomatic victory. Representing a government whose authority scarcely reached beyond its own capital and whose limited financial resources threw its diplomatic corps largely on their own, the members of the Chinese delegation secured advantages for China greater than any won at the time by the Soviet Union.[10]

In the international field the Chinese owed their strength to the same factors that weakened them at home: careful attention to form, the anxious cherishing of prestige and appearance, and a limitless patience which did not predispose the diplomats to violent action. Since the Peking regime, in point of military forces available for world-wide action, was on about the same level as Liberia, the fact that China remained a second-rate power instead of becoming a plain victim suggests the degree of her international prestige. The Peking government provided a background, however shadowy, for the Chinese Foreign Office, and the Foreign Office carefully nursed the fictions of China's international status. Moreover, some domestic machinery remained. Around the Peking government there clustered a group of administrations which were so purely bureaucratic and non-policy-making in character that they were tolerated even by the military, or else were under the protection of international agreements. The Maritime Customs in Shanghai was staffed in its key positions with Westerners. This feature arose out of conditions during the T'ai-p'ing rebellion; it was later given international status by Chinese assurances that under certain stipulations the customs were to retain their foreign personnel. The autonomy of the customs became a striking characteristic of the international legal and financial position of China, since most of the Chinese debts were secured by a mortgage on customs receipts.[11] The Salt Revenue Administration was similarly separated from the rest of the Chinese bureaucracy by international agreement, since loans had been secured upon this revenue. The surpluses from both services were paid for the greater part to the central government at Peking and provided a definite fiscal incentive for the maintenance of the Republic. The Chinese Post Office was also manned in part by Westerners, and it managed to preserve reasonably good postal service throughout the country despite the governmental anarchy which otherwise prevailed. These administrations were largely autonomous; they made up the deficiencies of the Peking government so far as it was within their power. Thus the regime could boast of an excellent written constitution, a first-class Foreign Office, several good revenue agencies, a good postal service, and almost nothing else.

In the age of the *tuchüns* the Peking regime had no domestic power to speak of; most of the time government was by courtesy only.

*The Governments of Sun Yat-sen in Canton*

In 1917, when the National Assembly was dissolved for the second time by the intervention of the *tuchün* Chang Hsün, a group of its members met first in Shanghai and then adjourned to Canton. Assembling as an Extraordinary Parliament, it elected Sun Yat-sen Generalissimo of the South. He was not given the title of president because he did not wish to create the appearance of national disunity. Sun was in the peculiar position of being placed in military command at the sufferance of regional military leaders. He even had to fight for support in the rump parliament which had elected him.

In this first Cantonese government, Sun's military objectives overshadowed all others. Attempts were made to promote a frontal assault on the army plague, and various expeditions were launched against the North. Sun Yat-sen had his experiences in the years of revolt before 1911 to hearten him. The Republican Revolution of 1911–1912 was not so much a carefully timed universal conspiracy as it was the seizure of a few pivotal points by small bands of revolutionists, backed by provincial support. Sun did not think in terms of nationalism as yet, for he felt that with the expulsion of the Manchus the Chinese had solved the major problem of foreign oppression. His course of action in the first Cantonese government was therefore that of a man fighting on a constitutional and democratic issue while leaning on a temporary military government. His new regime had acquired at one time an enormous reach of territory by bringing under its fold, through a process of negotiation and intrigue, the leading military figures of Southern China.

Sun was, however, working too much outside his own party. He had both the parliament and the Southern militarists to contend with. The task of maintaining a revolutionary movement with troops who were no more interested in it than the troops opposing them, transcended even Sun's optimism and courage. Despite demonstrations of his personal capacity and bravery, he felt that his work lacked momentum. In May, 1918, after his office as generalissimo had been abolished and he had been made one of a Supreme Committee of Seven, Sun left for Shanghai.

In Shanghai Sun had time to ponder organizational strategy, to conduct the world-wide operations of the Kuomintang officially now *Chung-hua Kê-ming Tang*, or Chinese Revolutionary Party, and to consider types of government and methods of propaganda. He worked with Judge Paul Linebarger, his sympathizer and supporter since 1906, on a biography similar to the campaign biographies of American presidential candidates.[12] At this time he was still devoting himself to the organization of the existing groups in Chinese society for revolutionary purposes. He saw himself as the moral leader of the revolution and simultaneously as the necessary advocate of constitutionalism. He was anxious to implement the ideological revolution but thought that the parliamentary democratic techniques had been designed in the West to accomplish just that end. While he was in Shanghai, the Canton regime carried on a fragmentary existence. In November, 1920, he returned to Canton after his military friends had cleared the way for him. On this occasion the Canton government came forth as a fully civilian regime. Sun was elected Extraordinary President of the Republic of China by the Southern parliament in April, 1921. Using the city of Canton as his base, Sun continued the long series of military expeditions he had led for years, trying to whip the *tuchüns* at their own game without becoming one himself. He personally went with forces into the field again. In 1922 treason on the part of his chief war-lord supporter drove him out of Canton. Back in Shanghai, he established contact with the representative of the Soviets, Adolf Joffe; both men stipulated the terms of the alliance between the Kuomintang and the Communists.[13]

In 1923 Sun laid new emphasis on one part of his program hitherto neglected: the doctrine of the three stages of revolution. The revolution had failed in fact because it had not provided adequate measures for democratic training. The revolutionists had assumed an organic political change, and militarists had profited by their mistake in taking over the Republic and using its forms to subvert what were the merest beginnings of democracy. Henceforth, the revolutionary group would have to emphasize a sequential process in democratic state construction: (1) the acquisition of political power by the missionaries of the revolution; (2) the teaching of the new ideology of democracy and the training of the people in the techniques of self-government; (3) the establishment of constitutional democracy.[14] When offered the opportunity of forming his third Canton government, he took no chances and himself assumed the title generalissimo and the command of the armies. In October, 1923, a plan was drawn up for the reorganization of the Kuomintang, with the advice of Borodin. Next January the First Congress of the Party opened. Sun Yat-sen, delighted with the new instrument for promoting the ideological revolution, allowed government problems to recede. The Party came to the front, and with the Party organization were to be solved the problems of a universe in revolution. During the fifteen months of life which remained to Sun Yat-sen, his third government at Canton was not to undergo any transformation. The strictly political purposes of the revolution had become mere adjuncts to the ideological and military features. The government continued to possess the now familiar parliamentary-democratic formulas which, misused and deformed as they were throughout China, had come to be the embroidery of might.

*The Nationalist Government, Soviet in Form*

The sorry picture of inadequacy in both the North and the South was interrupted by the launching of the Nationalist Revolution of 1926–1927. As a preparatory step to the acquisition of revolutionary power, Sun Yat-sen's followers reorganized the Canton government in June, 1925. This action followed Sun's death on March 11, 1925, in Peking, where he had gone to take part in a reunification conference with the leading *tuchüns* of the North. The conference had failed, but it is characteristic that Sun, embittered though he was, lent his last hours to formulating a compromise. The new Canton government took the name of *The Nationalist Government of China*, thereby disavowing succession from the ineffectual Republic which preceded it. It remained in Canton until the end of 1926; on January 1, 1927, it was transferred to Hankow, the greatest inland city of China, located some six hundred miles up the Yangtze River from Shanghai. Hankow is one of three sister cities collectively termed the Wu-han cities; hence this phase of the Nationalist Government is referred to as the Wu-han regime. It came to an end in the fall of 1927, enjoyed a momentary resurrection in Canton, and then passed into history, being succeeded by another Nationalist Government at Nanking.

In the last two years of his life, Sun had come to stress again his principle of nationalism. After the birth of the 1912 Republic he had for some years placed in the foreground democracy and *min shêng*, until he became aware that the problem of China's internal reconstruction could not be solved without an adequate adjustment of foreign relations. He saw that the *tuchün* wars were influenced by competing imperialisms, agreed upon resistance to the Chinese revolution while expressing pious hopes for Chinese unity. Accordingly, the Kuomintang began emphasizing its nationalist character, and Sun's followers, previously termed Republicans or merely revolutionaries, were called Nationalists. With a program of anti-imperialism, anti-*tuchünism*, and national unification, the Party began making great headway. The propaganda machinery which the Russian advisers had devised was turned against the vested interests. In addition, the rapid rise of the Nationalists must be explained through their party organization and the creation of agencies linked with the Party, such as youth groups, labor unions, peasant unions, and women's associations. Thus, instead of trying to superimpose a modern government upon preexisting social forms, the Nationalists built their government by molding the social groups necessary to its support.

The government was composed of a hierarchy of committees, similar to the Soviet system in Russia. The topmost committees of the government were subject to the control of the Central Executive Committee of the Party. The Party secured its authority through a policy of democratic centralism buttressed by the election of a Party Congress from the various branches of the party. Power thus followed a perfectly clear and traceable line; it did not depend upon mock elections or upon indefinite delegations of authority. The party members elected the delegates to the Party Congress; the Party Congress chose a Central Executive Committee; the Central Executive Committee or its Standing Committee controlled the Political Council (policy-making) and the Administrative Council (cabinet), together with the Military Council. These three were the supreme government agencies. The same party authorities appointed and removed all members of all other councils in provincial or municipal governments. There was not the faintest show of popular participation in the government; government had become the exclusive tool of the Party. But by being admittedly a tool, the government possessed definite power.

Party agencies opened wide the doors of mass participation, not in the government but in the movement. The Nationalist Revolution won with the assistance of the Communists in 1926–1927 rested on the extension of every conceivable agitational device to every group of the population. The government tied these devices together. Halfway on the road to victory the differences between the Right and Left Kuomintang, and between the Communists and the Kuomintang, became too acute to allow for further operation. In April, 1927, Chiang K'ai-shek, the Nationalist Generalissimo, established a Nationalist Government at Nanking. The Nationalist Government, soviet in form, remained in Hankow for a few more months, transferred again to Canton, and then expired. Even so, the councils of the Nationalist governments at Canton and Wu-han had served their purpose well; they had effected the concentration of power, instead of its division, in the course of a revolution when concentration was at a premium. With the approaching victory and peace, the council form of government began to appear to the Chinese as no less alien than parliamentarism. The Nanking government set out to reconstitute a government both Chinese and modern.

## THE REVOLUTION

#### NOTES

1. Sun Yat-sen, *How China Was Made a Republic* (unpublished manuscript written in Shanghai in 1919, now in possession of the present author), p. 40.
2. See above, pp. 43 ff.
3. Wu Chih-fang, *Chinese Government and Politics*, p. 361, Shanghai, 1934. Wu's work, and Kalfred Dip Lum, *Chinese Government*, Shanghai, 1934, are the two surveys in a Western language of modern Chinese government. Wu's work, while carefully done and containing a great deal of useful material, is patterned rather closely after Western works on Western government and makes no attempt to transpose Chinese politics into Chinese terms, nor does it give adequate documentation of Chinese sources; Lum's outline is based in great part on first-hand contact with Chinese politics and, while brief, is helpful, especially on Kuomintang organization and problems. M. T. Z. Tyau, *Two Years of Nationalist China*, Shanghai, 1930, is a statistical and official commemoration volume and useful within its obvious limitations; anonymous, *Twenty-five Years of the Chinese Republic*, Nanking, 1937, contains short essays and monographs, some excellent, some undistinguished, on the Nanking regime and its predecessors. See also Sih-gung Cheng, *Modern China: A Political Study*, Oxford, 1919, and the "China" issue of *The Annals of the American Academy of Political and Social Science*, vol. 152, Philadelphia, 1930.
4. Jermyn Chi-hung Lynn, *Political Parties in China*, Peking, 1930, gives the most detailed outline of political parties yet available. Bitterly anti-Kuomintang, the author became pro-Japanese in the autumn of 1937.
5. Harold M. Vinacke, *Modern Constitutional Development in China*, pp. 145–146, 150, Princeton, 1920.
6. See Wu, *op. cit.* in note 3, pp. 50–51, for the problem of constitutional succession.
7. Bertram Lennox-Simpson, who wrote under the pseudonym Putnam Weale, was an Englishman native to North China who spent his life editing newspapers, writing books, and playing the game of North Chinese politics. He was murdered in 1931. His books cover the period from the Boxer incident to the triumph of the Nationalists of Nanking, and—while not always reliable in detail—are stimulating contemporary documents. *The Fight for the Republic in China*, London, 1918, and *The Vanished Empire*, London, 1926, are very readable. His novels, which suffer from neglect, present some aspects of Chinese and foreign life in the North which are not dealt with by any other writer with the same qualifications.
8. A. N. Holcombe, *The Chinese Revolution*, pp. 96–101, Cambridge, 1930, discusses this point with clarity and vigor.
9. Jean Escarra, *Le droit chinois*, p. 133, Peiping and Paris, 1936.
10. W. W. Willoughby, the very competent and sympathetic adviser to the Chinese delegation at the Washington Conference, has written *China at*

*the Conference*, Baltimore, 1922, and *Foreign Rights and Interests in China*, 2 vols., Baltimore, 1927. For further treatment of recent Chinese foreign relations see, among others, R. T. Pollard, *China's Foreign Relations, 1917–1931*, New York, 1933.

11. For the origin of this system see John K. Fairbank, "The Creation of the Foreign Inspectorate of Customs at Shanghai," *The Chinese Social and Political Science Review* (Peiping), vol. 19, pp. 469 ff., 1935–1936.
12. Paul M. W. Linebarger, *Sun Yat Sen and the Chinese Republic*, New York, 1924.
13. See above, pp. 51 ff.
14. This program is very pithily put by Sun in his *Fundamentals of National Reconstruction*, issued the following year (to be found in M. T. Z. Tyau, *op. cit.* in note 3, pp. 439 ff., and L. S. Hsü, *Sun Yat-sen, His Political and Social Ideals*, pp. 85 ff., Los Angeles, 1933). The point is elaborated by Tsui Shu-chin, "The Influence of the Canton-Moscow Entente upon Sun Yat-sen's Political Philosophy," *The Chinese Social and Political Science Review* (Peiping), vol. 18, pp. 177 ff., 1934; and Paul M. A. Linebarger, *The Political Doctrines of Sun Yat-sen*, pp. 209–214, "The Three Stages of Revolution," Baltimore, 1937. See also Hou Yongling, *La vie politique et constitutionelle en Chine*, Peiping, 1935; Tsêng Yü-hao, *Modern Chinese Legal and Political Philosophy*, Shanghai, 1930.

*Chapter* VIII

## RECONSTRUCTION

The National Government of China set up at Nanking in April, 1927, was not definitively organized until late that year. Chiang K'ai-shek had to resign from the government before the Left Kuomintang group would accept the regime. In the following year, with the return of Chiang and the adoption of a new constitution (Organic Law of the National Government), the Nanking government was more firmly established than any previous government since the death of Yüan Shih-k'ai. A high price had been paid for stability: Northern military leaders had been allowed to join it, much as those of the South had supported Sun Yat-sen ten years before. The break with the Communists meant stopping a vast agrarian-proletarian revolution midway in its course, at a cost of many lives. The Nationalists, thrust into the role of governors, could not avoid turning against many of those who had helped to put them in power but wished to continue the revolution.

*The National Government of China*

Despite the difficulties which it faced, the National Government had many assets. In the realm of ideology, it had the advantage of possessing a state philosophy and a patron saint: the *San Min Chu I*[1] and its author, Sun Yat-sen. In the military sphere, it had at its disposal an army unequaled in China; in the economic, the support of the Chinese bourgeoisie, together with the friendly interest of the capitalist powers. In the province of politics, it carried with it much of the personnel formerly serving the Nationalist Government, soviet in form, to which it claimed succession. Its officials were accustomed to devote themselves seriously to government, so that from the very beginning the Nanking government was inclined to enforce its laws as well as promulgate them—thereby breaking with the usage of the shadow Republic at Peking. Finally, the new government secured full international recognition with the flight of Chang Tso-lin from Peking and the disappearance of the rival regime in the North (1928).

Sun's state philosophy fulfilled a cardinal function. Even in its most troubled phases, when military factors came closest to the surface of government, the new government did not lapse into fiction. There was a programmatic index against which Nanking's accomplishments could be tested, and a definite long-range plan to follow. The program enabled the National Government to utilize the forms of revolution for the purpose of stabilizing government—far less dangerous than the practice of their Northern predecessors, to use government in order to further disunited military despotism. The officers of the Kuomintang exhibited a meticulous respect for the dead Leader of their Party. Sun Yat-sen, known by his honorific pseudonym *Chung Shan*, was buried in one of the most magnificent tombs of modern times. In carrying out Sun's legacy, the Kuomintang was pledged to the principles of intraparty democratic centralism and party dictatorship over the rest of the nation. The formal party organization was not seriously effected by the change from a soviet form of government.

Government under the Kuomintang, despite the breakdown of morale which followed the disintegration of the Great Revolution (1927), was radically unlike that of the Peking regimes. In 1927, when Chiang K'ai-shek turned against the peasant unions and officialized the labor unions, a tendency toward outright military dictatorship became apparent. The developments of the following ten years did not at any time suggest that military power had meekly yielded to governmental power, but they did indicate that government was taking an increasing part in the control of society. The close interrelation of ideology and government, dating from the period of the Nationalist-Communist alliance, was to endure after the revolution had been transformed into a reconstructive process and rebellion had been superseded by administration. However much Sun and his teachings failed to create a new political Islam, they weathered criticism sufficiently well to provide a scheme of policy, political values, and broad objectives.

The influence of Sun Yat-sen was harmed, rather than reinforced, by the hysterical ritualists who seem to be the parasites of all one-party governments. The memory of the Leader and his teachings settled into the stabilizing roles of founding father and general dogma. Only a few veterans of the movement are still inspired by the fire of his words and the vigor of his personality. To the vast bulk of Chinese public opinion Sun Yat-sen is the human embodiment of virtuous, brave, and intelligent conduct, whose theories are acceptable in their general form and whose programs have proved pragmatically usable. The *San Min Chu I* failed to cause widespread political ecstasy; it succeeded in bringing direction and sanity, after a limited fashion. To spread allegiance the government fostered a Sun Yat-sen memorial ritual; every Monday morning, in every government office, college, school, police station, and other public building, there was held a service consisting of the reading of Sun Yat-sen's political testament and passages from his speeches clarifying his doctrines. The services seemed for a while to resemble a state religion; but the moderateness and formalism of Chinese life was inimical to the fervor necessary for political religion. The Kuomintang and its government came to see these limitations; although the services have remained, they are now severely secular in spirit.

The most dynamic part of the *San Min Chu I*, the doctrine of nationalism, had contributed to placing the Kuomintang in power. The new government was accordingly nationalist and centralistic; it opposed any type of regionalism—political, administrative, economic, or military. The Northern generals who sided with the government at the time of its formation were brought within the operation of the national military laws. When they revolted—quite properly, according to their *tuchün* standards—against reduction of their forces in the Disbandment War of 1930–1931, they were defeated. With the Southern and the Western military leaders Chiang was not as successful, until Japanese and Communist pressure brought first the one and then the other group into his fold. After actual autonomy for a number of years, the province of Kuangtung (Canton) submitted in 1936 to the authority of the National Government, thereby bringing to an end the generation-old division of North and South. Nationalism and centralism affected not only the armies but also the entire administration, whose service functions and police powers developed amazingly. Although the Nanking government had originally faced broad popular suspicion, it began to win genuine respect because of its accomplishments.

Was the Nanking government a dictatorship? Its record does not justify the assumption that it was merely to camouflage a military dictatorship commandeered by Chiang K'ai-shek. Moreover, the policy-making power was not by any means a prerogative of Chiang K'ai-shek. Chiang was nearly sovereign in technical military matters and possessed more political influence than did any other single individual. Yet the power of policy making rested with a small group of men not over a hundred in number. Some of the gentlest, sincerest, and quietest of these leaders had once been *tuchüns* in their own right; some of the most military and forthright had never handled anything more lethal than a cash register. The leaders tended to work within the party and government structure, so that the political organization, while not of great simplicity or clarity, accurately portrayed the distribution of power. No one can gauge the degree of interdependence between the leaders of a government system in its formative period, and between the offices which these leaders occupy. The Sian episode indicated that the Nanking government could continue without Chiang and that Chiang's incarceration was not the signal for immediate anarchy. But Chiang was not actually dead, nor was the government deprived of the support which his prestige had generated. From 1927 to 1937 the Nanking government remained under approximately the same leading officials.

The last test for the sources of Nanking's power may be found in considering the relation between the men in command and the authority which placed them there. The supreme organ of the party was the Party Congress. This body did determine the course of government policy frequently, and on such occasions clarified issues through action. The Congress elected the Central Executive Committee and the Central Supervisory Committee of the Kuomintang. The entire membership of the Congress would vote in the elections, any of the members being eligible. Since the Congress was composed of representatives from the various regional and functional divisions of the party, intraparty democracy was insured in theory and—though to a lesser extent—in practice. The two top committees elected smaller Standing Committees; the Central Executive Committee in addition elected the Central Political Council, which was the highest organ of government in China and the agency through which the party controlled the government. The Central Political Council did not seek to keep track of the detail of government; it outlined governmental policy, appointed major officials, and directed rather than supervised administration. It was a policy-making body in the strictest sense, and its action took effect upon the Council of State, which coordinated the government establishments.[2]

Had there been a schism between the Nanking government and the Kuomintang, it might have been possible to trace a political issue as it was fought out—all the way from the party membership up through the Party Congress and the Central Executive Committee, from party to government by action of the Central Political Council, and down through the Council of State and the subordinated government organs to the administrative network operating upon the broad masses of the populace. In fact, however, no issue saw the light, since the same group that dominated the party controlled the government. The relation between the leaders and the Party Congresses can perhaps best be compared with that between the leading personalities of a Republican or Democratic convention in the United States and the convention delegates. Convention action rarely transfers power or upsets leadership, nor do constructive plans or formulated policies emerge from convention sessions; and yet the conventions cannot be regarded merely as tools in the hands of the party leadership. A similar situation existed in China. Even when Chiang and the other leaders seemed to hold the bag, the meetings of the Party Congress did not lack importance, and the issues before the Congress were not considered predetermined. This was no personal regime in the Napoleonic sense. Party dictatorship expressed itself in defined forms, as a part of Sun Yat-sen's state philosophy. Benevolent oligarchy of patriotic modernists, acting with party sanction obtained through intraparty democratic processes, was not foreign to Sun's mind. The Nanking government further differed from fascist governments, and resembled the Russian, in that it was democratic in intent; its dictatorial character was avowedly temporary. Throughout the period during which the Kuomintang ruled from Nanking, democracy was regarded as a definite goal of governmental policy. The Japanese invasions culminating in open war made impossible the immediate abrogation of Kuomintang party dictatorship. Yet when war broke out in 1937, the National Government was on the verge of reconstituting itself as a democracy; but now the regime itself became itinerant, moving into the hinterland.

The Nanking government was organized under Kuomintang rule in a form unique among modern states. Its three most distinctive features were: (1) the concentration of power in the supreme agencies; (2) a fivefold division of power and function through the *yüans;* and (3) the absence of parliamentary chambers.[3] While the Organic Law was in effect as a constitution (1928-1931), the government was headed by a president wielding considerable power and a Council of State which served as the chief control agency. In 1931 a National People's Convention made up of representatives of the Kuomintang and of occupational groups adopted a Provisional Constitution.[4] Under this constitution the power of the president was sharply reduced, making him practically a titular officer. The Council of State became a more formalized agency, and the greater weight of government routine was placed in the Executive *Yüan.* Under the draft constitution proposed for the period after the end of party dictatorship a presidential system was to have been inaugurated.

The years 1931-1937 were characterized by the use of the Council of State as the supreme agency of formal government. The president of the National Government was little more than the chairman of the Council. The Council received instructions from the Central Political Council, and transmitted them to the five regular departments of government in the form of policies. Great as its powers may seem to be, the Council of State was largely an intermediary agency, although the personal influence of its members was extensive. The Council, with its administrative adjuncts, was of value in that it provided an institutional center for the government and gave governmental form to the commands of the party. There was no judicial check on the executive or the legislative branches.

The fivefold division of powers (adopted as the *yüan* system) is one of the most original points in Sun Yat-sen's political scheme. *Yüan* is an almost untranslatable Chinese term signifying a "public body" and used in modern China to designate the five great coordinate departments of government.

## PARTY MEMBERSHIP
### Party Congress
Central Executive Committee    Central Supervisory Committee
Standing Committee    Standing Committee
### Central Political Council
1. Secretariat for Civil Affairs
2. Secretariat for Military Affairs
3. Commission for the Disciplinary Punishment of Political Officials

### President of the National Government
#### Council of State
1. Commission of Military Affairs
2. Board of General Staff
3. Directorate-General of Military Training
4. Military Advisory Council
5. National Reconstruction Commission
6. Academia Sinica
7. National Economic Council
8. Sun Yat-sen Mausoleum Commission

### I. EXECUTIVE YÜAN
President
Vice-president
Secretariat
1. Ministry of the Interior
2. Ministry of Foreign Affairs
3. Ministry of Military Affairs
4. Ministry of the Navy
5. Ministry of Finance
6. Ministry of Industries
7. Ministry of Education
8. Ministry of Communications
9. Ministry of Railways
10. Commission on Mongolian and Tibetan Affairs
11. Commission on Overseas Chinese Affairs
12. National Health Service
13. Hopei-Chahar Political Council
14. Mongolian Local Autonomy Council
15. Weihaiwei Administration
16. Preparatory Commission for the Sikang Provincial Government
17. Boards of Trustees for Boxer Refunds
18. Committee on Efficiency

### II. LEGISLATIVE YÜAN
President
Vice-president
Legislative Members
Legislative Research Bureau
Bureau of Statistics

### III. JUDICIAL YÜAN
President
Vice-president
Commission for the Disciplinary Punishment of Public Functionaries
Administrative Court
Supreme Court
Ministry of Justice

### IV. EXAMINATION YÜAN
President
Vice-president
Examination Commission
Ministry of Personnel

### V. CONTROL YÜAN
President
Vice-president
Ministry of Audit

PROVINCIAL COMMISSIONS
*Hsien*      Municipalities
Villages

The Executive *Yüan* was headed, as were all the others, by a *yüan* president (*yüan-chang*), assisted by a vice-president, a secretary-general, and a director of political affairs. The *yüan* included all the major executive ministries, and the formal meeting of the Executive *Yüan* was a meeting of the *Yüan* officers, the heads of the ministries, and other directing officials. Such meetings took place once a week and corresponded to cabinet meetings in Western countries. The executive work of the entire government was performed by the Executive *Yüan* and—through characteristic Chinese devices—the *Yüan* Secretariat, divided into bureaus and committees, came to occupy a position of high strategic importance in Chinese government. All executive measures were funneled through the Secretariat, which cast them into proper form and determined whether or not they should be put on the *yüan* agenda. It thus occupied a position not unlike that of the Grand Chancery and Grand Secretariat of the T'ang dynasty or of the Office of Transmissions under the Manchus. The Executive *Yüan* combined within itself nine ministries: Interior (having charge of provincial and local government), Foreign Affairs, Military Affairs, Navy, Finance, Industries, Education, Communications, and Railways. Included were also a number of special commissions and agencies.

The Legislative *Yüan* consisted of a president, a vice-president, and eighty-six members, with an extensive administrative staff attached to it. The *yüan* was divided, as are parliaments, into committees, but it was not a representative body, nor able to enact laws independently of the other divisions of government. Its president's powers were so wide as to make the cameral organization of the *yüan* more apparent than real and to reduce the *yüan* to a legislative drafting and research agency. The Judicial *Yüan* was made up of four establishments: Supreme Court, Administrative Court, Commission for the Disciplinary Punishment of Public Functionaries (dealing with the government personnel below political rank), and the Ministry of Justice. The Examination *Yüan*, composed of two divisions (Examination Commission and Ministry of Personnel) gave expression to the Chinese tradition of separate examining agencies. Its function was to provide a merit system applicable to the whole government staff, except those relatively few positions which were political in nature. Because of the difficulty of developing elaborate machinery under unusual circumstances, the Examination *Yüan* did not establish for itself a high standard of accomplishment. Finally, the Control *Yüan* served as a chamber of censors entitled to bring suit against dishonest or treacherous officials, and maintained a central Ministry of Audit. In the last few years of the Nanking regime it brought over two hundred and fifty cases to bar each year.

An informative picture of the practical workings of one of the key parts of the National Government, the Secretariat of the Executive *Yüan*, is given by Tsiang Ting-fu, the Chinese ambassador to the Soviet Union and formerly one of the ranking officials of that *Yüan:*

> The Bureau of General Affairs keeps the internal machinery of the Secretariat going. It receives the dispatches and distributes them among the sections. It manages the funds and looks after supplies.
>
> The Bureau of Confidential Affairs handles confidential telegrams and keeps the secret codes.
>
> The Secretaries in the Drafting Bureau draft documents that require high literary finish, usually formal documents.
>
> The Reception Bureau takes care of callers and visitors and sees to it that dignitaries who come to the Executive Yüan for business or courtesy calls are accorded a due reception.
>
> The Meetings Bureau arranges for all meetings held in, or under the auspices of, the Executive Yüan.
>
> The Compilation and Translation Bureau watches over the periodical press, both Chinese and foreign.
>
> The real political work is done in the Sections. Let us take up first political correspondence. A minister, governor, or mayor sends a dispatch to the Executive Yüan, asking for instructions in regard to, let us say, a problem in raising funds. It goes to Section 5. The head clerk and his assistants look up regulations, precedents, and other relevant facts and write a memorandum. The dispatch with the memorandum goes to the secretary or councillor in charge of the Section, who writes a minute suggesting a solution or approving a solution suggested by the head clerk. Then the dispatch, memorandum, and minute go to the Director of Political Affairs, who, taking into consideration political factors, renders a tentative decision for final approval by the Secretary-General. The clerical staff

sticks to law, tradition, and precedent. Adjustments are usually made only by the ranks above. As the majority of problems are so-called routine problems, in connection with which the opinion of the clerical staff is usually sound, the ranks above usually accept the proposed solution. What is important and bothersome is the minority of unusual problems, for the treatment of which procedures are varied.

The sender of a dispatch dealing with an unusual problem may call, or send a representative to call, on the Secretary-General or the Director of Political Affairs before or simultaneously with the sending of the dispatch, giving a personal detailed explanation of the matter and sounding the opinion of the Executive Yüan as represented by the Secretary-General and the Director of Political Affairs. An agreed solution may be arrived at during the interview. In that case the correspondence will be only formal. But the parties involved may disagree, in which case the Secretary-General will courteously say that the matter must be referred to the President or to the Yüan meeting, and the Director has an additional solution of the problem by resorting to consultation with the Secretary-General. In some cases the Secretary-General and the Director will decide the matter during the interview whether the caller likes it or not.

Some unusual matters touch several jurisdictions, *i.e.*, two or three ministries; or a number of provinces or cities; or both. The Executive Yüan then calls a meeting of representatives of the jurisdictions affected and the matter is threshed out there. The conclusions of such meetings may be referred to the President or to the Yüan meetings.

In dealing with unusual problems of primary importance the Secretary-General usually consults the President, and the Director of Political Affairs consults the Secretary-General in most cases and the President in some cases where the work is specifically assigned to the Director by the President.

The average of dispatches (including telegrams) received and sent out daily by the Executive Yüan is about three hundred, of which number only two or three need to be referred to the President or the Yüan meeting, the rest being handled by the Secretariat without such reference.

The Secretariat on its part, by the order of the President as Chairman of the Yüan meeting, or on the initiative of the Secretary-General or at the suggestion of the Director of Political Affairs, sends dispatches to the ministries, commissions, provinces and municipalities, in the form of decrees, ordinances, instructions, inquiries and requests.

The energies of the clerical staff are devoted entirely to the incoming and outgoing correspondence. About half of the time of the secretaries and councillors is devoted to correspondence and half to conferences. The sub-committees created by the Yüan meeting are numerous and are almost always convoked by the Secretariat. In a few cases the Secretary-General and the Director of Political Affairs, usually accompanied by a secretary or councillor, attend; in most cases, however a secretary or a councillor is designated as the Yüan's representative. The conclusions of such sub-committees are always reported back to the Yüan meeting.[5]

Strange as the *yüan* system may appear, it seems to have been the most effectual form of government that the Chinese have devised in the Republican era. In times of military or revolutionary crisis, however, this elaborate scheme of bureaucratic departmentalization would prove too cumbersome for rapid readjustment and action; during the Japanese invasions, great reliance was placed on the creation of emergency commissions. In addition to the *yüans* there were a number of agencies which did not fit into the five-power scheme. Great independent establishments were attached directly to the Council of State. An Academia Sinica took the place of the Han Lin of imperial times as a national center for scholarship. A National Economic Council and a National Reconstruction Commission performed specialized functions effectively, with assistance from experts provided by the League of Nations. In fact, there was a scattering of foreign advisers throughout the government. Of these the highest in rank were placed at the disposal of the Council of State, some rendering actual technical service, others active in unofficial representation abroad, propaganda, lobbying in foreign capitals, or similar tasks. Other advisers were attached to the *yüans* and to the ministries.

Provincial government under the Nanking regime was subordinated to the Executive *Yüan* through the Ministry of the Interior. The provinces each possessed a commission form of government, with the commission chairman serving as titular head of the province. The actual operation of the provincial governments exhibited a great deal of variation, depending on the character of the area, the extent of its political development, and the tangible influence enjoyed by the National Government. The provincial commission combined the policy-making, policy-executing, and quasi-judicial functions, operating largely on the basis of instructions from Nanking and transmitting reports through the Secretariat of the Executive *Yüan* at the other end. Attached to each commission were a secretariat and four or more departments—mainly civil affairs, finance, reconstruction, and education. The department heads were members of the commission—a type of government not unlike that of American cities under the Galveston plan. The theory of Sun Yat-sen provided, however, that the province should decrease in importance with the growth of modern government in China, so that the dangerous regionalism in the country would eventually be denied overt political expression. He saw the future significance of the provincial governments only in their role as intermediaries for *hsien*-national relationships. Under the National Government while at Nanking, the tendency was to centralize control and to emphasize national guidance in those provinces squarely under Nationalist rule. In other provinces the provincial governments tended to follow local conditions and mirror the national standards as a matter of decorum only. The provincial governments were far less important in the life of the provinces than was the National Government for the nation. They had the national civilian and military authorities to cope with, in addition to the impositions of their own local military. Their sources of revenue were not ample, and their authority not well established. In some provinces the commission form was adopted only as a matter of legal compliance, leaving to local leaders the actual conduct of affairs. In fact, reform centered on the *hsien* rather than the province, partly because the province was a potential rival to the nation, and partly because the *hsien* was a more organic unit in Chinese society.

Between the provincial authorities and those of the *hsien* there stood Special Commissioners of Administrative Inspection, whose function was to relate the two administrative units and to work for the modernization of *hsien* organization. The *hsien* served, and still serves, not only a rural area but also the central municipality in which the *hsien* magistrate has his headquarters. The *yamên* (official building) occupies the center of the town, mostly a one-story edifice built around a courtyard; some *yamêns* still display the two flagpoles and the two stone lions that were required by the custom of the Empire. Usually the *yamên* contains:

"(a) the rooms occupied by the tax collectors and the administrative and judicial police; (b) the court and the assembly room; (c) the offices of the various bureaus; (d) the residence for magistrates and the dormitory for officers."[6] The conduct of *hsien* government is influenced by three main groups—the illiterate masses, the conservative gentry, and the younger progressives. In those *hsien* units where no reformist or revolutionary pressure is felt, the magistrate and the tax collector do little more than collect funds, and the administration is marked by the laxity which characterized old Chinese government in its inadequate form. The gentry, the scholar-administrators, and the tax collectors represent a single social group and manage to rule in their own economic interest. In other *hsien* units the influence of modern government is noticeable; the magistrate is in most cases a man determined to put into effect the standards of twentieth-century administration. The prestige and power of young men with modern educations have so increased that they are able to obtain a considerable number of magistracies, and if they are willing they may introduce a respectable measure of good government and reform.

The magistrate selects his secretary and four bureau heads, subject to the approval of the provincial authorities. The secretary performs the work usually expected of permanent officials, carrying on much of the routine so as to leave the magistrate free for political and quasi-judicial functions. The secretary is virtually a vice-magistrate and, if successful, keeps the governmental machinery of the *hsien* in smooth operation. When the magistrate is absent, he acts as the substitute. The four bureaus of the *hsien* correspond to the four chief administrative divisions of the province—civil affairs, finance, reconstruction, and education. An opium suppression bureau is often added, carrying on the anti-narcotic campaign. The civil affairs bureau has charge of the census, and supervises local areas within the district. Such matters as police, militia, sanitary administration, public buildings, classical shrines, and parks are frequently under its jurisdiction. The subordinate units of administration are provisional, but the *pao-chia* system has been restored at the lowest level. This is a device for the mutual guarantee, protection, and responsibility of citizens, in which ten families make a *pao* and ten *pao* make a *chia*. The tax bureau is one of the weakest links in Chinese local government, as in this office corruption is rife, and severe oppression of the farmers most frequent. In unreformed *hsien* units, the tax bureau is likely to be the political plum of members of the local gentry, who use it to extend their tenant farms, promote usury, and defraud the government. The provincial governments have begun to send out accountants and to install regular book-keeping systems—an undertaking which if completed would be one of the major reforms of local administration.

In the smaller *hsien* units the magistrate is assisted for judicial purposes by a judge; in the larger, separate courts are provided. Up to the outbreak of hostilities in 1937 the national and provincial governments were making great strides in reorganizing judicial administration and in the professionalization of police work. The judges are appointees of the provincial courts, a factor which may make for greater professional capacity and independence. The general importance of the *hsien* is illustrated by the fact that in Manchoukuo the Japanese have been forced to revive this system. They have, however, implemented it with a Japanese officer known as the *Kanjikan*, who is supposed to advise his Chinese colleague. The experiment is of great interest, as it provides the acid test for the Japanese attempt actually to administer a Chinese area. Without firm *hsien* governments beneath them, the Japanese puppet regimes are foredoomed to failure.[7]

Until the beginning of the undeclared war, the departmentalization and modernization of the *hsien* had proceeded most extensively in certain model districts selected for the purpose of political and administrative experimentation. Some of these had reached a level of efficiency which augured well for the future of Chinese government. With the coming of war, however, administrative interests had to yield in many cases to political or military ones, but in one significant respect *hsien* government was constructively affected. The evocation of popular interest in and cooperation with the government caused a great acceleration of progress toward local democracy, and focused attention on reaction and corruption in the inland regions. War propaganda among the masses of the people amounted to a call for public-spirited action; such action is bound to take the form of direct military enlistment or of collaboration in local patriotic and defense schemes.

Municipal government in old China was carried on largely by the officials of the imperial or provincial bureaucracy. Cities and towns were graded and even named according to the rank of the office for which they served as headquarters. The imperial administration thus extended to municipal affairs; each municipal government included a designated rural area surrounding the city. With the growth of modern government in China, plans were considered for a definite and systematic development of municipal administration. The foreign-controlled cities of the coast provided models of Western administration, and the Chinese were not slow to copy. A few years ago the cities of China were divided for administrative purposes into three categories: those administered directly by the national government; those placed directly under the provincial governments; and those for which no special category was provided, leaving them under the established bureaucratic hierarchy. In 1936 there were five cities of the first class (Nanking, Peiping, Shanghai, Tientsin, and Tsingtao) and eighteen of the second class, including the very important cities of Hankow and Canton. The municipal administration is headed by the mayor and the council. The mayor is appointed by the authority under whose jurisdiction the city is placed. The council is composed of two appointed councillors and the chiefs of the municipal bureaus—four or more. The four required bureaus are civil affairs, finance, public works, and education. Intracity organization was accomplished through the use of *ch'u*, or wards, subdivided into family groups of defined size. With the development of democracy it was intended for each of these to take part in the promotion of self-government; at each level representatives should be chosen by free suffrage. The family foundation has remained a significant feature even of municipal administration.

The chief political question before the National Government at the outbreak of hostilities in the summer of 1937 was the adoption of a permanent democratic constitution. This was to be accomplished in much the same way that the Provisional Constitution had been adopted in 1931—by means of a specially elected People's Congress. In the meantime, a draft constitution had reached a nearly final form. The outstanding features of the draft included the strengthening of the presidency, the abolition of the Kuomintang party dictatorship, the extension of a widely defined suffrage to operate on an unprecedented scale, and provision for periodically assembling People's Congresses to take, by and large, the position of the Kuomintang by exercising the four powers of the people: initiative, referendum, election, and recall. The elective offices would be reduced to a few. The installation and removal of the major government officers was a function to be divided between the People's Congress and the president, who was himself to be elected and recalled by the Congress.

The Japanese invasion led to the scattering and the partial suspension of government. Military needs began to rule the hour. The Kuomintang Party Congress held in the spring of 1938 elevated Chiang K'ai-shek to the newly-created position of *Tsung-tsai*—a term meaning Party Leader, which had been the office held by Sun Yat-sen under the more august synonym *Tsung-li*. Not only was this a partial recognition of the leadership principle[8] in a democracy at war and a testimonial to Chiang as the supreme military leader of the Republic, but it was also a substantial grant of power. Four new powers were given Chiang as Party Leader: (1) the position of Chairman of the National Kuomintang Congress; (2) the chairmanship of the Central Executive Committee of the Kuomintang; (3) the power to ask (impliedly, to demand) that the National Kuomintang Congress reconsider its resolutions, which amounted to the grant of a courteous but effective conditional veto; and (4) final authority on Central Executive Committee resolutions, by means of a parallel veto.[9] This apparent trend toward emergency one-man control was, however, offset by the convening on July 6, 1938, of the People's Political Council, an advisory all-Party representative body, designed to substitute temporarily for the again-postponed National Congress. Its appearance was the widest break in the formal front of one-party Kuomintang rule to occur in a decade, and was heralded as a signal for the practical democratization of the government.

### The Chinese Soviet Republic

After the suppression of the Marxists by Chiang K'ai-shek and the liquidation of the Nationalist government at Wu-han, the Chinese Communist movement took to underground agitation. It demonstrated its power, however, by proclaiming the Canton Commune on December 11, 1927. The Commune ended in bloody suppression. At the same time, in the far interior, the first Chinese Soviet had been established; from it, in Tsalin on the Hunan-Kiangsi border, was to develop the Chinese Soviet Republic.

On the fourth anniversary of the Canton Commune the Chinese Soviet Republic came into official being. A constitution was adopted, and soon in the Communist districts soviets began to spread during a period of relative peace. Nevertheless, the Soviet organization was always under considerable pressure because of the war waged upon it by Chiang. Although labor and agrarian legislation was adopted, the regime had to operate under conditions of extreme military activity, counterrevolution, and terror. Despite all these handicaps, the Communists kept their government intact; they were able to move it thousands of miles across China in the historic Long March from South Central to Northwest China, which began October 16, 1934, and ended October 20, 1935.

Under its constitution, the Chinese Soviet Republic is declared to be "the democratic dictatorship of the workers and peasants."[10] The suffrage was set at the age of sixteen. The government was formed in a manner similar to that employed in the U. S. S. R. before the adoption of the new Soviet Constitution: local soviets elect district or city soviets, which in turn elect provincial soviets, which elect a National Congress of Soviets. In practice, the pattern could not be followed closely, since elections were difficult to hold and territorial division not always certain. The Central Executive Committee of the Congress of Soviets was the chief political authority of the Communist regime; it had the familiar executive organization of the Soviet system: a Presidium of the Central Executive Committee and under it the People's Council, the equivalent of a cabinet. The strength of the Chinese Communists lay in their Party and adjunct organizations, in their land policy, and in their Red Army.

The central government of the Chinese Soviet Republic was no mere torso. It included the following agencies immediately subordinate to the People's Council: the Supreme Court, the Ministry of Inspection, the Ministry of Finance, the Ministry of Land, the Ministry of Labor, the Revolutionary Military Commissariat, the Ministry of Home Affairs, the Political Safety Bureau, the Ministry of Communications, the People's Economic

Commissariat, the Ministry of Health, the Ministry of Food, the Ministry of Education, and—strangely—the Ministry of Foreign Affairs.

As a result of the kidnaping at Sian at the end of 1936, the Nationalists and the Communists drifted toward a *rapprochement*. The next February the Central Executive Committee of the Kuomintang accepted the Communist offer of United Front collaboration, although disguising the acceptance by formal conditions for a Communist surrender. In September the Chinese Soviet Republic was ready to assume the name of *Special Administrative District of the Chinese Republic*. This left their governmental and administrative organization unaffected; nor did it mean the dissolution of the Red Army, now also under a new name, that of the Eighth Route Army. With the commencement of the Japanese advance, Communist leaders began taking part in the work of the National Government, first at Nanking and then inland.

*Other Governments in China*

As the National Government at Nanking rose to a dominant position in Chinese affairs, regional regimes outside its fold found it less easy to fit themselves into the framework of the new Chinese state. The Disbandment War of 1930–1931 had witnessed the defeat of the two most redoubtable *tuchüns* remaining in the North. On the other hand, it became increasingly evident that acceptance of the Nanking hegemony in name led to the infiltration of Nanking rule in fact.

Nothing but a register of encyclopedic proportions could list and describe the various political institutions which arose calling themselves *governments* in the troubled quarter-century of the Chinese Republican era. Some have bordered on the pathological: Islamistan, for instance, which was the work of an Englishman who proclaimed himself emperor of a new Moslem Empire in Central Asia. The provincial authorities of Chinese Turkestan (Sinkiang) drove him out by using airplanes borrowed from the Soviet Union. In Foochow, in 1932–1933, there arose a movement headed by exiled Left Kuomintang leaders and other ultra-patriots eager for immediate war with Japan. This government was the first in years which did not pay lip service to the

*San Min Chu I*, nor claimed legitimate descent from the movement of Sun Yat-sen and his revolutionaries—a surprising circumstance. Its very flexible constitution would have permitted collaboration with the Chinese Soviets—had the Red leaders not decided against it. The other main point in which it varied from the pattern set by the Nanking government was its profession of federalism. Known as the Federal Revolutionary Government of China, it lasted a few months only to be destroyed by Chiang, who had no scruples against using the weight of his modern armies, including planes and motorized troops. These vegetations of government can only interest the political botanist. Far more troublesome have been the opposition governments mentored or sponsored by outside forces. Tibet and Sinkiang (Chinese Turkestan) provided a fertile field of anti-Nanking agitation. Two "states" in China proper—Manchoukuo and an equally Japanese-controlled Peking Republic (1937)—find their counterparts in three others located in Chinese dependencies: the Communist republics of Outer Mongolia and Tannu-Tuva, and the ambiguous "state" in Eastern Inner Mongolia (sometimes called *Mêngkokuo*).

These Communist republics are under stable government, and, judged from reports which reach the outside, seem efficiently administered. They lie in the former Imperial Russian sphere of influence, south of the Sino-Russian border; except for the complications which would have arisen internationally, they might just as well have been in the Soviet Union as outside. Both governments maintain legations in Moscow. It might be mentioned that when the Russian Red Army invaded Manchuria in 1929 during the conflict over the Chinese Eastern Railway, a Barga Mongol Soviet was temporarily established. The Communist "states" cannot be compared with the Chinese Soviet Republic, which depended on no outside military support and resulted from a great ideological drive. They serve as advance posts of the Soviet Union—precedent for the creation of puppet states within China. Years later the Japanese manufactured a "state" in Eastern Inner Mongolia, with the cooperation of anti-Chinese Mongol princes, which Japan has publicized very little. Known in the world press as *Mêngkokuo*, it provides a Japanese buffer state to meet the Russian buffer of Outer Mongolia. On October 29, 1937, it reached its latest phase with the proclamation of the Autonomous Government of Inner Mongolia.

The Great Empire of Manchou, to use its present official name, arose as Manchoukuo. The word itself was a concession to world opinion, as Manchuria is known to the Chinese simply as the Three Eastern Provinces (Tung San Shêng); its population is overwhelmingly Chinese. With the development of Chinese national unity, the Japanese position in this area was threatened. They invaded Manchuria in September, 1931; the following year they proclaimed the independence of Manchoukuo, inviting the young man who as a child had been the last Manchu emperor of China to serve as the head of the state. In 1934 he was installed as Emperor Kang Têh of the Great Empire of Manchou. The Japanese have done a great deal toward bettering their own economic position in Manchuria, but the effect of their policies on the Chinese population is of doubtful merit. Equal motives underlay the rebirth of Peking, where on December 14, 1937, the Provisional Government of the Republic of China was proclaimed.[11] The old Peking-Republican flag was flown. The heads of the new regime were aged men who already twenty years ago had cooperated with the Japanese. Others served under duress and performed their mock routine in the cold agony of treason. The new administration is honeycombed with Japanese "advisers" and under the domination of the Japanese army.

To round out their collection of puppet governments, the Japanese established in the spring of 1938 a Reformed Government of the Republic of China in Nanking, and even went so far as to adopt—provisionally, at least—the constitutional form of the National Government, which had moved upriver. This regime was admittedly even more ephemeral than the others, and the Japanese announced their intention of consolidating it with the set-up they had organized in Peiping. For the time, it was to be subordinate for purposes of theory to the Northern regime, but the future of the whole Japanese adventure was in doubt, and that of their half-conceived instrumentalities even more dubious.

*The Growth of Government in China*

In the decade following 1927, Chinese government became more significant than it had been since the days of the founding emperors of the Ch'in and the Han. Power was based on a correlation of government with ideological and military forces. The Nationalist Party was the first to effectuate this correlation, in part as a result of lessons learned from the Soviet advisers in the period of collaboration.[12] The Nationalists utilized the doctrinal bases of the *San Min Chu I*, tested in the social revolution which arose from the Nationalist-Communist propaganda. The great personal prestige of Sun Yat-sen was one of the most important contributing factors to the growth of Nationalist administration in Canton.

The military ability and political leadership of Chiang K'ai-shek largely determined the success of the subsequent National Government. Chiang created a military machine superior to any other in China and coordinated army and government in such a way as to add strength to both.[13] But Chiang stood not alone. His wife became his *alter ego* for press relations, and important in her own right. His brother-in-law T. V. Soong, resourceful financier, and his sisters-in-law, Mme Sun Yat-sen (Sun's second wife) and Mme H. H. K'ung (wife of a later minister of finance), were strong influences at Nanking. Yet these members of the "Soong dynasty" did not shape the course of Nanking policies as a closed concern. They were part of a larger group sharing responsibility equally.

Once the National Government was established its success was largely the result of success. Improvements in the international status of China accrued to the prestige of the regime, and a new surge toward reconstruction, delayed intolerably long by the anarchy of *tuchüns*, occurred as the result of the Nanking hegemony. In the later years of the National Government, before the Japanese onslaught transformed it into a quasi-military regime fighting for its existence, the increased extent of the national police power was brought into sharp relief. With the extension of a unified gendarmery service over great parts of the nation, and the development of a court system which worked well except when under political pressure, the individual came to face government as a reality—more than ever before, under any dynasty. The government defied custom and tradition in promoting public health, in attacking epidemics, in sponsoring modern burial practices, and in deriding unhygienic superstitions. In the broad field of mores which adjoins public health, the influence of the government made itself felt—in reducing the cost of marriage, in promoting municipal cleanliness and tidiness in public places, in furthering temperance. The New Life movement combined the prestige of the government with the elasticity of voluntary association. In its closing days Nanking whipped up an unprecedented wave of public spirit among the masses.

As to government control of the economy, the Nanking government aimed at system, in place of the inchoate conditions which existed before its ascendancy. Chinese banks began to be as reliable as those of the West. The currency was standardized on a national basis. A national fiscal policy was adopted. A great achievement was the introduction of a managed paper currency in a country where specie alone had been respected for ages. Agriculture, however, was lagging behind.

Government disavowed its previous identification with a scholastic officialdom. It dispensed with a state religion, although the commemoration of Sun Yat-sen compensated in part for the change. Government disclaimed any vague totalitarianism and instead clarified its zone of functioning through the use of law. By narrowing the field of its authority, it increased its effectiveness. Nationalization, centralization, bureaucratization, the development of lawful process, the emergence of a half-Western state working for Chinese needs—thus may the growth of government be characterized in the period after 1928. Obstacles remained, enough to dismay any ruler; but they had become obstacles and were not impassable barriers of cynicism, incomprehension, and futility.

The Japanese invasion of 1937 had two immediate effects on the government. It shattered overnight the structure erected by the Nanking regime. The work of a decade was undone. On the other hand, the Japanese threat helped to drive the Communists and Nationalists together and forced into the national nexus those regional leaders who were maintaining the last vestiges of separatism. Most consequential of all: Japan's push—the greatest invasion the Chinese had known since the 1600's—thrust government and people toward each other. Foreign troops taught inland China what nationalism really meant.

They taught nationalism not merely with the fury of their guns, or with the cruelties of their hysterical troops in Nanking. The Japanese fostered nationalism most strikingly when they drove inland the protagonists of nationalism. Students, merchants, engineers, soldiers, administrators, physicians, and scientists of the coast were forced into the far interior. Villagers to whom the sight of these modern Chinese was as rare as the sight of a lama in Arkansas now had such refugees dwelling among them. The effect of forced cultural cross-fertilization is yet to be seen, but it may prove to be of extraordinary significance. Chinese able to hold their own with any representative of the Western world can now be found in the remote valleys and plateaus of the hinterland—twentieth-century China and timeless China, united in their hatred of the invaders, and deeply aware of their new national unity, their desperate need for power.

NOTES

1. See above, pp. 41 ff.
2. See Wu Chih-fang, *Chinese Government and Politics*, pp. 147 ff., Shanghai, 1934.
3. The outline given and the description offered are brief and generalized because the Japanese invasion will probably lead to recurrent reorganization of the government. Shih Chao-ying and Chang Chi-hsien (editors), *The Chinese Year Book*, 1936–1937, have an excellent series of short descriptions by acknowledged authorities of the organs of government. Some of these are: Tsui Wei-wu, "Kuomintang," pp. 223–229; Ray Chang, "Central and Local Administrative Systems," pp. 230–240; Tsiang Ting-fu, "Executive Yüan," pp. 241–246; Hsieh Pao-chao, "Legislative Yüan," pp. 247–292; Hsieh Kuan-sheng, "Judicial Yüan," pp. 293–336; Chien Chih-shiu, "Control Yüan," pp. 337–347; Chen Ta-chi, "Examination Yüan," pp. 348–362; and Chu Shih-ming, "Army," pp. 946–955. This annual, which is written by Chinese in English and edited by Chinese, is not to be confused with the British *China Year Book*, 1912–; the latter gives a broad outline of Chinese government.
4. Kalfred Dip Lum, *Chinese Government*, Shanghai, 1934. The author was himself a member of this convention; his work, therefore, possesses unusual interest.
5. Tsiang Ting-fu, *loc. cit.* in note 3, pp. 244–245.
6. A number of French doctoral dissertations by Chinese students deal with Chinese local government. Although they are of uneven quality, some give considerable material not otherwise available in a Western language. Among these are Chang-Yu-Sing, *L'Autonomie locale en Chine*, Nancy, 1933; Hsu Han-hao, *L'Administration provinciale en Chine*, Nancy,

1931; Ku-Yen-Ju, *Le Regime actuel le l'indépendance decentralisée en Chine*, Nancy, 1931; and Loo Kon-tung, *La Vie municipale et l'urbanisme en Chine*, Lyon, 1934. Among the most valuable and informing pictures of *hsien* government is "Hsien Government and Functions" by W. H. Ma, *The Chinese Recorder* (Shanghai), vol. 68, pp. 506–512, 1937. The quotation is from p. 506. The *Information Bulletins* published by the Council of International Affairs, Nanking, 1936–1937, include much material on Chinese politics and government. Especially interesting are E. C. Tang, *Five Years of the Control Yüan*, Nanking, 1936, and C. L. Hsia, *Background and Features of the Draft Constitution of China*, Nanking, 1937.
7. See "An Account of the Hsien and Banner Council System of Manchoukuo," *Contemporary Manchuria* (Dairen), vol. 2, no. 3, pp. 92 ff., 1938.
8. Compare the position of Chiang as Party Leader in China with that of the *Führer* in Germany, as described in Fritz Morstein Marx, *Government in the Third Reich*, 2d ed., pp. 62 ff., New York and London, 1937.
9. See the news reports in *The China Weekly Review* (Shanghai), vol. 84, pp. 150 ff., 1938.
10. See *Fundamental Laws of the Chinese Soviet Republic*, p. 18, New York, 1934. Edgar Snow's *Red Star Over China*, New York, 1938, is the best book on the Chinese Communists. P. Miff, *Heroic China*, New York, 1937, is a useful condensed history of Communism in China based on the material currently available in the Soviet press. Mao Tse-tung, Wang Ming and others, *China: The March Toward Unity*, New York, 1937, contains some of Snow's material and also translations of important speeches and manifestoes regarding the inauguration of a United Front policy. A considerable amount of Chinese Communist material is to be found in the magazines *The Voice of China* (now suspended), Shanghai, and *China Today*, New York.
11. For a description of the nature and organization of the pro-Japanese Peking regime of 1937–1938 see Andrew W. Canniff, "Japan's Puppets in China," *Asia*, vol. 38, pp. 151–153, 1938. The new Nanking regime is described in the *China Weekly Review* (Shanghai), Apr. 2, 1938.
12. Tsui Shu-chin, "The Influence of the Canton-Moscow Entente upon Sun Yat-sen's Revolutionary Tactics," *The Chinese Social and Political Science Review* (Peiping), vol. 20, pp. 101 ff., 1936.
13. For biographies of Chiang K'ai-shek see Chen Tsung-hsi, Wang Antsiang, and Wang I-ting, *General Chiang Kai-shek, the Builder of New China*, Shanghai, 1929; Gustav Amann, *Chiang Kaishek und die Regierung der Kuomintang in China*, Berlin and Heidelberg, 1936, which is only incidentally a biography of Chiang, since its scope is that of providing nation-wide reportage; Hollington K. Tong, *Chiang Kai-shek*, 2 vols., Shanghai, 1937; and Robert Berkov, *Strong Man of China*, Boston, 1938. The Japanese retired Admiral Ishimaru Tota published a sensational life of Chiang (which appeared in Chinese as *Chiang Chieh-shih Wei-ta*, Shanghai, 1937); since Mr. Ishimaru's other works have been translated into English, this one may soon be available for Western readers.

CONCLUSION

Government in China has in the Republican era undergone one of the most significant transformations to be found anywhere in the world's political experience. The oldest society on earth found itself forced to redefine its position and to reconstruct its ways of thought and internal means of organization. Pressure from without compelled China to adopt the modern state. Chinese society was required to incorporate this state and all implied institutions in its routine living. The earlier period of the Republic marks an epoch in which modern forms had been established in harmony with the accepted standards of the Western state system. Chinese society fell into chaos beneath the up-to-date superstructure. The later period witnessed the correlation of state and society by coordination of ideological, military, and governmental power. From the collapse of the Manchu rule in 1911 to the operative zest of the National Government at Nanking in 1937 there was a revolution in the processes of government which for completeness can compare with any century of Western transformation.

*The Collapse of the Imperial Society*

Western ideology has failed to enter China as a constructive whole, but it has smashed whatever reality there was to the old world view. Western-educated Chinese leadership has undertaken the task of governing a people which has learned only indirectly of the West. In carrying out a program of adaptation, contemporary Chinese leadership has relied on Sun Yat-sen's phrase, "modernization without Westernization." But a dilemma remains. How can the standards of the modern world be divorced from their Western origins? How can Western technology be used without the attitude of mind which has created it and brought it to operative efficiency? How can a world which never knew Rome or the Normanic *Curia Regis* know jurisprudence? How can modern government be made Chinese, when government itself has meant something far different in China from what it has meant in the West?

Further, the nature of Chinese leadership has not only been transformed from being literary and ethical in its orientation to being technical and legal; it has also been transformed socially in the replacement of scholars by soldiers. The ideal ruler of old was a humane classicist with a taste for historical studies; the contemporary Chinese ruler must be military, if not militaristic, and must have the inevitable background of engineering and management which modern war connotes. The soldier must collaborate with the modern administrator, while both recapture the high ideals of devotion typical of the old scholastic rule, even if they cannot use its substance. These imperatives are indispensable if China is to live.

Finally, the language system which did so much to create and then perpetuate the scholastic elite through thousands of years of Chinese culture has now submitted to changes deeper and more far-reaching than any in the past. The development of the *pai-hua* school of literature and the progress of mass education indicate that even with ideographs the Chinese can reach conditions of uniform literacy approximating those which prevail in the advanced Western nations. If the alphabetization of the Chinese language, which is now in the form of tentative experiment, should become a fact, even more striking developments could take place. Reading and writing, and on this basis the transmission of authoritative tenets, does not presuppose profound economic adjustments. The modern Chinese will know his classics increasingly through paraphrases no more difficult than a newspaper column. When it is realized that the simplification of intellectual activity is offered to a people schooled in the idolatry of books, the potentialities of educational and intellectual renaissance—already partially realized—become apparent.

With the disappearance of the imperial world society of the Confucians as a consequence of its encirclement by Westernized states, with the passing of the scholars and the rise of Western-trained soldiers, lawyers, and technicians, and with the alteration of the linguistic and intellectual foundation upon which the old society rested, what is there left of old China?

*The Nature of the Transformation*

In the first place, the ideological change is not complete. No Western idea can enter China unimpaired. Sun Yat-sen was influenced by the almost entirely contradictory notions of Western nationalism, democracy, and socialism. In the *San Min Chu I* their Western identity was destroyed, and the new doctrines had much in common with the past. Western ideas served largely as a mold; when the mold was removed, the form was Western but the content was still Chinese. Mazzini and Confucius might both approve of Sun's political doctrines.

Secondly, the extrapolitical agencies of Chinese life remain. Chinese society may be shattered in dogma, but it persists in fact. The family, though subject to legal redefinition caused by Western cultural and economic influences, nevertheless plays a role far greater than in the West. The village is still the fundamental grouping among the rural masses. The guild system is impaired by the Western impact, but the party organizations—Nationalist and Communist—have absorbed much of the strength which once lay in the *hui*. Under foreign domination, these institutions may play a determining role in the struggle against the intruder.

Thirdly, for modern government the Chinese have resources of their own experience on which to rely. But they also have Western devices and prescriptions. The National Government, while falling short of Western levels of government efficiency, nevertheless trained large numbers of Chinese to think in terms of the modern state. But no new pattern has as yet crystallized. Chinese political and military development may well present a flexibility beyond Western grasp.

Fourth, the Chinese have still ahead of them the choice of criteria of authority to prevail in society. Learning, office, property played a decisive part in the old society. Hitherto, the Republic has grown with three modes of power: ideological, military, governmental. The relation between them is not yet determined.

## The Problems of Government in China

Among the governmental problems confronting China the acquisition of national territorial sovereignty stands out. Ever since the establishment of the Republic the Chinese have grown acutely conscious of the fact that some of their most important economic centers have been lifted out of the national territory. Sun Yat-sen realized in the frustration of his first efforts toward republicanization and social policy that the problems of internal government could not be settled unless the people as a whole were free. Without general freedom there could be no question of democracy, no question of a coordinated plan for the realization of the *min shêng* principle.[1] Observing the intimate relation between the *tuchüns* and the foreign interests, which often favored them, Sun and his followers began to stress their nationalist role. With the Japanese invasion of the Northeast in 1931, of Shanghai in 1932, of Inner Mongolia and North China in the following years, and of China as a whole in 1937, the issue of territorial sovereignty has become the most important one of all. Until it is settled, all other questions must necessarily be considered in their relation to it.

Second, the question of economic sustenance and development is becoming pressing. Without an adequate economic base, the Chinese population lives under the constant threat of simply starving to death. Military difficulties emphasize this problem; in fact, military effectiveness and strategy will have to depend upon the physical existence of the people in and behind the lines. The Chinese masses have lived close to the edge of starvation for a long time. As a consequence, the Chinese cannot wage war but in close proximity to the point of economic paralysis—plain exhaustion of the physical necessities of life. The economic problem cannot wait for spontaneous self-cure.

Third, the Chinese will have to recognize the need for politicalization of public opinion. They must evolve the faculty of transforming group opinion into governmental or organizational action. They must acquire techniques for group collaboration which will allow them to break down traditional groups into more diversified units—a government commission, a factory workshop, an army unit—without reference to family bonds or village and *hui* connections. This is less a problem of doctrine or education than one of habit and practice.

Fourth, the restoration of national prestige is necessary to the security of the Chinese nation in the international sphere, and to the wholesome development of the Chinese people within their national boundaries as well. They cannot effectively borrow from the West if they do so reluctantly, overcome by the thought of inferiority or by shame. Unless they conquer their present handicap, the Chinese will continue to lack self-confidence.

Fifth, the army problem must be solved. In the last analysis, the excess of men under arms damages the Chinese military, as the number of well-equipped effectives remains disproportionately small. The hordes of half-armed soldiers constitute a heavy burden upon the society, reduce the general economic level, and—by affording one particular group a disproportionate opportunity for making its preferences felt—brutalize the operation of public opinion and discourage peaceable group pursuit.

Sixth, the Chinese state—if China is to solve political questions through governmental procedures—must be constituted as a clear and legal entity. The old imperial society of China was able to dispense with law through reliance upon social forces expressing themselves in a large number of small but stable units. If these disappear the question arises: How can the individual conceive clearly his relationships within Chinese society? Systematized modern organization requires a legal framework.

*The Question of Chinese Political Survival*

That the Chinese will survive, biologically, as a race—this no one doubts. That the Chinese will survive culturally is more open to question. The Chinese absorbed all their conquerors of the past because the country was large, because the people were extraordinarily homogeneous in ideology and habit, because the Chinese were wealthier than their conquerors and more cultured. Absorption or cultural extinction is not a matter of race; it is a question of ideology, of thought and the habits which arise from ways of thought. What ways of thought are there today that will absorb the conquerors? What ways of thought are there that the conquerors might tear apart from the long past, to change China into a mere geographical expression?

In the past, China has been conquered by invaders who accepted the Chinese estimate of China, and who reciprocated the Chinese self-esteem with a deep admiration for Chinese culture. China's modern invaders bring with them a veritable cult of national self-aggrandizement. Their fondness for the Chinese past is mixed with contempt for modern China. Will the Chinese preserve their national equanimity and sanity in the face of such an attitude? Much depends upon their military and political fortune and its effect upon their confidence.

Government in the Republican era demonstrates the fertility and inventiveness of the Chinese mind in building political and administrative institutions and in finding means of uniting and controlling the Chinese as a people. When the chaos from which they have been emerging is considered, their recent accomplishments are an attestation of political ability. The National Government and the Chinese Soviet Republic were worthy adversaries; each met disastrous odds, not the least of which was the other. Their governmental forms may be destroyed and yet reappear so long as the Chinese remain Chinese in the sense of their long past. Sun Yat-sen expressed his countrymen's elementary social and national consciousness, so different from the feverish nationalism of the West, in very clear language:

Suppose that we, Chinese, were naturalized English or Americans and helped England or America to conquer China on the principle that we accept cosmopolitanism, would our consciences, I ask you, be at rest or not? If our consciences troubled us, that would be a sign that we have nationalism; nationalism would trouble our consciences.[2]

Such nationalism may prove indestructible. With democracy and *min shêng* as nationalism's corollaries, China promises to contribute a gift of peace and political intelligence to the world, and may yet return to her ancient role as the pacific preceptress of nations.

### Notes

1. See above, pp. 41 ff.
2. Paschal M. d'Elia, S. J., *The Triple Demism of Sun Yat-sen*, p. 132, Wuchang, 1931.

# CHRONOLOGY OF DYNASTIES

This is the accepted time scheme in China. The dates are the Western equivalents of the most widely current Chinese computation, which is known to be incorrect or haphazard from the eighth century B.C. back. The periods given for the dynasties are chronological formulas rather than the exact expression of political realities. For a discussion of the materials of Chinese historiography, see Charles S. Gardner, *Chinese Traditional Historiography*, Cambridge, 1938. For an excellent short summary of Chinese history, see the "Historical Sketch" by Lei Hai-tsung in *The Chinese Year Book*, 1936–1937, Shanghai. Chronologies are to be found in the major Chinese-English dictionaries, and—among many others—in Leon Wieger, S. J., *La Chine à travers les âges*, Hsien-hsien, 1920, where they are accompanied by a great deal of the old-style, uncritical, but nevertheless informative, Chinese scholarship.

| | | |
|---|---|---|
| HSIA | ended 1765 (?)B.C. | prehistoric or semi-historic |
| SHANG | 1765(?)–1123 (?)B.C. | |
| CHOU | 1122(?)–256 B.C. | |
| Ch'un Ch'iu (Spring and Autumn Epoch) | 770–473 B.C. | |
| Chan Kuo (Warring States Epoch) | 473–221 B.C. | |
| CH'IN | 221–203 B.C. | |
| EARLY HAN (including Wang Mang) | 202 B.C.–A.D. 25 | |
| LATER HAN | A.D. 25–220 | |
| SAN KUO (Three Kingdoms) | A.D. 221–264 | China's "dark ages" |
| CHIN | A.D. 265–419 | |
| NAN PEI CH'AO (Northern and Southern Dynasties) | A.D. 420–588 | |
| SUI | A.D. 589–619 | |
| T'ANG | A.D. 620–906 | |
| WU TAI (Five Dynasties) | A.D. 907–960 | |
| SUNG | A.D. 960–1279 | |
| YÜAN (the Mongols) | A.D. 1280–1367 | |
| MING | A.D. 1368–1643 | |
| CH'ING (the Manchus) | A.D. 1644–1911 | |
| MIN KUO (The Republic) | 1912– | |

# INDEX

## A

Administration (see Hsien; Scholastic bureaucracy; and Yüan system)
Agrarian problems, 115ff.
Aircraft, military, 108ff.
Anfu party, after 1916, 47, 157
Armies, under the Han, 83ff.; Manchu period, 86ff.; Nationalist, 105ff.; national, 110ff.; tuchünal, 104ff.

## B

Barga Mongol Soviet Republic, 185
Borodin, Michael, 53, 162
Boxer uprising, 95, 117
Buddhism, 24, 131

## C

Canton governments (established by Sun in opposition to the Peking Republic), 156ff., 160ff.
Canton-Moscow entente (see Nationalist-Communist coalition)
Capitalism, 46, 69
Chan Kuo epoch, 473-221 B.C., 15ff., 82
Chang Chung-chang, the Dog-Meat General, 103
Chang Hsüeh-liang, 1898– (ex-tuchün of Manchuria, son of Chang Tso-lin), 108
Chang Hsün (monarchist tuchün), 156
Chang Tso-lin, 1876–1928 (tuchün of Manchuria), 103ff., 158, 168
Charioteers (Chou period), 80ff.

Ch'en Tu-hsiu, 1879– (excommunicated Communist leader), 65
Chiang K'ai-shek [Chiang Chieh-shih], 1888– (military heir to Sun Yat-sen; educated in Japan, further trained by Russians, advised by Germans; leading general in China after 1927, and outstanding figure in the National Government), 52, 105ff., 122, 164, 182
Ch'in Shih Huang Ti, 259–210 B.C. (king of Ch'in, legalist, despot, unifier, conquered all China by 221 B.C.), 80ff., 128ff.
Chinese Soviet Republic (established in Kiangsi, 1931; merged with National Government, 1937), 66, 182ff.
Ch'ing dynasty (see Manchu dynasty)
Chinputang (Progressive Party), 151
Chou, Duke of (died 1105 B.C.[?]; semi-historic state founder), 127
Chou dynasty, 1122(?)–256 B.C., 14ff., 80ff., 127ff.
Christianity, 48ff.
Chu Hsi, 1130–1200 (Sung philosopher; interpreter of Confucianism), 16
Ch'un Ch'iu epoch, 770–473 B.C., 15, 81, 128
Communism, 51ff., 63ff., 72ff., 182ff.
Communist Party, 54ff., 68, 182ff.
Concessions, foreign, 140
Confucius [K'ung Ch'iu], 551–479 B.C. (China's most important philosopher, spent his life teaching, with intervals of practical administration), 15ff., 128

199

Constitutions: Constitution of 1923, 158; Constitutional Compact, 1914, 153; Draft Constitution, 1937, 181; Nanking Organic Law, 1928, 172; Nanking Provisional Constitution, 1931, 172; Provisional Constitution of 1912, 148ff.
Council of State (*see* Yüan system)
Customs, Maritime, 159

### D

Democracy (*see* San Min Chu I)
Double Ten Day, 145

### E

Emperor, in old China, 18ff., 130ff.
Empress Dowager Tzŭ Hsi [Yehonola], 1835–1908 (actual ruler of China in the latter days of the Ch'ing), 141
Extraterritoriality, 140

### F

Family system, 3, 136ff.
Federal Revolutionary Government, 1932–1933 (Foochow), 184ff.
Fêng Yü-hsiang, 1880– (the Christian general, later pro-Soviet, joined the Nationalists, revolted in 1930, took part in anti-Japanese agitation), 103ff.
Feudalism, 80ff.
Foreign Office, 139, 159

### G

Genyosha (ultra-patriotic Japanese group), 71
George, Henry, 118
Goodnow, Professor Frank, 154
Gordon, Charles George, 1833–1885 (British commander of the Ever-Victorious Army), 93

### H

Han dynasty, 202 B.C.–A.D. 220, 82ff., 116, 129
Han Lin (Imperial Academy), 130, 177
Hsia dynasty, 2205(?)–1765(?) B.C., 13
*Hsien* (district) system, 178ff.
Hsüan T'ung (last Manchu emperor of China; abdicated in his boyhood; now Kang Têh, Emperor of Manchoukuo), 156, 186
Hu Han-min, 1886–1937 (leader, Right Kuomintang), 59
Hu Shih, 1891– (philosopher, literary critic, language reformer), 76
Huang Hsing (early military leader of Republicans), 96
*Hui* (guild, league) system, 3, 136ff.
Hundred Days, the (*see* Reform Movement)

### I

Ideology (*see* San Min Chu I)
Imperialism, 119ff.
Islam, 24ff., 94
Islamistan, 184

### J

Japanese-Chinese conflict, 34, 69ff., 74, 122ff., 154, 188ff.
"Japanese Monroe Doctrine," 70
Joffe, Adolf (Soviet agent in China), 51ff., 161ff.

### K

K'ang Yu-wei, 1856–1928 (monarchical reformer), 140
Kuang Hsü, Emperor, 1871–1908 (modernist and reformer), 95, 140ff.
Kublai Khan, 1214–1294 (emperor, Yüan dynasty), 88

# INDEX

K'ung, H. H. [K'ung Hsiang-hsi], 1881- (industrial and financial administrator; Kuomintang leader), 60
Kuomintang, 31ff., 38ff., 50ff., 57ff., 72ff., 161ff., 167ff.

## L

Lao Tzǔ, traditionally 6th century B.C. (founder of Taoism, mystical philosophy antistate in effect), 24, 128
Li Hung-chang, 1822-1901 (Ch'ing viceroy), 92, 142
Li Yüan-hung (military opportunist; once President), 146, 155
Linebarger, Judge Paul (adviser to Sun Yat-sen), 161
Local government (see *Hsien*)

## M

Manchoukuo, 28, 72, 185ff.
Manchu (Ch'ing) dynasty, 1644-1911, 32, 86ff., 135ff.
Mandarins (see Scholastic bureaucracy)
Marxism (see Communism)
Mêngkokuo, 185
Militarism (see Armies; *Tuchünism*)
*Min shêng* (see San Min Chu I)
Ming dynasty, A.D. 1368-1643, 17, 85
Missionaries (see Christianity)
Mohammedanism (see Islam)
Municipal government, 181

## N

Nanking government (see National Government of China; "Reformed Government")
National Government of China (Nanking, 1927-1937; inland thereafter), 114, 164, 167ff.
Nationalism (see San Min Chu I)

Nationalist-Communist coalition 1923-1927, 54ff., 161ff.
Nationalist Government at Nanking (see National Government of China)
"Nationalist Government" of Peking, 1930-1931 (rebellious coalition of Northern *tuchüns* and Left Kuomintang; suppressed), 59, 107
Nationalist Government, soviet in form (Canton, 1925-1926; Wuhan, 1926-1927), 162ff.
Nationalists (see Kuomintang)
New Life movement, 61

## O

Opportunist movements, 44ff.
Outer Mongol People's Republic, 185ff.
Overseas Chinese, 35ff.

## P

Pan-Asianism, 47, 70ff.
Pan-Mongolism, 47
Parliamentary Republic at Peking, 1912-1928, 114ff., 149ff., 157ff.
Party Congress, Kuomintang, 170ff.
Political doctrines, Sun Yat-sen's, 41ff.
Pro-Japanese movements, 47
Propaganda, 23ff.
Provincial government, 134, 177ff.
"Provisional Government" at Peking, 1937- , 186
Provisional Government of the United Provinces of China, Nanking, 1911-1912, 146

## R

Red Army, Chinese, 107, 182ff.
Reform Movement, Manchu, 140ff.
"Reformed Government" at Nanking, 1938- , 186
Republicans (see Kuomintang)

## 202  GOVERNMENT IN REPUBLICAN CHINA

Revolution, doctrine of, 59, 162; of 1911–1912 [the Republican Revolution], 38, 97ff., 145ff.; of 1926–1927 [the Great Revolution], 55, 105ff., 168

Revolutionists (see Kuomintang)

### S

Salt Revenue Administration, 159ff.

San Min Chu I (the philosophy of Sun Yat-sen, since 1927 the official state dogma of China), 36, 41ff., 59ff., 72ff., 120, 167ff.

Scholastic bureaucracy, 5, 86, 129ff., 188

Settlements, foreign, 140

Shang dynasty, 1765(?)–1123(?) B.C., 14, 80, 126

Shih Huang Ti (see Ch'in Shih Huang Ti)

Siam, 69

Sian, kidnaping of Chiang K'ai-shek at, 62, 66ff.

Sino-Japanese War of 1894–1895, 34

Soong, T. V. [Sung Tzŭ-wen], 1894– (brother-in-law of Sun Yat-sen; Kuomintang leader; finance administrator), 59ff., 121

Soviet Republic, Chinese (see Chinese Soviet Republic)

Soviet Russia (see Nationalist-Communist coalition)

Sun K'ê [Sun Fo], 1891– (son of Sun Yat-sen; Kuomintang leader; railway administrator), 59ff.

Sun Yat-sen [Sun I-hsien; Sun Wên], 1867(?)–1925 (agitated for a republic; first President, 1912; author of the San Min Chu I; elected Leader, Tsung-li, of the Kuomintang; known after death as Chung Shan), 31ff.

Sun Yat-sen, Mme., 59

Sung Chiao-jen, Nationalist, 152

Sung dynasty, A.D. 960–1279, 1, 16

### T

Taikwa reforms, 645 A.D., 132

T'ai-p'ing rebellion, 1849–1865 (Christian agrarian jacquerie), 32ff., 117

T'ang dynasty, A.D. 620–906, 1, 85, 132ff.

Tannu-Tuva People's Republic, 185

Taoism (see Lao Tzŭ)

Toa-shugi [Far-Easternism], 71

Treaties, with Western states, 48, 139ff.

Treaty ports, 140

Tsao Kun (Northern tuchün), 103

Tsêng Kuo-fan, 1811–1872 (Ch'ing viceroy), 82

Tuan Chi-jui (Northern tuchün; once President), 103

Tuchünism, 45ff., 76ff., 107ff., 114ff., 157

Tungpei troops (Chinese soldiers exiled from Manchuria), 67

### U

United Front policy, 1937–    , 60, 67ff., 72ff., 184

### V

Village system, 3, 136ff.

### W

Wang Ch'ing-wei, 1885–    (leader, Left Kuomintang), 59

Wang Mang, 33 B.C.–A.D. 23 (Utopian who usurped the throne, dividing early and later Han), 17

War, in Chinese thought, 79

War lord (see Tuchünism)

Ward, Frederick Townsend, 1831–1862 (American adventurer in Manchu service), 93

Whampoa Military Academy, 105

INDEX 203

Wu Chih-hui, 1864– (Kuomintang leader with anarchist leanings), 59
Wu P'ei-fu (*tuchün* of the Yangtze valley), 28, 103ff.
Wu-han regime (*see* Nationalist Government, soviet in form)

## Y

Yellow Turbans, 3rd century A.D. (farmer rebels), 63
Yen Hsi-shan, 1881– (the "Model Governor"; Northern *tuchün* who joined the Nationalists, revolted in 1930, subsequently retired), 103
Yen, Dr. James [Yen Yang-chu], 1894– (mass-education leader), 76
Yüan Shih-k'ai, 1859–1916 (administrator, soldier, politician; served the Manchus, leading in army modernization; became President, attempted usurpation, failed, and died), 38, 44, 94ff., 146ff.
*Yüan* system (five-fold division of powers), 172ff.

www.ingramcontent.com/pod-product-compliance
Lightning Source LLC
Chambersburg PA
CBHW032110090426
42743CB00007B/309